THE AGE OF
INSECURITY

THE AGE OF INSECURITY

LARRY ELLIOTT
AND
DAN ATKINSON

VERSO
London · New York

First published by Verso 1998
© Larry Elliott and Dan Atkinson 1998
All rights reserved

Verso
UK: 6 Meard Street, London W1V 3HR
USA: 180 Varick Street, New York NY 10014–4606

Verso is the imprint of New Left Books

ISBN 1–85984–843–5

British Library Cataloguing in Publication Data
A catalogue record for this book is available from the British Library

Library of Congress Cataloging-in-Publication Data
A catalog record for this book is available from the Library of Congress

Typeset in Perpetua by M Rules
Printed and bound in Great Britain by Biddles Ltd, Guildford and King's Lynn

CONTENTS

CONTENTS

THE AGE OF INSECURITY

The central struggle of our time is that between laissez-faire capitalism, which represents the financial interest, and social democracy, which represents democratic control of the economy in the interests of ordinary people. These ideologies are incompatible, in that at the heart of social democracy is the one economic feature specifically and unashamedly ruled out by the resurgent free market: security. Social democracy offers nothing if it does not offer security; the free market cannot offer security (to the many at least) without ceasing to be itself. Instead it provides security to the financial interest at the expense of the majority, upon whom is shifted the entire burden of risk and 'adjustment' whenever the system hits one of its periodic crises.

But the insecurity suffered by those who need to sell their labour to survive goes beyond the workplace; it extends to fear of loss of home and mortgage, the fear of being robbed or burgled, the fear that our children are being poisoned by carbon-monoxide fumes or hamburgers, and – if the deluge of articles containing intimate advice about how to conduct relationships is anything to go by – the fear that we are now unable even adequately to reproduce the species. Far from being a nation at ease with itself, we are a nation in therapy.

Beyond this, we are also a nation under surveillance. The creed of laissez-nous faire applies only to finance and big business. The age of insecurity has brought forth its own instrument of political control, the new command economy, in which capital is free and working people have been nationalized. The citizen now fears not only the P45 and the UB40, but the knock on the door from the child-welfare inspector.

Our theme throughout this book is that we need social and economic justice, that it can be delivered, and that those who currently prevent us from having it include false friends as well as sworn enemies.

Larry Elliott and Dan Atkinson
London, January 1998

INTRODUCTION

HAPPY CHRISTMAS, WAR IS OVER

Who controls the past controls the future, as George Orwell memorably put it, and who controls the present controls the past.[1] We have moved on a little since Orwell's time, with the battle for control of the historical narrative now focused exclusively on the flat landscape of the ever-unfolding, amnesiac Present, the zone called Now. It is a battle waged with computers, communications devices and the latest in camera technology, all wielded by highly professional opinion formers and publicists, with their 'rebuttal' and 'attack' units, in the service of the big corporate and political interests. The French philosopher Régis Debray has compared the life of a nation with a novel written by its leader: 'all of us . . . are minor characters in a work of fiction beyond our understanding'.[2] Or, as the British army has put it in times of stress: 'who's writing the script?'

The drama that was Britain in 1997 was scripted to perfection, with the strong underlying theme of a grand synthesis, of (yet another) 'end of history'. Britain and, to a varying extent, other developed countries, had called a halt to the 200-year-old war between left and right. Its youthful leader Tony Blair had presided over a triumphant Armistice Day, in which both sides had, in time-honoured round-table fashion, been invited to make a contribution to a historic settlement. The right offered its economics, the left its compassion and the centre its tolerance. Those outside this Arthurian political system were primitives, barbarians or cynics; worse, they were 'irrelevant'. It is never pleasant to be shivering on a dark hillside when the youthful king is feasting with his courtiers in a warm banqueting hall. The temptation must be to make peace with the new order, to get back on stage with the rest of the cast, to work with the script rather than against it, to get 'on message'.

Nevertheless, there is – in the hackneyed schoolmaster's phrase – 'always one who has to spoil it', and there are those (ourselves included) who believe this spoiling role has a valuable function. In this spirit, we offer a potted alternative narrative concerning the events of 1997, a year that marked not a grand synthesis, a salvaging of all that was best from exhausted political traditions, but an intensification of the war to establish laissez-faire international capitalism as the single world social and economic system, beyond challenge. The compassionate yet dynamic New Britain (or New France, or New Europe) existed nowhere beyond the cover of *Time* magazine or the vacuous thousand-word newspaper features about 'Cool Britannia' or the post-Diana 'floral revolution'. The casualties of international capitalism's drive for supremacy were only too real. We believe the rival narratives represent different perspectives. The first is wishful thinking, the second the position on the ground. The left's supposed gains in 1997 were largely illusory, beginning with the chronological illusion bolstered merely by the fact that it was twenty years since the right's monetarist argument had begun to roll over the demoralized post-war consensus and that the wheel must have turned back by now.

In this scenario, two decades had elapsed since the collapse of the post-war system. In Britain, this had meant both the International Monetary Fund-imposed spending cuts of 1976 and, equally importantly, with the Bank of England's manoeuvres in the summer of 1977 to obviate the IMF Letter of Intent (which had stipulated the maintenance of manufacturing competitiveness) by keeping interest rates so high that sterling had to be uncapped. It had also affected the United States (where Jimmy Carter's 'new liberalism' – a forerunner of Bill Clinton's 'New Democrat' thinking – paved the way for deflationary policies); France (where President Giscard first 'locked in' the initial generation of long-term unemployed); Germany (where the hidden army of Turkish 'guest workers' took the strain of Chancellor Helmut Schmidt's anti-inflationary position).

Put simply, life had been pretty beastly since the mid-1970s and was now coming good again; even the distant bonfire of Northern Ireland, which had blazed so fiercely since the end of the 1960s, was about to be extinguished in the new mood of optimism, hope and compassion. It had to be so: the calendar does not lie.

Indeed, not since the late 1960s had the Great Ones of the Earth seemed so at one. Mr and Mrs Clinton dined with Mr and Mrs Blair in a trendy

London restaurant; Mr Blair lunched with Premier Lionel Jospin while holidaying in France; German Chancellor Kohl visited Chequers; Tony Blair appeared as himself in a Russian radio serial during a visit to President Boris Yeltsin; the handover of Hong Kong to Chinese rule allowed both Britain and China to appear 'positive' on the world's TV screens.

After two decades of confrontation, inequality, war, ideological conflict and intolerance, it was suggested, the pendulum had begun its long journey back again: once more, love (or a virtual approximation of the same) was all you needed.

Few suggestions are as welcome to the war-weary as the hint that an honourable draw – indeed, a sort of quasi-victory – is at hand. The suggestibility of exhausted veterans is twice as great when the tide of battle has been running strongly in the enemy's favour for some time.

In such a state of heightened suggestibility have been the defenders of the most successful socio-economic system the Western world has ever seen: the system known variously as social democracy, the mixed economy, 'social Gaullism', the Christian social tradition, the American free enterprise system (with the emphasis on the qualifying first and fourth words) and the post-war settlement. For eight long years, since the collapse of East European Communism, they have been fighting the one battle they thought they had won – that against laissez-faire capitalism – having unexpectedly triumphed in what they had imagined would be 'the main event', the struggle against Soviet totalitarianism and its Western proxies. Much as Harold Godwinson had to march from the victory of Stamford Bridge to engage a fresh army at Hastings, so Western social democrats have had to drag themselves from one front to another. And, as with King Harold, the second fight is not going well.

It does not help that laissez-faire's opponents are divided amongst themselves as to strategy; that some of their strongest garrisons hold forts that are not worth defending; that, by contrast, some of the most vital points in the line are wide open and that the rag, tag and bobtail high command – which includes disgruntled Old Labour peers, a few patrician Conservatives, an amalgam of former European Communist henchmen, the Pope, Prince Charles and the always-about-to-break-through green guerrilla leaders, not to mention unsavoury opportunists from the French right and American Republican Party – is unlikely to inspire confidence. In such a position, the idea that the struggle may, in contrast to appearances, be progressing fairly well is one likely to find a ready audience. And the hint that the enemy has actually sued for some sort of accommodation is more welcome still. From the first appearance of the Trojan horse to the ringing declaration of President de Gaulle to the Algerian colonists – 'Je vous ai compris' – history is rich in examples showing that the battle-scarred are easy to woo. But it is similarly rich in cautionary tales of the folly of the wooed.

In 1997, social democrats in Britain and, to a lesser extent, elsewhere in Europe lifted their heads above the trenches and heard news of a grand settlement. The war was, if not over, then at least in suspension, as a new breed of leaders from the 'dynamic centre' – principally Britain's Tony Blair, France's Lionel Jospin and the indulgent uncle of dynamic centrism, President Clinton – declared the ideological ceasefire permanent. To their surprise, the social democrats learned that their life-and-death struggle had never been very important in the first place and ought to be terminated without further casualties. Miles from the front line, the new centrist politicians had carved up a peace deal with international capitalism. True, there were big concessions to the latter: free movement of capital, complete deregulation of all investment, the permanent enthronement of sound-money financial policies, the dismantling of burdensome welfare systems and labour-market flexibility. But the dynamic centre had made gains as well, in terms of a more compassionate, tolerant, open and socially hygienic society.

A cursory inspection of these items would disclose the unavoidable fact that all the concrete concessions are on one side and all the empty expressions of good intentions on the other. Nor is this an academic point: working people – by whom we mean everyone who is reliant entirely upon their ability to sell their labour – lose not just once but possibly twice over in such a settlement. Their over-riding need is for physical, financial and material security, precisely those things that are signed away in such an agreement, whereas their cultural and class background may well make them the targets rather than the beneficiaries of the drive for social hygiene.

Put bluntly, few are likely to regard a Freedom of Information Act or a written constitution as fair compensation for the loss of job security. Crusades against drinking, smoking and fatty foods are more likely to add to their woes than to lighten their burden. And the display of conspicuous compassion for the generally poor victims of fashionable diseases is something they leave to celebrities and would-be celebrities.

In 1989, Austin Mitchell declared: 'Socialism is not about making everyone white collar and middle class like Labour MPs.'[3] Sad to say, that is now, in the Blair era, all that it is about. Given the lop-sided nature of the peace deal on offer, it would be pleasing to be able to report an outbreak of scepticism in the trenches, a refusal to abandon positions or weapons, a standing fast along the front. Regrettably, our social democrats, like the Trojans before them, caroused all night before falling into an alcohol-induced sleep. Only now are they perhaps becoming dimly aware of the shadowy figures clambering down from the belly of the wooden horse.

So how is the phoney peace going? A few dispatches from the various theatres of war may be helpful in assessing the peace terms on offer.

DISPATCH ONE: THE DOMESTIC FRONT

The Mall on 6 September 1997 saw scenes unprecedented since VE Day in 1945. As the funeral cortège moved north towards Diana's final resting place in the Midlands, Britain was at a standstill. Just one week after the French Interior Ministry stunned the world with the announcement that the Princess of Wales had perished in a car accident in central Paris, the final and climactic act in an extraordinary drama was being played out before the world's media. Normal life had been turned upside down: on the morning of the funeral there were few shops open, television and radio were given over almost completely to the tragedy (as they had been all week), and so extensive was the reorganization of London's road system to accommodate the event that it was some time before the funeral cortège came anywhere near an ordinary public highway. One million people lined the Finchley Road alone; these were the people who had queued through the night to sign books of condolence in St James's Palace. Floral tributes lay in great drifts outside Diana's home, Kensington Palace, placed there by a nation said to be unbuttoning itself at last.

As therapists and other 'experts' appeared in print and on the airwaves to instruct the British people in the appropriate manner of mourning, there were mutterings in some quarters about the 'grief police'. Even the Royal family bowed to the demands of 'emotional literacy': that they had grieved was not enough, the Royals had to be seen to grieve. The Queen duly appeared on television to confirm her sorrow at Diana's death and Prince Charles was required to appear outside Balmoral to inspect the wreaths with his two sons. Emotional literacy, it seemed, was another way of describing emotional fascism.

But the political Establishment had few doubts about the desirability of 'unbuttoned Britain'. One government minister quoted in the *Sunday Telegraph* on 7 September said: 'The British have had two hard decades. Tony and Diana have allowed them to get in touch with their emotions.' Three weeks later 'Tony' held centre stage at Labour's annual conference in Brighton, the first time in nineteen years that the movement had been addressed by a Labour prime minister. There was little sign of the 'unbuttoning of Britain' in the security arrangements for the gathering; rather, large chunks of the seafront and streets stretching a hundred yards inland were sealed off to ensure a sterile zone including the conference centre, the Grand and Metropole Hotels and the Odeon cinema complex. Overhead a police airship hovered in a security crackdown bigger than anything Mrs Thatcher ever demanded. Inside this impregnable fortress, the Prime Minister announced the beginning of the 'Giving Age'.

The Giving Age was to be strictly a spiritual experience. New Labour's early moves had included the abolition of student grants and the introduction of tuition fees; suggestions shortly after the conference that patients were to be charged as much as £10 a time to visit their doctors were not denied and Frank Field, one of Mr Blair's first appointments, laboured in the Department of Social Security to 'think the unthinkable' on welfare reform ('unthinkable' in this context translates as fully thought-out proposals for dismembering social security, proposals well trailed by right-wing think tanks). By the beginning of December, the government was embroiled in its first serious backbench revolt, triggered by its plans to cut benefits for lone parents. The disabled were next in line.

In November, Chancellor Gordon Brown's 'Green [discussion] Budget' had encapsulated the new thinking. No mention was made of controls of any sort on capital; such restrictions had long been abandoned by the Labour Party as neither possible nor desirable. But if it was impossible to control the movement of billions of pounds in and out of the country, no such inhibitions were expressed with regard to the control of alcohol and tobacco. Mr Brown had inherited a roaring black market in these goods, caused by the disparity between high British duties and the lower rates prevailing on the continent. Under single-market law, anyone could bring in any amount of such goods provided they could prove they were intended for personal consumption. Labour's response to the epidemic of bootlegging was to propose new coercive powers for customs. But then the Giving Age seemed unlikely to be intimately connected with a civil libertarian outlook. Labour ushered into law the Police Bill, bequeathed it by the outgoing Tory government, a measure allowing the law enforcement community to break into people's houses and tap their telephones without a court warrant, while simultaneously shifting towards an American-style no win, no fee system of litigation, outlawed in Britain in the Middle Ages. A few days after Labour's conference the rump of the Conservative Party boarded its clapped-out Virgin trains at Euston for its Blackpool post-mortem on its election defeat. Ex-ministers were given the opportunity to discover at first hand the reality of their railway privatization programme: dirty trains, endless and unfathomable delays, rivalling the darkest days of the British Rail era. Labour had not only accepted privatization, but was pledged to continue the process. During the 1997 election campaign it floated the idea of selling off air-traffic control to raise £500 million, and in October it announced its first sale: the Commonwealth Development Corporation, created by the Attlee government in 1948 to give priority in aid to the poorer countries of the Commonwealth.

Britain in the 1980s had been the world's test-bed for privatization, and the downsizing of the public sector was, in common with much of the Thatcherite legacy, embraced by Tony Blair. Few would deny that there had been successes among the many privatized entities, chiefly in those business areas where the government ought never to have been involved in the first place. Obvious examples are luxury hotels, duty-free shops, railway-station buffets. Nor can it be doubted that a second category of companies were arguably better off in the private sector as and when commercial and technological circumstances allowed: British Telecom, British Shipbuilders, British Petroleum and others. But absent from the Thatcher–Blair approach was any notion that the private sector was just that — a sector, not the whole of life.

Intimately linked with growing public disquiet over the results of inappropriate privatizations of common service organizations, such as water, electricity supply and railways, was national outrage as the former public servants, now turned 'entrepreneurs' in charge of the floated entities, indulged in an orgy of greed, gorging themselves on share options, bonuses, lavish pension deals and a range of other 'incentives'. Indeed, it seemed the less appropriate the initial privatization and the poorer the service to the public – water being the prime example – the more egregious the boardroom excesses.

Bosses across industry as a whole hurried to join in the party. Well-meaning attempts in the mid-1990s to regulate the feeding frenzy via committees of the great and good of British commerce were a dismal failure. In October 1997, the business ethics watchdog, PIRC, disclosed that the 'performance hurdles' set by industry bosses in both privatized and pre-existing big private companies were so laughably easy to jump in many cases that incentive plans would pay out even were the firms in question to be lagging badly behind their competitors. PIRC declared the pay-outs – due around the turn of the century – would spark fury amongst the general public.

All in all, the bosses of industry were rather like First World War generals, sitting comfortably in a château forty miles behind the front line, sipping fine wines culled from the cellar, while handing out orders to those in the mud and slime of the trenches to think of King and Country as they went over the top. The only difference this time was that the poor bloody infantry was urged instead to face longer hours or the dole queue, bearing in mind the company's need to survive ferocious global competition.

It was not so much the Giving Age as the Taking Age – at least for the favoured few. Even on its own terms, the Giving Age was turning sour by the end of 1997. The hysteria generated by the case of 'English nanny' (in fact an au pair) Louise Woodward, convicted by a jury in Massachusetts of murdering a baby in her care, exposed the darker side of 'Cool Britannia'. Americans sympathetic to the nineteen-year-old's plight, and concerned that the life sentence passed was unjust, were nonetheless appalled as the judge's quashing of the verdict triggered triumphalist scenes in her local pub back home, scenes beamed into living rooms across the United States. The tolerant 'New Britain' was exposed as a febrile, self-deluding sort of country in which the life of a child of mixed race counted for very little against the urgent need to get 'one of us' home from the clutches of one of the most liberal states of the union, transformed in the tabloid imagination into a Saudi Arabian-style autocracy.

Meanwhile, the Queen and Duke of Edinburgh ended the year quietly celebrating fifty years of marriage, while the despised 'buttoned-up' John Major basked in the interest of local and national journalists in the ornamental pond he was constructing in his garden in Great Stukeley. So rapid had been the 'cool' fever that its most high-profile victims seemed to be ending the year on something of an up, while its biggest beneficiary – Tony Blair – struggled with the aftermath of a 'sleaze' scandal of his very own, the now infamous decision to exempt Formula One motor racing from a proposed ban on tobacco sponsorship. In what was to seem a typical response to the disclosure that a leading Grand Prix promoter had given £1 million to the Labour movement only months before the election, Blair's government simultaneously protested its innocence, blamed the fund-raising system, suggested taxpayers ought to foot the bill for political activity and hinted at compulsory no-smoking areas in pubs and restaurants of a type that would drive hundreds of smaller establishments out of business.

As for the Formula One promoter, he received his money back from an embarrassed party. It gave the Giving Age a whole new meaning. As 1998 arrived, Labour was left thankful that the Conservatives remained divided and demoralized. William Straw, the seventeen-year-old son of Home Secretary Jack Straw, was arrested for supplying cannabis to a *Daily Mirror* reporter in a London pub. Mr Straw said it would make no difference to his opposition to legalization of cannabis. Meanwhile, the first stirrings of opposition to Labour's 'nannying' approach to health were prompted by the decision to ban the sale of beef on the bone because of a minuscule risk of contracting the human form of 'mad cow' disease. The centrepiece of the government's plan to celebrate the millennium, a giant £700 million dome in Greenwich, was also continuing to arouse hostility, particularly in the light of benefit cuts.

DISPATCH TWO:
THE EUROPEAN THEATRE

Continental bourses shuddered under a financial artillery barrage of a type they had never seen before. In a few frenzied days in the early autumn of

1997, a wave of cross-border mergers rocked Europe's once sleepy stock exchanges. It was a big push for laissez-faire against what had once been the bastion of the 'social tradition', the Rhineland corporate scene. Sympathetic war correspondents gloated that even France had now embraced the hostile takeover along with previously alien concepts such as 'shareholder value'.

Once again, the industrial infantry took enormous casualties as the financial interest cleaned up. In October 1997 alone, European companies axed thousands of jobs: international electrical engineering company ABB announced 10,000 job losses, equivalent to 8 per cent of its workforce; the rail transport joint venture Adtranz, supported by ABB and Daimler Benz, announced 3,600 job losses; and Sweden's rolling bearing maker SKF scrapped 2,000 posts. All this came on top of substantial employment losses at Siemens, the German electrical group, Electrolux, the Swedish household goods manufacturer, car makers Peugeot and Renault and tyre group Michelin. To add insult to injury, sacked continental workers learned from the bond gurus and think-tankers on capitalism's general staff that they had only themselves to blame for their plight; it was not the ferocity of the fighting that had felled them, but their own 'backward', pampered, flabby condition brought about by the now defunct European social model.

Capitalism's shock troops had every reason to press ahead on Europe's bourses, for they knew their not-so-secret ultimate weapon, the European single currency, the Euro, was in the final phase of construction. Governments in France, Germany and Italy pushed ahead with the 'reform' of their welfare states demanded by the monetary union criteria. By the end of 1997, few were bothering to pretend that the Euro was anything other than an instrument for Europe-wide deflation and the entrenchment of a monetarist agenda. By 22 October, even the US Deputy Secretary of the Treasury Larry Summers felt it sufficiently uncontroversial and diplomatic to disclose to readers of the *Financial Times* Washington's view that:

Policymakers cannot afford to allow EMU [Economic and Monetary Union] to distract them from pursuing fundamental reforms. As we have seen in the recent flood of cross-country mergers and acquisitions, the European private sector is already responding to the new situation. Governments need to build on the growing consensus in favour of reform and put it to work achieving genuine changes on the ground.

The 'consensus' of which Mr Summers wrote applied, of course, only among US and European elites.

On 22 October1997, Martin Walker wrote in the *Guardian*:

The budgetary austerity and 'reform' of the traditional welfare state which are now being imposed to let Italy, France and Germany meet the financial qualifications for the euro represent a form of Thatcherism by stealth. . . . Mass unemployment in Germany and France go hand in hand with a wild stock-market boom. Inflation appears tamed, but the real incomes of most Europeans have been stagnant or declining while corporate profits and stock prices have been soaring.

DISPATCH THREE:
THE PACIFIC THEATRE

Not since Joseph Stalin finally accepted, some days after the event, that his 'ally' Adolf Hitler had invaded the Soviet Union had there been a falling out as spectacular as that between the 'Asian tigers' and international capitalism in the summer and autumn of 1997. Malaysia's Prime Minister Dr Mahathir, promoted for more than a decade as an oriental Mrs Thatcher, ranted publicly about Jewish conspiracies as Kuala Lumpur's stock market dived and the ringgit collapsed, thanks in part to the man with the golden gun, billionaire speculator George Soros. Neighbouring Thailand had been the first victim of a scramble for the exit by the same international capitalists who had long lauded 'Asia Pacific' as a dynamic place where tomorrow was happening today. So severe was the Thai crash that the government had been forced to beg International Monetary Fund assistance. Hit also were Indonesia and the Philippines as speculators decided the previously praised economic management of these 'tigers' had in fact been irresponsibly over-expansionary.

The contagion seemed at first to be containable, confined as it was to the 'new tigers' – alias the 'little dragons' – and far away from those Far Eastern economies that were the founder members of the tiger club: Singapore, Hong Kong, South Korea and Taiwan. That illusion was shattered by the end of October 1997: South Korea and Singapore staggered under a wave of speculation and, in the week ending 25 October, Hong Kong found itself the centre of the storm. As Beijing-appointed chief executive C. H. Tung wooed investors and industrialists in London, the Hang Seng Index registered its biggest ever fall as interest rates were jacked up to hold the Hong Kong dollar in line with the US currency. Mr Tung declared his willingness to spend the whole of the territory's foreign-exchange reserves: $86 billion.

But the crisis was far from being contained; by the end of November South Korea had faced the ultimate humiliation of having to approach the IMF for a loan some said could total $100 billion. The country's once-touted system of industrial combines clustered around banks was found to be riddled with sour loans. Most seriously of all, the first and greatest of the Asian economies – Japan – ended 1997 in a state of near collapse. One of its big four brokers – Yamaichi – went bust. Commentators suggested half the country's banks had serious solvency problems and the government was forced to release enormous sums of liquidity to prevent the Tokyo market from going into free fall. Whereas the West could shrug its shoulders at the crisis in Thailand, by the time the domino effect threatened to topple Japan, alarm bells were ringing across Europe and America. Politicians and financial gurus were dusting off their histories of the 1930s and noting that the Great Depression had started with the collapse of one small Austrian bank.

This atomic cloud of financial destruction was matched in the real world by a huge pall of carcinogenic smoke drifting from Indonesian Borneo across the region. Slash-and-burn capitalism at its most basic had run out of control as landowners friendly with the Indonesian government, allowed to set fire to the rainforest as the cheapest way of clearing land for cultivation, had continued this practice despite a recent drought with the entirely predictable result that much of the island became a raging inferno. Nobody denied this was the biggest environmental disaster of all time, easily dwarfing the 1986 Chernobyl nuclear power station meltdown in terms of long-term effects. Medical services struggled to treat children damaged for life by the smog as the authorities dispensed face masks as a rough and ready protection against the filthy air.

What was the response of the West to these twin crises? Was it to begin work on capital controls and tough environmental standards? On the contrary; at the IMF conference in Hong Kong in September, Thailand's finance minister and central bank governor were paraded before the world's press to confess their economic sins and promise to sign up for whatever austerity package was on offer. Meanwhile, in October, after ferocious lobbying by the oil and car industries, the United States postponed until between 2008 and 2012 measures that would cut greenhouse-gas emissions to their 1990 levels.

No such delay was to be tolerated by the United States when it came to the latest free trade proposals. Quite the opposite. Both a new deal to liberalize financial services and a charter permitting inward investors free rein across the world were matters of the highest priority in Washington, DC. The White House, acting on behalf of Wall Street, demanded that the world agree by midnight on 12 December to the deregulation of all financial and banking services. At 11 p.m. on 12 December the world duly obliged. The next step was to be a Multilateral Agreement on Investment, a multinationals' charter that would leave countries such as Thailand even more exposed than they were already to the vagaries of international capitalism.

Some poorer countries, particularly after their experience of the World Trade Organization (WTO) – the body that polices nation-states to ensure they are obeying free trade rules – may have doubts about signing away more economic control to such multilateral bodies. One example would be the banana-producing current and former British and French colonies of the Caribbean, which have enjoyed preferential access to the European Union. In 1997, spurred on by Chiquita, a US-owned company with banana plantations in Latin America, Washington fought and won a WTO case forcing the EU to drop its quota system, even though this spelt economic ruin for many small Caribbean producers such as the Windward Islands, which were one-commodity economies. As a footnote, the day after Washington lodged the case with the WTO in Geneva, Chiquita handed $500,000 to the Democratic Party.

These, then, were the armistice terms on offer: anything damaging to international capital and big business can be shelved or dismissed as impractical (in terms of capital controls, for example). Anything helpful to the financial interest is to receive action without delay.

One's view of a battle depends on one's perspective of the spectator. We accept that there will be those who urge social democrats to seize the peace terms as the best, or even the only, terms on offer. These are people who have accepted the bulk of the right's defence of the free market and believe that any unfortunate side-effects can be tweaked out of existence by benign legislation, concentration on education and training and 'international co-operation'. Whereas once they saw capital as the universal wolf which had to be caged, they now see it as a frisky thoroughbred stallion that can be broken in by a suitably caring and understanding trainer. The right itself differs only in that it believes that the beast is ready-trained and has no need of the caring ministrations of the centre and centre-left. Elimination of all capital controls, complete free trade in services as well as goods, and the deregulation of both labour and product markets are not the problem but the solution. Only backsliding by those who would try to stand in the way of the invisible hand of the market can prevent the world from entering into a new era of undreamed-of prosperity. Everything, from this perspective, is going swimmingly.

This book takes the opposite view. We do not deny that the twenty years from the late 1970s to the late 1990s have seen the triumph of capital and big business values, and indeed the first chapters explain how this has come about. But we would argue that the system thus created has failed, even in its own terms, and left the global economy chronically unstable and poised on the brink of a social and environmental chasm. Nor, as we shall show in the coming pages, are we enamoured of the various ways proposed by the new business-friendly left to accommodate itself to the international capitalist order: we identify an unappetizing menu of leftist options, comprising two overseas sources of inspiration – Bill Clinton's America and the European Union – and two domestic recipes – constitutional reform and social authoritarianism. We argue not only that there is scant chance of any of these having the desired effect, but also that there is little, if anything, about them that is left-wing, in the traditional meaning of the term.

Our objection to the new world order is twofold. First, at a practical level, it does not function properly. But even if it did, it would be objectionable in moral terms, since at the heart of the laissez-faire system is the unjust sharing of risk that both in the developed West and, far more acutely and often fatally, in the poor countries of the south, has created an Age of Insecurity for ordinary people.

The answer, we conclude, is to put the wolf back in the cage. And, this time, to keep it there.

CHAPTER ONE

RIGHT ON: THE RISE AND FALL OF ENTERPRISE CULTURE

It is a civilisation in which children grow up with an intimate knowledge
of magnetoes and in complete ignorance of the Bible.
George Orwell, 'The Lion and the Unicorn'

Libraries should open during evenings and Sundays, according to the first
Government report on the service for more than 30 years. It concludes
that they are part of the entertainment world and must compete by
providing high-tech reference sections and low-brow books outside
usual working hours.
The Times, 20 February 1997

'You know . . . I think government has to be very careful about throttling
small businesses.'
'The bank's not actually a small business.'
'It will be if we throttle it, Bernard.'
from *Yes, Minister* (BBC TV, 1980–82)

Scene: The bedroom of a family-run hotel in Torquay. It is morning, but the
room is in semi-darkness because the curtains are drawn. A man in pyjamas
is sitting up in bed with his head slumped on his chest. He is obviously dead.
Enter Basil Fawlty bearing a breakfast tray.

BASIL: 'Another car strike. Marvellous isn't it? The taxpayers pay them millions each year
so they can go on strike. It's called socialism. If they don't like making cars why don't
they get themselves another bloody job, like designing cathedrals or composing violin

concertos? That's it, the British Leyland concerto in four movements, all of them slow, with a four-hour tea break in the middle.'

Basil Fawlty is arguably the funniest character ever created for British television. He epitomized the frustrations and discontent of the middle classes in the 1970s, the pivotal decade of the post-war period. As played by John Cleese, Basil was symbolic of a nation on the edge of a nervous breakdown, where nothing seemed to work properly, the established order of things was under threat from assorted 'rubbish and riff-raff' (as Basil politely described guests who failed to live up to his high expectations) and the external world was both frightening and hostile. There were only two series of *Fawlty Towers*, twelve half-hour shows in all, but the first was broadcast in 1975, when inflation reached a post-war peak of 27 per cent, and the second in early 1979, during the Winter of Discontent. In fact, only five of the six episodes of the second series were shown at that time; the sixth was blacked out by an industrial dispute among TV technicians, something Basil would no doubt have seen as entirely typical of the new anarchic world of 'socialism'.

In the 1990s, Basil Fawlty remains the classic portrait of the middle class under stress. Years before the concept of 'road rage' was imported from America, the manic hotel proprietor was thrashing his decrepit Austin 1100 with a branch snapped from a roadside tree because it stalled and refused to restart. He spoke for all those members of the bourgeoisie who, in the 1970s, saw their standard of living squeezed by inflation, their sense of class superiority challenged by the influence of the trade unionists parading in and out of 10 Downing Street for 'beer and sandwiches', and their sense of decency affronted by hippies, punks and those – to quote David Bowie – who were not sure if they were boys or girls. Basil does his best to keep up appearances with his attempts at false sophistication – 'some of the people we get in here wouldn't know the difference between a bordeaux and a claret'. Guest: 'A bordeaux is a claret' – but stumbles from disaster to disaster. To middle-class eyes, to those people who founded the National Association for Freedom in 1975 and were convinced that Harold Wilson was a Communist, Fawlty Towers was the Britain of the 1970s: riven by conflict, indifferent to the needs of customers, held back by shoddy workmanship. Interestingly, perhaps, the only person who could make the hotel work was Basil's gorgon of a wife, Sybil. Like another woman coming to prominence in the mid-1970s, she was middle-aged, blonde, shrill, philistine and utterly ruthless.

SIGNS OF THE TIMES: MARIANNE FAITHFULL TO ROAD RAGE

Culture matters. This is not, and is not intended to be, a cultural history of post-war Britain. But cultural change has been an important harbinger of a changing economic and political climate. Of course, there are times when political change produces cultural change, but more often the causality is the other way round. The three-year period from 1973 to 1976 marked the end of the post-war system: a period of unprecedented growth, peace and stability in the West that had seen living standards rise rapidly for all sections of the population and for all countries. In its place came the Age of Insecurity, built on the idea that workers had had it too easy for too long and that lasting prosperity could be guaranteed only if people accepted the need to knuckle down and change the habits of the previous thirty years. From the standpoint of the late 1990s, the laissez-faire counter-revolution seems to have an air of inevitability about it. But that was not how it seemed at the time. The Conservatives had just suffered four election defeats out of five and were being written off as a south-east England regional party; in America the Republicans were tainted by defeat in Vietnam and the sleaze of Watergate. Had the new-right counter-revolution amounted only to the economics of Milton Friedman, the philosophy of Friedrich von Hayek and the politics of Margaret Thatcher, it is unlikely that it would have made much more than a dent in the Keynesian post-war edifice. The fact is, however, that Thatcher and Ronald Reagan were cutting with the grain of cultural change, and were able to fashion a new consensus of their own from the fears of the middle classes and the aspirations of the blue-collar working class. Although the *coup de grâce* for the post-war system was the economic crisis that stemmed from the Yom Kippur war in the autumn of 1973, changes to where people lived, how they spent their leisure time and how they perceived themselves, all lay behind a gradual erosion of the collectivist cement that held the West together in the era of Beveridge and the Beatles.

It is our contention that the 1990s could prove to be as pivotal a decade as the 1970s, but this time the winds of cultural change are blowing from a different quarter. Once again, the system seems to be on the point of break-down, but this time it is the right's model that is being found wanting. Where Basil Fawlty merely indulged in some mild flagellation of his old jalopy, now motorists are forced off the road and stabbed to death. Where once crime seemed to be confined to the criminal classes, now everybody lives in fear of random psychopaths, serial killers, and the rootless underclass. Where once the epitome of Western moral decay was Marianne Faithfull and her alleged antics with a Mars Bar, now it is fashion models too stoned on heroin to work. Where once Big Government's failure to protect the environment was measured by how many hedgerows disappeared, now the ecological tragedy of small government is seen in disappearing rainforests and global warming.

In short, the coalition that supported laissez-faire and the rise of big busi-ness from the mid-1970s is now looking as vulnerable as Keynesian social democracy did then. In the 1980s, Thatcherism appeared to be an unstop-pable juggernaut – combining as it did the support of intellectuals, the private-sector bourgeoisie and large chunks of Labour's old blue-collar con-stituency. But in the 1990s, parts of the juggernaut started to drop off, until in the end all that remained was a piece of rusting bodywork, going nowhere.

The political consequence of this cultural shift has been some spectacular political victories for the left, not just in Britain but also in France, Canada and the United States. There is the possibility that the first few decades of the twenty-first century will see a left-wing hegemony that will haul the West back from the brink of social, economic and environmental disaster. But for the moment that looks unlikely, primarily because of a lack of courage and a lack of vision on the part of nominally left-wing parties. Blair and Clinton talk of 'young' and 'new' countries, suggesting that they are aware of some of the cultural cross-currents of the 1990s, but their instinct is to change little. They talk the language of big business, of globalization and of mone-tarism and seek to construct a homogeneous all-inclusive global politics to match a homogenized global culture.

This is woefully misguided, and risks squandering a once-in-a-lifetime opportunity for the left. The free-market right did not spend the thirty years after the war finding ways of accommodating to Keynesianism; it fought col-lectivism all the way from Hayek's *The Road to Serfdom* in 1944 to the founding of the Centre for Policy Studies thirty years later. It went with the grain of cultural change, not against it, and as a result, was perfectly placed to capitalize fully when Keynesianism ran aground in the mid-1970s.

We intend to take some time examining the cultural reasons behind the rise of the free-market right, an ascendancy which, as we shall see, was prefigured by changes in sport, entertainment, technology and movements of population. For, unless the left is content to have merely the trappings of power, it is important that it understands how and why the right was able to push through its radical manifesto over the past twenty years.

CREATIVE TENSION: THE BIG MAC AND THE END OF HISTORY

The main lesson for the left from the rise of the market is that not only does culture matter, but that it functions through a fundamental antagonism. The energy of rock 'n' roll came both from the clash and fusion of two different musical traditions, black rhythm and blues and white crooning, and from the way it immediately set teenagers against the parents. The best comedy is also based on competition: between the funny man and the straight man as in *Morecambe and Wise*, or between working class and middle class as in *Whatever Happened to the Likely Lads?*. Cultural struggle is permanent; there is no preordained, deterministic end-point, in which McDonald's, Walt Disney and Coca Cola inevitably exert a totalitarian grip on the way we live. Globalization and the reach of multinationals have certainly produced a model based on cultural homogeneity, but it is as inherently unstable as the post-war system, and perhaps even more so given its reliance on inequality and its cavalier attitude to unemployment and the environment. Just as in the early 1970s the right's almost total capitulation to the orthodoxy of ever higher public spending on maintaining full employment was a sell signal for Keynesianism, so the 'end of history' as proclaimed by Francis Fukuyama in his book coincided with the first stirrings of a cultural backlash against the insecurity engendered by the policies of the new right. This is acknowledged by the new right itself. As Richard Cockett concluded in his book on laissez-faire think tanks: 'Far from it being the End of History, we are now at the point where the counter-revolution against liberalism will start.'[1] The remainder of this chapter will seek to explain some of the cultural tensions that helped shape the politics and economics of the modern world. There is, for example, an obvious antagonism between the local and the global which takes in a separate battle between environmentalism and materialism. There has been an ebb and flow in the struggle between the individual and the collective, as there has between freedom and control, nostalgia and modernism, workers and bosses, and consumers and producers. However, the focal point of cultural antagonism over the coming years – and one which will touch upon all the others – will be between the desire for 'home' and the dictates of 'business'. The left cannot be on both sides of this fundamental struggle, much though it would love to give the impression that it can. We have no doubt on which side of the fence it should come down; nor, sadly, on which side it will.

HOMEWARD BOUND: CULTURE RETURNS TO BASE

Even a cursory glance at toddlers playing hide-and-seek illustrates how powerful the idea of 'home' is in our culture. Home is where they have to race back in order to be safe. It is an instinct that stays with the child as he or she grows up; for both the young couple buying their flat-pack furniture in IKEA and the pensioner refusing to go into sheltered accommodation, home means security and independence. Nye Bevan provided one of the best expositions of this need when he said: 'The assertion of anti-socialists that private economic adventure is a desirable condition stamps them out as profoundly unscientific. You can make your home the base for your adventures, but it is absurd to make the base itself an adventure.'[2]

Two key elements stand out in this passage. First, and most obviously, there is the mention of 'home', a metaphor for employment, steady income, decent housing, health and welfare. Here is one of the planks of the post-war system: security, at any cost, and as an over-riding objective of policy. Less obvious is the second element, Bevan's 'adventures'. He was not prescribing, as a sort of trade-off for security, the adoption of a subdued, stolid, social persona of the type associated (however unfairly) with the Scandinavian social democracies. The 'safe' home was to be the platform from which individuals would be able to pursue the great adventure of life. This adventure was to be every bit as thrilling as it had been in days gone by but without the terror of poverty, starvation or the dole. The title of the book from which the quote has been extracted encapsulates this aim: *In Place of Fear*. Eight years before the dawn of the 1960s, Bevan trumpeted a new social and cultural ideal: adventure without risk. The home–adventure alliance provided the cultural foundation for the post-war system. It lay behind the creation of the cradle-to-grave Welfare State in the late 1940s and it was the guiding light for a generation dedicated to the pursuit of rising living standards and greater self-expression. There was a compact, unspoken perhaps, between the unionized working class, to whom the 'home' concept was a guarantee of personal security, and the newly liberated intellectual middle class, to whom the promise of adventure was an invitation to explore new lifestyles.

For thirty years after 1945 the home–adventure alliance proved successful not just in Britain but across the Western world. Indeed, as the 1950s drew to an end, it gradually dawned on the British political Establishment that other countries – France, Germany and America – were doing much better, and that Japan was starting to catch up fast. This sense of relative decline was to preoccupy both Conservative and Labour governments in the 1960s, and in the 1970s turned into a fear that Britain might be facing not just mid-table mediocrity but relegation to a lower division. Even so, in comparison to any previous or subsequent period, 1945–73 was a veritable Golden Age. Unemployment, which had hit 22 per cent during the Depression, stayed well below 500,000, and only started to edge up in the late 1960s. Inflation moved up and down according to the economy's position in the stop–go cycle, and although the trend became clearly upward as the post-war system started to creak under the strain, it mainly stayed within a range of 0–4 per cent. Growth rose by 3 per cent on average, productivity likewise, investment grew by around 6 per cent a year from 1950 until the 1960s, tailed off to 2 per cent from 1968 to 1973, and then virtually stagnated for the rest of the 1970s. Although in the 1940s and early 1950s, with memories of the Depression and the privations of the Second World War still fresh, it is hardly surprising that the emphasis was on 'home', from the mid-1950s onwards there was a reaction against the oppressiveness and conformity prevailing in Eisenhower's America and Eden's Britain. The 1960s saw the 'adventure' part of the equation become more prominent. The state became more liberal in social policy, passing the civil rights and Great Society legislation in the United States; abolishing the death penalty, legalizing abortion and homosexuality, relaxing censorship, and making divorce easier in the UK. In short, the government increasingly saw its job as being tough on big business, and soft on the people. But there were limits. There was not the 'anything goes' mystique that the current right-wing mythology would suggest. The Summer of Love reached its zenith on 25 June 1967 when pictures of the Beatles garbed in psychedelia and singing 'All You Need is Love' were beamed around the world in the first-ever global satellite link-up. Four days later two members of the Rolling Stones, Mick Jagger and Keith Richards, were jailed for possession of drugs. William Rees-Mogg, then editor of *The Times*, attacked the sentence as heavy-handed in an editorial which took Pope's 'Who Breaks a Butterfly on a Wheel?' as its inspiration. But there is little evidence that the mass of the British public were inclined to support Mr (now Lord) Rees-Mogg. It was generally held that the Beatles – particularly John Lennon – had gone a little weird after they grew moustaches, and when the group's manager, Brian Epstein, admitted that he had taken LSD the outrage was so great that the matter was raised on the floor of the House of Commons, and the Home Office, run by the arch-liberal, Roy Jenkins, issued an official statement saying it was 'horrified' that so important a figure had been dabbling in mind-bending and dangerous hallucinogenics. Similarly, the authorities came down with a crushing show of force on pirate radio stations in the same year, with Tony Benn pushing through the Marine Broadcasting (Offences) Act in August 1967, and the state reflected public abhorrence at the Moors murders, the gangland wars between the Krays and the Richardsons, and the murder of three policemen by Harry Roberts with life sentences that, in all three cases, are still being served.

The bargain had been that the government would take care of jobs and welfare, leaving individuals free to organize their own private lives – provided that they did not go too far. Moderation and tolerance – both values that the British considered themselves to be rich in – were needed if the post-war order was to survive. Once people started to overstep the mark, as they did when the 1960s melted into the 1970s, it was doomed.

ENTERPRISE INITIATIVE: FREE ECONOMY, STRONG STATE

Within a decade, 'home–adventure' had been supplanted by 'business culture', and the role of government had been turned on its head. The language of business culture was all about economic freedom – giving management back the right to manage, shaking off the 'dead hand' of the state, liberating the talents of the people, rolling back the frontiers of collectivism, and so on. But its weapons were order, discipline and control. The fundamental philosophy behind the rise of the managerial counter-revolution was that the Welfare State had made the nation soft and flabby, and in particular that the workforce was more likely to be found on a wildcat strike or hidden in a corner of a factory engrossed in a card school than doing the jobs for which its members were being generously paid. Britain's continued economic woes (in comparison to its competitors) and – as we shall see – a backlash against bureaucracy and some of the illiberality associated with union power meant that 'business culture' swept all before it in the 1980s and early 1990s. Central to the philosophy, part of the return to Victorian values, was a new formality. The home–adventure concept was too loose and flexible; there was plenty of 'give' provided that nobody went too far. The language of the Keynesian era was one of partnership and tolerance, even when participants were at each other's throats. By contrast, the 'business culture' was coldly formal; it was defined by rigid codes of behaviour, established performance targets and strict surveillance. Companies, even government departments, were given given mission statements to define their role, and staff were trained and retrained to think in the 'right' way. The talk was all of 'downsizing' and 're-engineering'; the sole judge of performance was the 'bottom line'. No organization was immune from this revolution; the NHS started to talk about customer through-put when it meant getting patients out of hospital as soon as was decently possible (and sometimes sooner), the BBC was colonized by management consultants intent on breaking the unified Reithian structure into autonomous 'profit centres'. One leading cleric, speaking a month or so after the death of Diana, Princess of Wales, said that a 'lack of resources' was making the Church unable to cope with the numbers of people seeking spiritual help. Presumably, had it not been for a 'lack of resources' – only five loaves and two fishes – the Good Lord would have been able to feed the entire population of Galilee and not just the five thousand.

Academia, too, was invaded by the business ethic, with dons spending time courting corporate sponsors to make up funding deficits or else trying to raise their media profiles with 'sensational' new discoveries in science, history or literature. Tom Stoppard, an arch-critic of the home–adventure coalition in its dying days, had turned his fire on the new order by the early

1990s. In his play *Arcadia*, an English professor cuts corners to prove that Byron killed a rival in a duel at a country house.[3] He is scornful of a rival's old-fashioned scholarship, which involves actually investigating the evidence properly, and preens himself on the way he is about to astound both his colleagues in academia and the wider public. His paper, he boasts, will be 'Very dry, very modest, absolutely gloat-free, and yet unmistakably "Eat your heart out, you dozy bastards". But first it's Media Don, book early to avoid disappointment.' His rival warns: 'Bernard . . . you're arrogant, greedy and reckless.' She is proved right, but not before he has been given airtime on the 'Breakfast Hour' to promote his crackpot theory.

The 'business culture', too, is arrogant, greedy and reckless: arrogant because it brooks no opposition – there is only one model and workers have to be drilled until they get the message; greedy because it has swallowed up traditional ways of doing things, seeing no reason why, for example, education should be an end in itself rather than simply a functional mechanism for providing business with plentiful and adequately docile supplies of labour; and reckless because, in the end, the 'business culture' has been blind to its own contradiction, namely that there is a disparity between the individual as consumer with unlimited choice and the knowledge that he or she is always 'right' and the individual as producer, to be subjected to ever more stringent control. A typical business in the 1990s wants its own workforce to be cowed by de-unionization, labour-market flexibility and the threat of the sack, but the workforce of every other business to spend until it drops, taking advantage of financial deregulation to gear up its borrowing. Little wonder, then, that the decade has given rise to a radical culture of insecurity, in which individuals are not sure whether the advice given in the glossy magazines about the need for parents to spend more time with their children might put them in the boss's black book, and in which the 'nothing is for nothing' world seems soulless, empty and cold.

OH WHAT A LOVELY WAR: THE 1940S AND THE HIGH NOON OF COLLECTIVISM

In the mid- to late 1990s, the political consequences of this cultural upheaval have become evident. There has been a swing, albeit gradual, back towards a belief in more active forms of government. In an anxious age, people have turned to the state for reassurance. Before we explore in this book whether they are likely to find the helping hand they are looking for, we need to find how the dynamics of post-war culture have changed.

Clement Attlee showed what could be done. It was he who presided over the high noon of British collectivism although, contrary to popular belief, this occurred during the war, when Attlee as deputy prime minister was left in charge of the home front while Churchill was preoccupied by military strategy, rather than during Labour's six and a half years in power following its landslide election victory in July 1945. The very real threat of invasion in 1940 and the need to mobilize the nation for total war meant that Attlee, Dalton, Bevin and Morrison were free to prosecute the purest form of socialism ever seen in Britain. Industries seen as vital to the war effort were taken under public control, Bevin's Ministry of Labour became the engine of industrial production, converting factories to war use, planning centrally, directing labour. Keynesian ideas — and Keynes himself — were permitted access to the Treasury, where pre-war thinking about balanced budgets and laissez-faire had as much salience between 1940 and 1945 as the ideas of the Munich appeasers. The role of the Chancellor of the Exchequer — few could now name any of the holders of this great office between September 1939 and July 1945 — was much diminished. Moreover, as almost every chronicler of the period has detailed, there was a mood of national unity, of sacrifice for the common good, of fair shares for all. The high point of collectivism was between the evacuation of Dunkirk in June 1940 and the publication of the Beveridge Report in November 1942, but there was little evidence of any significant ebbing of the tide until the end of the war, indeed well into 1946. The culture of the period reflected both the strength of purpose and the refusal to accept a return to the conditions and insecurity of the 1930s. The sense that Britain, essentially a deferential culture, had been let down by its ruling elite, comes through powerfully in the 1943 Ealing film, *Went the Day Well?*, in which a small English village is taken over by German paratroopers disguised as British infantrymen. At first, the trusting villagers are taken in by the plausible Germans, but they gradually realize not just that they have been duped but that the local squire, to whom everyone has looked for guidance, is a fifth columnist in league with the enemy. Despite being in a seemingly helpless position, the villagers band together, with everyone down to the local poacher having a part to play in thwarting the Germans. The class message of the film is blatant; it is the poacher, society's outcast, who ensures that the alarm is raised, it is the squire who in the film's climax is shot by his girlfriend for his treachery.

By the war's end, the British wanted to see the advances made between 1940 and 1945 consolidated. They wanted to see the Beveridge Report put into action; they wanted homes and jobs, they wanted to see the commanding heights of the economy in safe state hands rather than risk a rerun of private ownership. As one of the demobbed soldiers puts it in J. B. Priestley's 1945 novel *Men in Three Suits*:

'We don't want the same kind of men looking after our affairs as pre-war. We act as if we've learnt something. . . . We don't go back on all we said when the country was in danger. We stop trying for some easy money. We do an honest job of work for the community for what the community thinks we're worth. We stop being lazy, stupid and callous. . . . Instead of guessing and grabbing, we plan. Instead of competing, we co-operate.'[4]

Attlee's strength in 1945 was that millions of people across Britain shared Priestley's dream. The Conservatives had been pushed back to their rural and seaside redoubts, with Labour winning six out of seven seats in Norfolk and cathedral towns such as Winchester and St Albans for the first time. The call was for a fresh start, to ensure, first, that there was no repeat of the post-1918 betrayal that culminated in the General Strike of 1926, but also to offer the hope of a better future to returning servicemen. The new Labour government had its problems, however, not least that Britain had been bankrupted by war. A quarter of the nation's stock of wealth had been eaten up, exports had all but vanished as production was concentrated on machine guns, tanks and planes, and overseas indebtedness had soared. Barely had the bunting come down after VJ Day than Keynes was dispatched to Washington with HMG's begging bowl. The great economist had described the incoming government as facing 'a financial Dunkirk' and eventually (but not before some stringent conditions, notably the convertibility of sterling, were imposed by American officials for whom the distinction between socialism and Communism was doubtful) negotiated a $3.75 billion loan to help Britain avoid a balance of payments crisis.

A subsidiary problem was one that has troubled every Labour occupant of

10 Downing Street: how to hold together the coalition of class interests that had brought Labour its 146-seat majority. The middle classes may have been prepared to forgo their creature comforts in wartime; there was no guarantee that they would continue to be self-sacrificing once the fighting was over. This, then, was the tension that ran through the Attlee government during the late 1940s and early 1950s. The economic crisis, exacerbated by the fuel shortages in the unusually harsh winter of 1947, meant that rationing was even more draconian in peacetime than it had been when the U-boats were stalking Allied convoys. Rationing influenced the collectivist timbre of the age, because there were few consumer goods in the shops to buy. By 1950, only 10 per cent of people in Britain had access to a TV set, so it was the heyday of the dance hall, the pub, the cinema and mass spectator sports such as football and cricket. In the era of Ealing comedies in 1949, cinema audiences were running at 30 million a week, and there were more customers at the Odeons and Gaumonts in a fortnight than there were in an entire year when the industry hit its nadir in the early 1980s. Football audiences also reached all-time peaks, while the handful of die-hards who today turn up at county championship cricket matches would be taken aback by the 'Ground full' signs outside Headingley or Old Trafford to watch Len Hutton opening the batting in one of the two annual Bank Holiday Roses matches between Yorkshire and Lancashire, and by the willingness of London office workers to rush off to Lord's after work in the hope of catching a glimpse of Denis Compton at the crease in his *annus mirabilis* of 1947.

As Neville Cardus wrote:

In 1947, summer sun so blessed England, which was still licking its war wounds. Never have I been so deeply touched on a cricket ground as I was in this heavenly summer, when I went to Lord's to see a pale-faced crowd, existing on rations, the rocket bombs still in the ears of most folk — to see this worn, dowdy crowd watching Compton. The strain of long years of anxiety and affliction passed from all hearts and shoulders at the sight of Compton in full flow, sending the ball here, there and everywhere, each stroke a flick of delight, a propulsion of happy sane healthy life. There was no rationing in an innings by Compton.[5]

The signs of stress become visible in Cardus's essay. The working-class segment of Labour's coalition was dependable; it remained faithful to the idea of fair shares and was kept sweet by the increased spending on health, education and pensions which, by and large, it did not have to pay for itself. But the middle classes grew increasingly restless at the lack of consumer choice and the puritanical zeal with which the government policed its controls, necessary though they were for economic revival.

The working class stayed loyal with good reason, for the Labour government stayed loyal to it. When Hugh Dalton came to write his account of the post-war Attlee government, he said this:

> So we went, each of us to his battle station, and I to the Treasury, to encounter most grave problems, wide opportunities, heavy strains, hard choices. But through it all I was to be sustained by the strength and comradeship and understanding of our great Parliamentary majority. And we all knew that, within us, and because of us, and around us, something had suddenly changed.
>
> > England arise, the long, long night is over:
> > Faint in the East behold the dawn appear.[6]

The phrase 'hard choices' was repeated fifty years later by Tony Blair, when he too formed an administration with an overwhelming mandate. But whereas for Blair 'hard choices' means cutting benefits to single mothers, imposing tuition fees on students and 'thinking the unthinkable' on the Welfare State, for Dalton, Cripps and Attlee it meant something quite different. Hard choices meant safeguarding spending on welfare, even at a time of large-scale overseas commitments, and if necessary increasing taxes on those who could afford them. Soundbites were not part of the lexicon of politics in 1945, but had he adopted one, Attlee's would not have been 'hard choices'. It would have been 'fair shares'.

Dalton, the first post-war Chancellor, made it clear where his priorities lay when he announced in 1946: 'Twice in our lifetime we have banished unemployment in wartime. Now we must banish it in peace. I will find, with a song in my heart, all the money necessary for sound constructive schemes.' Dalton's first decision as Chancellor was to nationalize the Bank of England. According to his biographer: 'We're going to nationalize the Bank', the new Chancellor told his private secretary on the Monday after his appointment. 'We don't know how, but we're going to do it. Get the appropriate fellow to draw up the plans.'[7]

Ironically, the first decision of Gordon Brown, when he arrived at the Treasury in May 1997, also concerned the Bank of England. Mr Brown, however, decided that the Bank should be given back control over setting interest rates. He did not need 'an appropriate fellow' to draw up the plans. His senior adviser had them already prepared.

In 1997, the Bank acted as central banks tend to, putting up interest rates. Dalton, by contrast, followed a policy of cheap money. Base rates remained unchanged at 2 per cent between 1945 and 1951 (indeed they had been at 2 per cent since 1931 apart from a brief rise on the outbreak of war in September 1939) and this helped not just to foster economic recovery but also to redistribute wealth and finance cheaply the building of the Welfare State. 'Budgetary policy, during Dalton's "cheap money" era, had a strong social component, including the financing of family allowances and national assistance, the easing of restrictions on house building, and heavily subsidized rents for council house tenants', one chronicler of the Attlee government, Kenneth Morgan, noted. 'Food subsidies, by which large sums were paid from the Exchequer to food producers and suppliers, specifically to keep down the cost of living for poorer people, and thus to relieve any pressure on wage inflation, were manifestly redistributive in their effects.'[8]

The same philosophy guided the Treasury under Dalton's successor, Sir Stafford Cripps. Austere the Cripps regime may have been, but it was built on fairness. Food subsidies were maintained, the Chancellor did his utmost to exempt social services from any expenditure cuts, and the hefty over-runs in the NHS budget after its inception in 1948 were largely accommodated. To help balance his books, and unencumbered by Mr Brown's pledge to spare the rich from any increase in income tax, Cripps used his 1948 budget to impose a one-off capital levy on the better-off.

For all the problems that beset it – some of them of its own making – the record of the 1945 government was impressive. By the time it left office in October 1951, unemployment stood at 1.8 per cent; a region such as the north-east which had seen a jobless rate of 38 per cent at the depth of the Depression boasted a rate of only 3 per cent in the late 1940s. In addition, the breathing space provided by the American loan, the beneficial impact of the devaluation of 1949 and strong American growth helped to turn round the balance of payments, at least until the Korean war intervened in 1950. In his book, Morgan quotes the 1949 Economic Survey as describing the previous year as one of 'substantial progress in nearly every part of the economic life of the United Kingdom'. It was, he says, the best year for the economy since the

First World War, with exports up 25 per cent on 1947 and 150 per cent up on 1938. Industrial production increased by 12 per cent on 1948.

But Labour's success was as much social as economic. 'All the indices – for instance, the statistics of medical officers of health, or of school medical or dental officers – suggest that the standard of health and of robust physique steadily improved during the entire 1945–51 period, from infants, whose survival rates continued to improve, to old people, whose expectation of a long and happy retirement steadily lengthened.'[9]

The price paid for this period of post-war consolidation was severe rationing, which in some respects became even more draconian after 1945. But Labour's bedrock support held up. Despite winning 393 seats in 1945, it managed to hold onto them all in the by-elections of the subsequent six and a half years.

Rationing was at the heart of the archetypal Ealing film of the period: *Passport to Pimlico*, released in 1949 but set in the heatwave summer of 1947. The detonation of an unexploded bomb reveals that under a medieval treaty which has never been rescinded, Miramont Square in Pimlico is actually still part of Burgundy, therefore exempted from all official restrictions and controls. Ration books can be torn up, the pubs can remain open all hours, the ladies' dress shop can order the finest French fashions, the timid bank manager can tell his head office that he will run his branch his own way. A party atmosphere ensues, with Miramont Square revelling in its notoriety and freedom. Then things start to go wrong. Every spiv in London arrives in Pimlico, and the decent, law-abiding citizens find their community descending into anarchy. The Metropolitan Police are unable to intervene because Pimlico is officially now a foreign country. The spivs are eventually ousted, but only when frontier conrols – barbed wire – are imposed by Whitehall. As Charles Barr says in his seminal book on Ealing: 'The Burgundians, from this point, engage in a diplomatic war: they recover the spirit, the resilience and local autonomy and unity, of wartime London.'[10] In the end a very British compromise is reached and an open-air dinner, complete with new ration books laid out as part of the table setting, is held to celebrate the return of Pimlico to the fold.

The standard right-wing interpretation of all this is that *Passport to Pimlico* was the expression of a nation straining to be freed from petty officialdom and, in Mrs Thatcher's phrase, 'the whiff of controls'. But it is a far more complex film than that. Certainly, there is the deep suspicion of a bullying bureaucracy and a quite justifiable desire for some of the material comforts that were expected to come with peace. Yet the over-riding message of the film is that the community works best when it pulls together rather than acts as a series of atomized individuals, a message that Blair has repeated himself on many occasions since becoming Labour leader.

The difference, however, is that the people of Miramont Square have no time for laissez-faire; the influx of hawkers from outside threatens the order and security of the community's settled way of life. They have to be dealt with, swiftly and forcibly. The 'business culture' would be anathema to these people and, significantly, the only person in Miramont Square to utter a syllable of modern business-speak – the publican Garland, who declares 'it's every man for himself' – is the one man who cannot stomach the sacrifices required to last out the siege and scuttles off across the frontier.

For all his talk of hooking every school up to the Internet, Tony Blair's vision of a New Britain would look something like Miramont Square, although without the repudiation of laissez-faire shown in New Burgundy. People would draw individual strength from communal solidarity, would think of others as well as themselves, would be polite, tolerant and considerate. There is nothing wrong with this vision. It is preferable, frankly, to a society in which people have to log on to a computer in order to feel part of a collective movement. In the end, however, *Passport to Pimlico* is something of a cop-out, as is Blairism, though for different reasons. Ealing could obviously sense the way the post-war wind was blowing; it regretted that the collectivist spirit was retreating in the face of individualism and the demands of consumer power, but the studio tried to pretend that the answer could be a recrudescence of the mood that had seen Britain through the Blitz. There was simply no chance of that happening, and within a decade of making *Passport to Pimlico*, Ealing Studios had ceased to exist. Blair would like to give the impression that all will be well if the government – with the help of business – knocks a few of the rough edges off the laissez-faire model.

Tony Blair is not the first Labour leader to ponder on the consequences of cultural change. Attlee clearly saw no future in attempting to maintain the wartime orthodoxy. There was certainly much moral fervour behind Crippsian austerity and, as Morgan discloses in *Labour in Power*, there were even attempts to introduce the notion of a social crime to stand alongside criminal offences and civil wrongs. When Hugh Gaitskell urged citizens to observe the regulations on petrol rationing he did so by stating that evading the law was 'social sabotage and, therefore, immoral'. But this strictness existed alongside an easing of controls designed to prevent former Conservatives from gravitating back to their old party allegiance, a policy championed by Herbert Morrison who, as a London MP, knew that Labour was in danger of losing its tenuous grip on the suburbs. He urged a relaxation of rationing, a halt to nationalization and an abandonment of the class war rhetoric exemplified by Bevan's comment that the Tories were 'lower than vermin'. Morrison's analysis, which is reflected in the Ealing films and is still held by the Labour leadership today, is that the British people (or at least the bulk of them) are decent and upright, believe in common sense, are rooted in a commitment to fairness, and are generally suspicious of snooping bureaucrats. Britain is a reformist, not a revolutionary, culture, with a natural aversion − as Orwell made clear in 'The Lion and the Unicorn' − to totalitarianism of either the right or the left. But in the late 1940s, reform meant just that: reform. Reform under Blair has quite a different meaning: doing nothing that big business would find objectionable.

The Blue Lamp is a prime example of how Ealing characterized the British in the immediate post-war years. Like Passport to Pimlico, The Lavender Hill Mob, Whisky Galore and The Ladykillers, The Blue Lamp was set in a precise locality, this time the streets of Paddington. The story centres on a young PC who comes to work at the station and finds lodgings with the sergeant (George Dixon), who has lost his own son in the war. It is a world of order and stability, where the police are shown as being part of the community, playing as much a pastoral as a punitive role. So, when Dixon is shot and killed by a young hoodlum people draw together in the hunt for the murderer. In the end he is trapped at a packed greyhound meeting (gambling being another way workers could dispose of their excess income in 1950), where the bookmakers use their secret tic-tac language to chart his movements around the stadium, and he is carried by the departing crowd into the arms of the police. As Barr says, The Blue Lamp is really about belonging to a family. The young PC is admitted to an actual family, but he also has a professional family at the police station, where the film places much emphasis on the unifying spirit engendered by the darts team and the choir. Finally, there is the idea of nation as family 'which may have its tensions and rows but whose members share common standards and loyalties; in a crisis, the police can call upon a general respect and will to co-operate.'

The darts team and the communal choir of *The Blue Lamp* would no doubt have appealed to Richard Hoggart, who produced a classic book on popular culture, *The Uses of Literacy*, in 1957. Hoggart's view was that the working class was gradually becoming coarsened by the new mass culture, mainly – indeed, almost exclusively – imported from America. Here, for example, he starts a chapter with a discourse on the 'juke box boys': 'This regular, increasing and almost unvaried diet of sensation without commitment is surely likely to help render its consumers less capable of responding openly to life, is likely to induce an underlying sense of purposelessness in existence outside the limited range of a few immediate appetites.' These 'juke box boys' hang out in milk bars characterized by nasty 'modernistic knick-knacks' and 'glaring showiness'. Hoggart concludes that 'compared even with the pub around the corner, this is all a peculiarly thin and pallid form of dissipation, a sort of spiritual dry-rot amid the odour of bottled milk'.[11]

Several things stand out in this passage. First, there is the idea that culture is becoming mass-produced and imposed from above rather than rooted in the people. Second, there is the strong strain of anti-Americanism; Hoggart elsewhere is scathing about young men adopting 'an American slouch', playing American records on the juke box and 'living to a large extent in a myth world compounded of a few simple elements which they take to be those of American life'. Third, there is the sense of teenage emancipation; whereas the young men in *The Blue Lamp* were happy to take their lead from their elders, by the mid-1950s they were striking out on their own. *The Wild One*, a 1954 film starring Marlon Brando, was originally banned in Britain for its scenes of teenage revolt, even though it looks pretty tame today. But one scene seems to sum up Hoggart's view that the youth of the 1950s were going off the rails. Brando's Johnny is asked by a bemused adult: 'Johnny, what is it you're against?' Brando sneers dismissively and replies: 'Whaddya got?' Fourth, there is the puritanical distaste for the hedonism that has replaced the moral fervour of wartime and the immediate post-war years. Finally, there is the knowledge that Hoggart, however prescient he may have been, was wildly overstating his case. Britain in the 1950s was still an ordered and, to a large extent, deferential culture, as even a cursory glance at the new medium of television showed clearly. Film clips of the time show that politicians were treated with what now seems fawning respect, with questioning along the lines of: 'Is there anything else you would like to say, Mr Attlee?' Mr Attlee: 'No.' Interviewer: 'Thank you.' This may have been connected with the fact that in its early post-war days, TV was very much a middle-class preserve. The Coronation in 1953 and, two years later, the arrival of a commercial channel to rival the BBC provided a major boost to the new medium. By the time the travails of the Macmillan government were being lampooned by *That was the Week that was* in 1963 only 10 per cent of homes were without TV.

The common view of the 1950s is that it was a decade of stability, perhaps the only such decade that the West – and in particular Britain – has enjoyed since the war. It was certainly a time of rising prosperity; the need to rebuild from 1945 onwards and the pent-up demand left by years of austerity ensured full employment, rising profits and higher living standards. Harold Macmillan announced on the last day of 1953 that the Conservatives had achieved what Labour had never managed: they had built 300,000 houses in a single year. Moreover, the budget of that year was the first since the Second World War which neither announced new taxes nor increased those that already existed. The Chancellor 'Rab' Butler instead knocked sixpence off income tax and 25 per cent off all levels of purchase tax.

For the first half of the decade – when Churchill was Prime Minister, Everest was conquered, Stanley Matthews won the cup for Blackpool, Gordon Richards at last rode a Derby winner, the Ashes were regained and there was a new Elizabethan Age to wallow in – there was a sense of palpable progress. Only in the late 1950s did the weaknesses of the era start to come to the surface, disclosing some of the bitterness and suppressed rage of the period. In retrospect, it was a wasted decade for Britain, when its share of world trade halved, its position as the biggest exporter of cars was lost to Germany, and its obsession with the grandiose led to the political disasters of Suez and the industrial blind alleys of nuclear power and Blue Streak. While Germany and Japan were refocusing their economies on the production and export of cars, cameras, washing machines and stereos – things ordinary people may want to buy – Britain was trying to sell, government to government, such items as gas-cooled nuclear reactors and military hardware, and was developing the biggest white elephant of all, the Concorde supersonic transporter.

Films of the 1950s – from *The Man in the White Suit* at the start of the decade to *I'm All Right Jack* at the end – depict just how slow industry was to face up to the fact that times had changed. The 1950s finally saw the flowering of a technology that had been in existence for more than half a century: the motor car. Henry Ford had pioneered mass production in the USA in the early years of the century, and the technique had been brought to Britain by William Morris after a visit to America in 1914. But the Depression and war delayed the growth of car ownership so that by 1950 40 per cent of Americans still did not own a car. However, once the pent-up demand was released, ownership expanded rapidly and prompted the building of the inter-state freeways in the USA and the motorway network in Britain. The car's predominance not only hastened the demise of the railway – as seen in the 1954 Ealing film, *The Titfield Thunderbolt* – but encouraged the growth of the suburb and the dispersal of families. Smaller families living further from urban centres, in turn, helped to stimulate demand for the full range of domestic appliances – from TV to refrigerators – which were lovingly dwelt upon by the camera in the many films set in the suburbs during the 1950s, *Father of the Bride* starring Spencer Tracey and Elizabeth Taylor being but one example.

Britain could have been at the forefront of this industrial revolution. Immediately after the war, Stafford Cripps had told the scions of the British motor industry that there was an urgent need for a 'cheap, tough, good-looking car', with 50 per cent of production sold as exports. The very next year the industry was presented with an unprecedented opportunity to fulfil this need when, as part of the spoils of war, it could have transplanted production of the VW Beetle from Wolfsburg in Germany. Familiar excuses were paraded for refusing the offer: the car was too small for the American market and did not really have the potential to be a long-term success. Far from grabbing this heaven-sent opportunity with both hands – the VW Beetle became one of the five top-selling cars of all time – the British motor industry's only response was to ask whether it could strip Wolfsburg of its machine tools so that Germany's industrial recovery might be hindered.

This is the industrial mentality satirized in *The Man in the White Suit*, where the bosses fear that the indestructible cloth invented by a young scientist (Alec Guinness) will lead to a drop in demand and profits. Boardroom finds common cause with shopfloor, which is fearful about the implications for jobs, to sabotage the project which, in the end, proves to be less of a break-through than originally believed. The Boulting Brothers film *I'm All Right Jack* displays similar connivance between management and unions, even though the cosy relationship is couched in the language of confrontation and class war. On the one side there is the humourless Marxist shop steward, Fred Kite (brilliantly played by Peter Sellers), forever calling the proletariat out on wildcat strike on the flimsiest of pretexts; on the other the louche ex-army major (Terry-Thomas), stuck with the task of trying to keep the workers ('an absolute shower', he calls them) sweet with endless concessions. Stuck in the middle is the unworldly nephew of the boss (Ian Carmichael) who tries to improve efficiency and productivity but is seen as a menace by both sides. Kite, based on a union official in the film industry who had actually crossed swords with the Boultings, is portrayed as the archetypal British small-minded, petty official, down to the pens in the lapel pocket of his ill-fitting suit and his Hitler moustache. But Kite is a figure of fun as much as a real threat. The British working class never had much time for the Soviet Union – 'all those cornfields and ballet in the morning', as Kite puts it – and has found the attractions of America far more difficult to resist. Kite's bimboesque daughter (Liz Fraser) is totally bemused by her dad's monomaniacal obsession with politics and wants only to spend her wages on having a good time.

REBEL YELL: THE DETONATION OF THE 1950s

Britain was a long way behind America when it came to the emancipation of the young. By the mid-1950s, America's 16.5 million teenagers were buying 40 per cent of all radios, records and cameras, more than half of all cinema tickets and 10 per cent of cars. While their parents stayed in to watch TV, teenagers went out. America quickly developed its own teen heroes, kicking hard against the stolidity of suburban life and the authority represented by parents, school, the system generally. Brando was the first rebel icon, but he was followed by James Dean, Montgomery Clift and Elvis Presley. Britain had no Brando, no Dean, and certainly no Elvis Presley. While America was in at the birth of rock 'n' roll, the best Britain had to offer as an anti-hero was Jimmy Porter, a quintessentially conservative figure. 'I must say it's pretty dreary living in the American age – unless you're an American of course. Perhaps all our children will be Americans. That's a thought, isn't it', he says in *Look Back in Anger*.

Much the same criticism could be levelled at the other 'Angry Young Men' – Amis, Wain, Waterhouse – whose work self-consciously rejected modernism in favour of provincialism and whose characters' only solution to the dreary 1950s was escapist fantasy. However, *Look Back in Anger* remains the classic text, because it was supposed to represent the voice of youthful radicalism. In fact, it does no such thing. Jimmy is an armchair philosopher, a pipe-smoking bore who would have seen modern jazz as a heresy, and might have marched to Aldermaston with CND but then voted for Macmillan in 1959 in the privacy of the polling booth. Moreover, he puts into perspective the idea that self-absorption was a trait that emerged only in the arriviste and solipsistic 1960s. Is there actually a more extreme example of whining self-pity and bullying egomania than Jimmy Porter? Indeed, the subtext of *Look Back in Anger* is far more interesting than its main character. There is, for example, the fact that Alison, Jimmy's long-suffering wife, feels trapped in her poky Midlands flat and cut off from her family, with whom she communicates only by letter. The message was clear: families were no longer the thriving units seen in *The Blue Lamp*; rather, they were splintering and becoming dysfunctional. Women, who by now had become bored with their labour-saving devices, felt trapped, as shown in this passage written by Betty Friedan in 1963:

The problem lay buried, unspoken, for many years in the minds of American women. It was a strange stirring, a sense of dissatisfaction, a yearning that women suffered in the middle of the 20th Century in the United States. Each suburban wife struggled with it alone. As she made beds, shopped for groceries, matched slipcover material, ate peanut butter sandwiches with her children, chauffeured Cub Scouts and Brownies, lay beside her husband at night, she was afraid to ask even of herself the silent question: Is this all?[12]

Here, then, was a new complication, something else to rumple the smooth security blanket that was thrown over the 1950s. The economy was underperforming relative to the rest of the West, a fact that was being reflected in a series of gloomy tomes, such as Michael Shanks's *The Stagnant Society*. An era of mass production and consumerism was leading to a more individualistic culture that was gradually casting itself off from its traditional family and community moorings. Teenagers were enjoying more economic freedom, yet bridling at the restrictions imposed from above – home by midnight, two years' national service, censorship of what could be seen and read. Women, encouraged to work to help the war effort, were back in the home, watching the significantly named *Watch with Mother* and waiting for the breadwinner to come home for his tea. As one chronicler of the period expressed it: 'Beneath the wiped and polished surface of British culture around 1960 lay a festering mass of sexual ignorance, prejudice and repression only slightly ameliorated since the 19th Century. . . . Britain was stiff with a psychic tension which was bound, sooner or later, to explode.'[13]

INTO THE KALEIDOSCOPE: THE 1960s

Explode, of course, it did, not in 1960 but in 1963, the year when the 1960s truly began. In February, Harold Wilson was elected leader of the Labour Party; in March, Thomas Beeching, the transport supremo, took his axe to hundreds of branch lines in his shake-up of the railway network; in April, Martin Luther King was arrested on a civil rights march in Birmingham, Alabama; in May, Timothy Leary was sacked by Harvard for experimenting on his students with LSD; in June, Minister of War Jack Profumo resigned after belatedly admitting that he had lied to the House of Commons about his relationship with Christine Keeler; in July, the Beatles recorded 'She Loves You'; in August, £2.5 million was snatched from the Glasgow night mail train in the Great Train Robbery (still the most famous crime of the entire post-war period despite later, more lucrative, heists); in September, the Denning Report castigated the Macmillan government for the Profumo scandal; in October, Macmillan suddenly resigned and was replaced, mysteriously, by Alec Douglas Home, who had to renounce his peerage to become prime minister. Harold Wilson meanwhile promised that the Britain of the future would be forged in 'the white heat of the technological revolution'. In November, the month John Kennedy was shot in Dallas, Texas, the Beatles appeared at the Royal Command Performance, where John Lennon slyly poked fun at the Queen Mother and Princess Margaret by saying: 'Will the people in the cheaper seats clap your hands. The rest of you can just rattle your jewellery.'

In film, 1963 was the year when to be working class was to be fashionable: Lindsay Anderson's *This Sporting Life*, Tony Richardson's *The Loneliness of the Long Distance Runner*, John Schlesinger's *Billy Liar* were all released. On TV, there were the first episodes of *Ready, Steady Go* and *Doctor Who*; in fashion the designer Pierre Cardin declared that clothes were 'a form of protest'.

In the early 1960s the static unbending world of the 1950s cracked apart. The challenge, primarily from the young, but also from the increasingly affluent working class and the frustrated middle class, was intensified by the problems the Establishment brought upon itself; not just the debauchery of the Profumo affair, which resulted in Cabinet ministers being obliged to have their testicles examined to prove that they had not been guests at masked orgies, but also the Lady Chatterley obscenity trial, where the prosecuting counsel asked a somewhat perplexed jury 'Is this really a book you would want your wife or servants to read?', and the fact that the aristocratic Conservative Prime Minister (Douglas Home) cheerfully admitted that his economics was based on the use of matchsticks. There were, of course, fears that the freedoms won in the 1960s by this coalition of forces would lead to moral decay; the counterpoint to the satire boom and the relaxation in censorship was Mary Whitehouse and the National Viewers and Listeners Association (NVLA). But somehow it all held together. The 1960s saw the post-war system enjoy its finest hour; the British pop music explosion was the full flowering of an alliance between art school and back street, and a detente between the old and the new. As Ian McDonald put it:

Anyone unlucky enough not to have been aged between 14 and 30 during 1966–67 will never know the excitement of those years in popular culture. A sunny optimism permeated everything and possibilities seemed limitless. Bestriding a British scene that embraced music, poetry, fashion and film, the Beatles were at their peak and were looked up to in awe as the arbiters of a positive new age in which the dead customs of the older generation would be refreshed and remade through the creative energy of the classless young.[14]

All this is true. Yet the Beatles, for all their youthful verve and genius, relied heavily on the production skills of George Martin for the polished studio albums that epitomized their talent. And Martin – ex-Fleet Air Arm in the war, producer of *The Goons*, vehemently anti-drugs – was a classic 1950s figure. Martin was the base for the Beatles adventures, the man who found a way of splicing two separate takes of 'Strawberry Fields Forever', recorded in different keys, into a finished song where the join is only evident to the trained listener. Moreover, the Beatles, even when they moved into mock tudor mansions in the Surrey stockbroker belt or fashionable villas in St John's Wood, remained firmly rooted in their past. The double A side, 'Strawberry Fields'/'Penny Lane', was seen, rightly, as the classic psyche-delic single, yet both songs were set in the Liverpool of their childhood, Penny Lane being a rather nondescript suburban street and Strawberry Fields a gloomy Victorian children's home.

The Beatles symbolized the high point of the home–adventure alliance. Their songs were about exploration and excitement, but also about nostalgia and the need to belong. For every 'Ticket to Ride', there was a 'She's Leaving Home'; for every 'Day Tripper' an 'Eleanor Rigby'. The Beatles, the 1960s and Britain peaked in 1966, the year that *Time* magazine wrote admiringly of Swinging London, Twiggy and Mary Quant were the talk of the catwalk glit-terati, England won the World Cup, and Labour strengthened its grip on power with a general election win that increased its parliamentary majority from four to ninety-seven. Yet at the very moment of triumph the seeds of destruction were being sown. The Beatles, weary of travelling and disgusted by the sloppiness of their inaudible live concerts, retreated into the studio and, apart from a brief rooftop concert in Savile Row in January 1969, never played in public again. At the time, the Beatles' decision to stop touring was seen as professional suicide but, as in many other areas of the music business, the Beatles were the harbingers of change. The late 1960s was the period when the collectivist spirit of rock/pop was manifested in the great open-air festivals (Monterey, Woodstock, Hyde Park and the Isle of Wight). Thereafter, more and more bands followed the Beatles' lead, spending more time perfecting their sound in the privacy of a recording studio. The murder by Hell's Angels of a fan at the Rolling Stones concert in Altamont, California, in December 1969 showed how short-lived the optimistic mood of Woodstock four months earlier had been.

Disillusionment, when it set in, spread to all the main components of the post-war coalition. The working class, cosseted by rising real wages until 1966, was alienated by the deflationary measures imposed by Wilson that July in a vain attempt to fend off a devaluation of sterling, and by the squeeze that followed the government's long overdue recognition in November 1967 that the pound had to be brought down to a more realistic level. One problem, as David Marquand pointed out, in his book *The Unprincipled Society*, was that Keynesianism was an economic doctrine and suffered from its inability to put down any political roots. This became abundantly clear in the 1970s, but was already becoming evident when the Wilson administration called for belt-tightening for the common good in the late 1960s. The other weakness of Keynesianism was that it presented the working class as the source of Britain's economic difficulties; they needed to work harder and strike less.

Unemployment was on a gentle upward trend, rising from 1.4 per cent in 1955 to 2.2 per cent in 1960, 2.6 per cent in 1964 and 3.1 per cent in 1968. Inflation, having started the 1960s at 1 per cent, nudged up to 3.7 per cent in 1964, the year of Chancellor of the Exchequer Reggie Maudling's dash for growth, hit 4.1 per cent in 1968, then climbed to 7.1 per cent in 1973.

In the last five years of the post-war boom, 1968–73, Britain had the worst inflation record of the Group of Seven industrial nations and, together with the United States, the slowest growth. Without the devaluation of November 1967, growth would have been even more sluggish, but as in 1949, the benefits of the cheaper pound came at a price. Despite the scorn heaped on Robert Maxwell's 'Back Britain' campaign, exports did rise sharply, but consumption was squeezed. The working class was far less willing to accept privations than twenty years earlier and various parts of the middle classes were also disgruntled. One lesson from history for Blair is that the middle classes are political libertines. Provide them with security and affluence and they rail against consumerism; impose policies that slow down the pace of economic growth and they complain about higher taxes and a political culture that is anti-enterprise. Of course, there were times when everything worked, as on the last day of the fifth and final test against Australia in August 1968 when spectators from both the cheap and expensive seats at the Oval spent three hours mopping up the outfield after a downpour to give the spinner Derek Underwood the chance to square the series: a perfect example of collaboration between the Establishment and the people. But generally the mood became more sullen as the decade wore on and the forces of reaction started to regain some of the confidence lost at the time of Profumo. The Beatles, untouchable in the mid-1960s, were targeted when they grew their hair long, went public with their drug taking, adopted radical politics and – in the case of Lennon – offended the racist mood of the time

by having a Japanese mistress. Apple – the Beatles' attempt at hippie capitalism – was an unmitigated disaster; as in *Passport to Pimlico* twenty years earlier,
every huckster and rip-off artist in London (and beyond) turned up at Savile
Row for some easy pickings. This time, however, they were allowed to clean
up. Pop culture had over-reached itself; it could not run multinational businesses nor could it achieve any of its more political objectives, whether the
legalization of cannabis, workers' control of industry or an end to the
Vietnam war. Indeed, its main legacy was the legitimization of the pursuit of
aggressive individualism, and to that extent McDonald is right when he says
that the 1960s was a transitional period between a 'society weakly held
together by a decaying faith' and a 'rapidly desocialising mass of groups and
individuals united by little more than a wish for quick satisfaction'.[15] Put
simply, without the 1960s there would have been no Thatcher, no Reagan, no
1980s counter-revolution. Most of the key themes of the 1980s – self-
expression, freedom, the 'inevitable' onward march of technology, the
decline of organized religion and the rise of the cult, even the challenge to
print from the new electronic media championed by that most 1960s of figures, Marshall McLuhan – were there, quietly gestating. And while the
avatars of the post-war system were in retreat, a new right-wing coalition was
taking shape. We mentioned above that pop culture and the left failed to
achieve their political objectives, but this was not merely the case of missed
opportunities, however much it may have seemed like that in the spring of
1968. It is certainly true that those who sought to bring down capitalism in
that year did not really understand how badly the political Establishment
was rattled by their activities. But the fact was that in Britain and America –
if not in France – the political Establishment in 1968 was fronted by parties
of the left, trying as ever to keep together an uneasy class coalition. Wilson
and Johnson, in effect, did the right's dirty work for it: crushing peace
protests, proposing legal clamps on unions, coming down hard on drugs,
stripping Muhammad Ali of his world heavyweight boxing title as a warning
to blacks of what would happen to them if they tried to dodge the draft.
Looking back, the real significance of 1968 was not the Paris riots, nor those
in the Watts district of Los Angeles, nor even the hundreds injured when
Mayor Daley's police ran amok to quell disturbances at the Democratic convention in Chicago, but the election of Richard Nixon, the march through
London of dockers demonstrating in support of Enoch Powell, the huge

losses inflicted on Labour in the local government elections, de Gaulle's landslide in French parliamentary elections held a month after the Paris riots and, last but by no means least, the sight of Red Army tanks rumbling through the streets of Prague to put down Dubček's protest against Communism.

The cultural avant-garde was rapidly losing faith in the future at the same time as a large chunk of the traditional bourgeoisie was looking for reassurance that its way of life was not about to be swept away by banner-waving, drug-taking students. There was also class jealousy, and the sense that the working classes were getting just a bit too uppity. Writing about the Ad Lib Club, one of the favourite haunts of the Beatles, the Stones and the rest of rock's aristocracy, George Melly stated: 'It's essentially to do with being young, and those people who attack it are in many cases motivated by envy at the sight of young people, many of them of working-class origin, with the means and poise to enjoy themselves.'[16]

By the end of the decade night clubs had become rather passé for pop's millionaires languishing in their squierarchical mansions, uncertain, in Lennon's case especially, whether they wanted revolution or not. The less wealthy members of the European intelligentsia also announced their defection, in order to begin a sustained assault on the post-war system, using newly fashionable neo-Marxist critiques of 'society as spectacle' and 'one-dimensional man'. This detachment of the intellectual wing was to lead, in its most extreme form, to violent attacks on 'bourgeois' (i.e. social-democratic) institutions in the early 1970s by groups including the Angry Brigade in Britain, the Weathermen in the USA and the Baader-Meinhof gang in West Germany.

Alan Sillitoe had encapsulated the mood of the working classes at the start of the 1960s in *Saturday Night and Sunday Morning*. There was no indication, a decade on, that its hero, Arthur Seaton, had changed much. He still wanted a good time, more money and the state off his back. He had no desire to man the barricades and thought those who did could do with a haircut and a bath. As Lennon put it in his interview with *Rolling Stone* magazine in 1970 shortly after the Beatles broke up: 'A lot of people grew long hair, but nothing changed.'

Lennon was wrong. Some things had changed, not least the position of women. Rising job opportunities in the growing service sector, the pill and a reaction against the boredom of family life laid the foundations for feminism. By the start of the 1970s a young woman was more likely to be flicking through the pages of *Cosmopolitan* than staring vacantly at *Watch with Mother*.

The 1960s had also seen a technological shift. America's paranoia at the end of the 1950s about the Russian space programme meant that NASA had spent billions of dollars so that Neil Armstrong could be the first man to set foot on the surface of the moon in July 1969. The MCC cricket team that played in Australia in 1962–63 was the last to go by boat. This was the decade that saw the development of satellites, the jumbo jet, Concorde, the spread of telephones, the stirrings of the computer age. Some of these developments were off-shoots of military technology, but others – the rapid progression from radiogram to stereo systems – were driven by consumer demand and individual tastes. Record labels that had been loss-making adjuncts of defence companies such as Decca and EMI were now big money-spinners in their own right. Personal preferences were manifesting themselves not just in the high street but in politics as well, where there was a loss of faith in the mainstream left and a noticeable growth in single-issue groups calling for racial and gender equality, gay rights and environmental protection.

The mild anti-Establishment satire of *That was the Week that was* had been replaced by the harder-edged antics of *Monty Python* and the calls for full lifestyle liberation emanating from *Oz*, *International Times* and the rest of the burgeoning underground press.

GREY NEW WORLD: THE 1970s

But *Monty Python* and *Oz* were minority tastes. What were the cultural trends in the early years of the 1970s? First, the new decade was really the fag end of the 1960s, only more aggressive and much more cynical. Second, pop music was taking itself far too seriously. Indeed, pop music was really only for adolescent girls screaming at the Osmonds or David Cassidy or for working-class louts who followed Slade. Musicians were now 'rock' stars, and let it all hang out in endless concerts (now renamed gigs), records (albums, definitely not singles) and hagiographic interviews in the 'heavy' music press. Often they ended up looking bombastic and ridiculous, although nobody seemed to think so at the time.

TV had become unrivalled as the medium of the age, and had started to go nostalgic. *The Forsyte Saga*, made at the end of the 1960s, spoke of a time when the Empire was expanding rather than giving up all commitments east of Suez; *Upstairs Downstairs* was a period piece screened in an era when high personal taxation and domestic appliances had killed off domestic service. Contemporary accounts of Britain in the early 1970s were rather hard to find; perhaps the best was John le Carré's *Tinker Tailor Soldier Spy*, published in 1974 but set a couple of years earlier. The novel's theme — the hunt for a Russian mole inside MI6 — is itself appropriate to a time when the prevailing mood was one of profound disillusionment with the direction in which the country appeared to be heading. But it is the way le Carré captures the mood of rottenness, cynicism and decay that makes the thriller one of the most vivid descriptions of post-war Britain. The pensioned-off spy, Jim Prideaux, is showing off his beloved Alvis to the pupils at a rather run-down prep school in the West Country. 'Best car England ever made', was how Jim had introduced his car. 'Out of production, thanks to socialism'. After an inter-rogation, the master-spy George Smiley and his legman, Peter Guillam, stop off at a roadhouse that has obviously seen better days. They order some food and a bottle of wine.

The boy reappeared swinging a bottle of Burgundy like an Indian club. 'Would you please let it breathe a little?'
The boy stared at Smiley as if he were mad.
'Open it and leave it on the table,' said Guillam curtly.[17]

Later, Smiley explains how fifteen years earlier he had tried but failed to persuade his nemesis, the Russian spymaster Karla, to defect to the West with an ill-judged presentation of the delights on offer in Britain. 'I behaved like a soft fool. The very archetype of a flabby Western liberal. But I would rather be my kind of fool than his for all that.'

Le Carré does not think that Britain's decline is terminal; the fact that Smiley eventually tracks down the mole is proof of that. But the warning signs are clearly there, as in the passage where Smiley fails to enlist the sup-port of an old colleague Roy Bland in his search for the mole. 'As a good socialist I'm going for the money. As a good capitalist, I'm sticking with the revolution, because if you can't beat it spy on it. Don't look like that George. It's the name of the game these days: you scratch my conscience, I'll drive your Jag, right?'[18] Le Carré's MI6 has been led astray by its willingness to believe uncritically in big-bang solutions, and needs to return to the old values of loyalty, honesty and hard work if it is to restore its reputation for quality. Appropriately, the TV adaptation was transmitted in 1979, just as Mrs Thatcher was coming to power.

If anything, comedy was even more important to 1970s culture than drama, and at the root of most 1970s comedy was class. There was no attempt to hide the fact that Britain was a country in which class divides were as deep as ever. The key relationship in *Dad's Army* was that between Captain Mainwaring and Sergeant Wilson; the tension and the humour stem from the bourgeois bank manager lording it over the patrician Wilson both at work and in the Home Guard platoon. Similarly, *Whatever Happened to the Likely Lads?* has the edge over its 1990s equivalent *Men Behaving Badly* as comedy because of the class distinction drawn between the aspirational Bob and the doggedly proletarian Terry. In the original *Likely Lads* series set in the mid-1960s, both Bob and Terry had been cheeky-chappy apprentices, but by the early 1970s Bob was about to marry a librarian, had a steady job, a mortgage, a three-piece suit and a Kevin Keegan-style bouffant hair-do, while Terry, fresh out of the army was, in the words of the theme song, 'looking forward to the past'. Bob would have voted for Mrs Thatcher in 1979 without question. *The Good Life* showed that even those who would have considered themselves to be part of the progressive wing of the bourgeoisie, the *Guardian*-reading supporters of the Welfare State and redistribution, had lost faith in the ability of government to deliver. Tom and Barbara opt out of the rat race, turning their backs on the consumer society to set up a small holding in their Surbiton back garden. In the aftermath of the Barber boom — when consumer spending went up by 14 per cent in a single year and house prices by 50 per cent — it was a reasonably common fantasy. The success of *Small is Beautiful* and the emergence of the environment as an 'issue' were indicative of a small but active back-to-nature movement. The edge to *The Good Life*'s humour was provided by the contrast between Tom and Barbara and their next-door neighbours, Jerry and Margo, who remain committed to their traditional bourgeois values of class superiority, keeping up appearances, the quest for promotion, comfort, security. The sympathy of the viewer was intended to be with Tom and Barbara as they mucked out the pigs and milked the goats, but many would have instinctively felt for Jerry and

Margo as their suburban lifestyle was squeezed between the nutcracker jaws of high inflation and militant trade unionism. *The Good Life* is the one sit-com from the Golden Age of comedy in the 1970s that could be transplanted to the 1990s without too much difficulty. The new Toms and Barbaras would be the downshifters, those fortunate enough to have made enough in law or the City not to have to worry about money for the rest of their lives, who are now intent on 'finding themselves'. The new Jerrys and Margos would be much like the old Jerry and Margo, but with rather more reason to be worried. In the 1970s there was really not much threat to Jerry's comfortable perch on the corporate ladder; he could expect to keep Margo in fondue sets, foreign holidays and a new – if ghastly – wardrobe for every season. But in the 1990s he would be forever looking over his shoulder to see whether the management consultants called in by his new Japanese or American owners were about to downsize him.

If *The Good Life* was an eerily prescient foretaste of the 1990s, *Fawlty Towers* was very much of its time. Victor Meldrew, the crotchety pensioner in *One Foot in the Grave*, is Basil in retirement, but there is nothing in late 1990s sit-com that is remotely comparable. British Leyland no longer exists, strikes in the car industry (and elsewhere) are a rarity and it would be unthinkable for a hotel inspector to allow Basil and Sybil to keep trading after finding dead pigeons in the water tank, given the public paranoia about legionnaire's disease, E-coli bacteria and BSE. Anybody under thirty-five watching *Fawlty Towers* for the first time today could be forgiven for asking: 'Was it really like that?' The answer is, given a bit of artistic licence, 'Yes, it was.'

THE BIG MIRRORS: SPORT, CINEMA AND CULTURAL CHANGE

Sport, too, had been through some changes since the 1940s. By the early 1970s, mass-participation sports were in serious decline; attendances at football matches dropped sharply after the temporary boost provided by the World Cup victory. Harold Wilson always believed that England's defeat by West Germany in a World Cup quarter final on a Sunday in Mexico in June 1970 cost him the general election four days later; but even that performance, disappointing though it was, was better than the abject failure even to qualify for the finals in 1974 and 1978. One England manager, Don Revie, upped and left with no warning for a lucrative job in the Middle East; his previous club side, Leeds United, was the epitome of early 1970s football – cynical, tough, malicious, sly. Cricket was in an equally poor state. One sign of how times had changed since the mopping-up operation at the Oval in 1968 came in August 1975, when England was again playing Australia and, as the last day dawned on the final test at Headingley, had a chance to square the series. However, an inspection of the pitch found it unusable after it had been vandalized during the night by campaigners protesting the innocence of George Davies, in jail at the time for armed robbery. When play was possible, it was clear that things had changed on the field as well, with defeat after defeat for England and the domination of the game by a more aggressive form of play. Batteries of fast bowlers softened batsmen up with short-pitched bowling, while fielders tried to disturb their concentration with a running commentary of insults commonly known as sledging. It was perhaps fitting that in the summer of 1976 – with the International Monetary Fund trampling all over Whitehall and post-war Keynesianism about to be interred by Jim Callaghan – that England should send out 45-year-old Brian Close and 39-year-old John Edrich to face the most hostile quartet of fast bowlers ever fielded by the West Indies or indeed by any team. Close, who had first played for England as a teenager in the late 1940s, came off after one session with his body black and blue from deliveries that had thudded into him. He admitted later that he had been unable to see the ball and simply allowed it to hit him. With football and cricket in secular decline – football's hastened by widespread and frequent outbreaks of hooliganism – other, more individualistic sports grew in popularity. Bob and Thelma in *Whatever Happened to the Likely Lads?* play badminton; snooker enjoyed a renaissance not just because it had a suitably 1970s anti-hero in Alex Higgins but because the game was perfect for the small screen. Squash, too, enjoyed a boom.

The cinema, increasingly the exclusive preserve of youngsters who did not want to stay at home with their TV-watching parents, seemed to take an unnatural delight in unearthing the savagery that lurked just beneath the surface of Welfare-State man. Sam Peckinpah's *Straw Dogs* featured an American writer anxious to please his rustic West Country neighbours but driven to defend himself in the most violent way when they turn nasty. *Get Carter* broke new ground in that director Mike Hodges apparently felt no obligation to provide audiences with a single sympathetic character. Set in Newcastle, its characters were depicted as the real moving forces behind the permissive society; not pleasant, hippie-ish, right-on liberals but murderous gangsters and child pornographers. Far from settling their differences around the table, in the approved Ted Heath fashion, they shot people, threw them from multi-storey car parks, injected them with fatal drug doses and stabbed them to death.

Alexander Walker, the film critic, noted: 'The first few years of the 1970s brought home to British cinema and society just what bad times lay ahead.'[19] Commenting on *Sunday Bloody Sunday*, he notes its setting in a morning-after London, sliding from its swinging euphoria into its 'hangover period' — from 'what's it all about?' to 'what will you settle for?' The chief characters, played by Glenda Jackson and Peter Finch, have cut a deal with Murray Head, who plays their joint lover. In what could be seen as an expression of middle-class disillusion with the post-war system, the Glenda Jackson character concludes that the terms of the deal are 'lousy'.

Cinema also displayed a misogynistic streak, evident in the explicit rape scenes in *Straw Dogs* and Stanley Kubrick's *A Clockwork Orange*, and in Martin Scorsese's *Taxi Driver*. In the latter film, made in 1976 and as telling a portrait of New York after Watergate and Vietnam as *Tinker Tailor* was of post-1960s London, Scorsese himself plays a punter who hails Robert de Niro's cab. He orders the driver to stop outside an apartment, points to a window where a woman is undressing, comments that the woman in question is his wife and discloses that she is having an illicit affair with a black man. Scorsese's character then threatens to blow her vagina apart with a .44 Magnum, which, as Clint Eastwood explains in *Dirty Harry*, is the most powerful handgun in the world. Michael Pye and Linda Myles, writing about Hollywood in the 1970s, say: 'It is probably the ugliest scene of misogyny that has been filmed.'[20]

Although few women were subjected to sexism quite so crude as that in *Taxi Driver*, the 1970s was still a male-dominated decade. Advertising portrayed women as housewives or bimbos and even at the end of the decade a film like *Saturday Night Fever* was unapologetic in its view of woman as sex object. If the Mini was the car that summed up the classless, androgynous 1960s and the VW Golf the hedonistic yuppie 1980s, the car of the 1970s was the phallic Ford Capri. Organized labour, already going through a painful divorce from the middle classes, was not yet ready to take the plunge and start a relationship with women on the basis of equality. Norman Stag, deputy general secretary of the Union of Post Office Workers, commented on the Heath government's plans to promote equality of opportunity at the workplace: 'The Green paper doesn't affect us a great deal. We have had equal pay, and equal opportunity for promotion since the early 1950s. It is true that there are no women postmen, because the grade of postman is a male grade and always has been.'

This cultural legacy bore fruit in the election of 1979. The votes of women, alienated by a society in which the dominant image of the nation at work was a male chauvinist trade union leader cutting deals with an impotent government, were crucial in getting Mrs Thatcher into power. In a decade which had more than its fair share of warmongers, terrorists, dictators and bullies – from Amin to Nixon, from Pol Pot to Pinochet – the only female contender for the pantheon of evil was Indira Gandhi, responsible for a forced sterilization programme. The rest were men, and for many women that was a good enough reason to give Mrs Thatcher a chance.

The intellectuals who had supported Wilson in 1964 and 1966 were also deserting to Mrs Thatcher's camp. In part this was prompted by disgust at Labour's trimming, in part by the Russian invasion of Czechoslovakia, in part by the reaction against the perceived threat to freedom from the closed shop. Stoppard, himself Czech in origin, was instrumental in altering the terms of debate in the theatre, burying the notion that a serious playwright should strive either to write about issues (in a predominantly left-wing sense) or to break down barriers, or preferably both. Plays such as *Jumpers* (1972) and *Travesties* (1974) were unashamedly intellectual, individualistic and elitist. *Professional Foul* made explicit Stoppard's personal crusade against East European Communism, while *Night and Day* railed against the union closed shop and the way in which Stoppard considered language to have been brutalized and debased by trade union militancy. Paul Johnson, on the long march from left to right, warned of the dangers of compulsory union membership in an article for the *New Statesman* in September 1976: 'How easy is it for the [union] bureaucrat to expel a member?' he asked. 'The simple answer is: the easiest thing in the world'.

Other writers, inimical to the left in any form, had been emboldened to take the gloves off and have a swing at what remained of the statist Keynesian consensus by the extraordinary interest generated by the exile from the

Soviet Union of Alexander Solzhenitsyn in March 1974. His arrival in the West after years of incarceration in the gulags was hailed by anti-Soviet liberals such as Bernard Levin, who picked up on his theme of a moral sickness in the West. This malaise, according to Solzhenitsyn, rendered Westerners less capable than oppression-hardened Soviet dissidents of fighting the totalitarian menace.

POST-WAR CULTURE: A BACKWARD GLANCE

In retrospect, it is clear that the post-war alliance collapsed because one of its two main pillars – made up of the intellectuals, liberal professionals, civil servants, writers and academics – turned against their former allies, the unionized blue-collar workers, and against the state bureaucracy that had hitherto provided the arch linking the two pillars. Indeed, in many ways the bureaucracy took as many shots in the battle for ideas in the late 1970s as did the trade unions, and as this battle progressed the two entities blurred into one, with the bureaucrats depicted as trade union-minded, trade union-appeasing and generally trade unionist in conduct, and the unions portrayed as lumberingly bureaucratic.

The cultural manifestation of this growing obsession with bureaucratic structures was best illustrated by films and TV shows that fictionalized crime. Both *Death Wish* and *Dirty Harry* were the stories of loners – the one a vigilante motivated by the murder of his wife, the other a policeman – who have no time for the normal rules of engagement. To the audiences that watched *The Blue Lamp* in 1950, the amorality that lay at the heart of these films would have been anathema, yet audiences whooped with delight a quarter of a century later when Charles Bronson gunned down muggers, and identified with Clint Eastwood when he looked down the barrel of his Magnum at the young hoodlum and said his prey had to ask himself one question: 'Do I feel lucky?'

In Britain the TV shows were slower to reflect this mood than were the hard-edged Hollywood movies. As late as the early 1970s – and despite the well-publicized cases of serious wrongdoing and corruption, particularly in the Metropolitan Police – the archetypal TV copper was George Dixon (resurrected after his untimely death in *The Blue Lamp* and now starring in *Dixon of Dock Green*) or Inspector Barlow in *Softly Softly*. Their role was to reflect the way society felt about the police rather than real police activity, with a secondary aim of mirroring the way in which the British still saw themselves: unified, good-humoured, prone to the odd bout of temper and generally decent. Very much the same set of values as George Orwell had adumbrated in 'The Lion and the Unicorn' at the start of the war, in fact.

The public liked to think of the police as enjoying a bit of a knees-up on Jubilee Day in June 1977, not getting involved in skulduggery, corruption or brutality. Signs of change came with *The Sweeney*, in which Regan (John Thaw) and Carter (Dennis Waterman) are hindered as much by police red tape and Scotland Yard's bureaucracy as they are by the villains. Regan's sole aim is to 'get a result', despite the obstructiveness of his superiors. And, in episode after episode, he gets one. But he rarely used a firearm and never departed entirely from the liberal police-series tradition of *Z Cars*, *Softly Softly* and *Dixon of Dock Green*. The change came a little later, with *The Professionals*, in which a hit squad was government sponsored but exempt from all bureaucratic (i.e. normal) controls. The squad's charter allowed it to use 'any means necessary' and week after week millions of viewers relished the sight of the two main characters driving high-performance cars and shooting dead a motley assortment of terrorists and psychotic criminals. But this was 1977. George Dixon had finally been pensioned off the previous year, the year of the sterling crisis, the IMF intervention and Jim Callaghan's warning that it was no longer possible to 'spend our way out of recession'. The economy, too, was to be given a dose of the 'any means necessary' treatment.

The year 1976 was one of catharsis for Britain, not just economic crisis, although few realized it at the time. The Callaghan government was unashamedly reactionary; its response to the continuing low-level civil war in Northern Ireland was to meet fire with fire; its reaction to the Sex Pistols and their punk rock contemporaries was to harry them at every turn. The hippies who had regarded Wilson as the iron fist in the velvet glove when dealing with the 1960s counter-culture were lucky; Callaghan did not even bother with the velvet glove. In the week of the Queen's Silver Jubilee in June 1977, the Sex Pistols were at number two in the charts with 'God Save the Queen', a record that could not be heard on the radio, could not be bought in most high-street record chains and could not be performed live because of a blanket ban on live performances by the group. There was a retreat into economic orthodoxy, monetary tightening, public spending cuts and an incomes policy, but the reaction went deeper than that. There was a full-scale counter-offensive by an older generation who had never been seduced by the cult of youth, who had always harboured doubts about comprehensive education, and who believed that it was the duty of a good citizen to obey authority. These were promising foundations for the new right to build on, but there was more. The technological paradigm that had dominated twentieth-century industrial society was reaching its limits, with new products largely a refinement of existing goods; the video as the successor to TV, the personal stereo as the logical extension of the hi-fi system. But significantly, both these products – the Sony Walkman arrived in Britain a month after Mrs Thatcher's 1979 election victory – accentuated the drift away from collectivism towards a go-it-alone approach. There was a retreat into the private realm, with the strong demand for home ownership among the baby-boomer generation only restrained by incomes policy and mortgage rationing. Heathism had been the last desperate throw of the post-war system, in which a big-bang solution was sought as the answer to every problem, from an underperforming economy to local government reorganization and industrial relations. Unfortunately for the post-war system, Heath was the least effective champion it could possibly have had and the unchallenged candidate for worst prime minister of the post-war era. But in truth, had Heath and the OPEC cartel not hastened the demise of the post-war system, it would have died anyway, but a longer, slower death. Callaghan provided the overture for Thatcherism, pioneering many of her themes – aggressive policing (the use of riot shields on the mainland for the first time at the Ladywood by-election in 1977), the bussing in of strike-breaking workers at Grunwick, a national debate on standards in education – and a lot of her social conservatism, including surprise that any decent citizen would not be in bed by eleven (when responding to a question about a late-night TV blackout caused by industrial action).

The post-war system had been built upon a delicate balance of conflicting forces: Thatcherism replaced it with a much simpler message that seemed to chime with the prevailing mood: look after yourself and your family, keep your nose clean, respect authority and save a bit for a rainy day. It was crude, it was limited, but for the millions watching Basil Fawlty's rantings, it struck a deep chord.

THE 'WE' GENERATION?: CULTURE ON THE TURN

What evidence do we have of another shift in the cultural climate since the mid-1970s? In almost every area we have touched upon in this chapter there have been signs of a different mood. In cinema, audiences have been rising steadily since at least the mid-1980s, and the output from Hollywood has changed also. Romance has once again become fashionable, just as it was in the troubled 1930s. The modern Disney films invariably contain a right-on message: women's liberation (*Aladdin*), protecting the environment (*Pocahontas*) and minority rights (*The Hunchback of Notre Dame*).

Pop music, after a dismal and barren period in the 1980s when the scene was dominated by ageing superstars like Phil Collins, has been reinvigorated. Significantly, much of the output of bands such as Oasis harks back with deference to the 1960s, while the revival of the big open-air concert also harks back to an earlier age. In sport, soccer has gained in popularity, with the Euro 96 tournament – the first international tournament in Britain since the 1966 World Cup – an unalloyed success. Where Lindsay Anderson's *Britannia Hospital* captured in satire the decay and near-anarchy of Britain in the early 1980s, hospital dramas in the 1990s – *Casualty* being the prime example – verge on being straight propaganda for a properly funded NHS. Barely a week goes by without a TV drama decrying the lack of money in the health service.

It would be wrong to overstate these changes, just as it would be wrong to exaggerate the extent of the cultural shift in the 1960s and 1980s. Football's renaissance is, in essence, the result of the game becoming trendy with the middle classes. That was certainly true of the trouble-free Euro 96, and was also reflected in the growth of 'laddish' magazines aimed at making members of the metropolitan bourgeoisie feel comfortable about dropping their aitches at Stamford Bridge and Highbury.

Some people were rightly suspicious of the retro nature of the music business, not only in the homage paid to the Beatles and the Stones but also in the cynical repackaging in CD box sets by record companies of duff tracks, out-takes and badly-recorded concert performances by any artist of note from the 1960s and 1970s. The idea that the 1990s were a rerun of the 1960s could be overdone. To be sure there is a renewed fascination with alternative religions and with cults, and with a willingness to engage in various forms of single-issue protest. At the same time carpet-baggers have been depositing small amounts of money in mutual organizations in the hope that they will be allocated free shares if the building society or insurance company is floated on the stock exchange.

But the possibility for change is there. The most popular leisure pursuit for the young is now clubbing. After decades of drift to the suburbs, the 1990s have seen some sections of the middle classes and the better-off start to head back to the cities. The big amorphous estates, built on farmland at the edge of towns and without any core or centrality, have become as bleak and soulless as tower blocks seemed in the 1970s. The new suburbs, full of cul-de-sacs, symbolize the right's own dead-end. A move is afoot to recolonize space that was surrendered years ago. The question is: can the left do the same?

CHAPTER TWO

CASH IS FACT OR HOW I LEARNED TO STOP WORRYING AND LOVE BIG BUSINESS

If you are running a company nowadays, suppose you are running
Marks & Spencer or Sainsbury, you will be constantly trying to work out
whether your customers are satisfied with the product they are
getting . . . I don't think there is anything wrong with
government trying to do that.
Tony Blair, Prime Minister, BBC Radio, 29 July 1997

[S]ervice level agreements (SLAs) are being introduced between the
in-house service providers . . . and integrated divisions. The
agreements strengthen a customer service approach in
support of the core work of the Office.
Serious Fraud Office annual report to the Attorney-General, July 1997

'Well, sir, here's to a fair bargain and profits large enough for both of us.'
Dashiell Hammett, *The Maltese Falcon* (Cassell edition, 1974)

THE CAPITALIST LAZARUS: WHY EVERY DAY IS MARKET DAY

The market, protested Alvin Toffler, the American sociologist, is a tool, not
a religion, and no tool does every job. Writing in the early Reagan years, he
had detected an alarming enthusiasm for 'market solutions' in areas of life in
which the market had nothing to offer. He might as well have saved his

energy. Today, the tool has become a religion, the sole 'undistorted' external judge of doings in the human world. As one City of London analyst, Terry Smith, has declared: 'Cash is fact. Everything else is opinion.' He spoke truer than he may have known. (Incidentally, religion has moved the other way, becoming a tool, judged useful only insofar as its practitioners 'get something out of it' or 'find what they are looking for'.)

This dominance of market values is at the centre of the dominant business ethic which prevails not only in this country but around the world. This ethic is all-pervasive, to the extent that it does not even require the existence of any actual businesses in the legally constituted sense, in order to occupy a ruling cultural position. For different reasons, neither the People's Republic of China nor the wilder fringes of post-Communist Russia enjoy the property rights and other law-based underpinnings essential to proper business formation, yet both exhibit the business-market ethic at its most enthusiastic and ferocious.

Thus, the triumph we seek to analyse is not of large-scale private business *per se* but of its values and ethos. In the mid-1970s, big business justified itself in social-welfare terms; today, social-welfare organizations justify themselves in business terms. The spokesman for commerce in the mid-1970s was never happier than when discussing the services contributed by business to the common weal, in particular jobs, living standards and consumer goods. He would turn wryly defensive when talk moved on to the red meat of capitalism: profits, interest, monopoly, inequality. Human nature being what it is, he would aver, it is unlikely that the services of the 'private sector' (a term handily conveying a cramped, marginalized image of capitalist operations, in contrast to the broad acres of the 'public sector') can be dispensed with. In a perfect world, he would suggest, he would not exist. Auberon Waugh's fictional businessman declared: 'there is still a majority of the workers. . . . They know what they want – more money and more leisure to enjoy it. We can give them that, not these socialists or these philosophers and beatniks.'[1] Business cast itself as servant of the workforce, delivering the goods and tolerated on that basis.

Today, the reversal is striking. Core functionaries at the very heart of the state machine – police, diplomats, defence officials – are required to produce commercial justifications of their activities. Their colleagues in social-welfare operations – teachers, professors, doctors, nurses and librarians – have long been accustomed to 'market testing', a process designed to introduce the 'discipline' of the open market into traditional public service operations. This dominance of the business/market ethos is very recent and is only tangentially connected with privatization, the 1980s process whereby governments around the world divested themselves of industrial holdings that had more to do with wartime and the pre-war Depression than with any over-arching philosophy.

But what exactly is this ethos? It comprises three interlocking parts, acceptance of each leading to acceptance of the next:

1. The market, ranging from the localized market for, let us say, Chinese leaf in Derbyshire right up to the trillion-dollar foreign-exchange market, forms in total an objective, external reality against which all human activity can be judged. The market authenticates and validates activity. Non-market criteria are 'artificial' and likely to 'distort' this reality.
2. Human actions made in conformity with this reality are likely to prove more fruitful than those made in defiance or ignorance of it. And we mean all human actions. Thus the *Guardian* of 16 October 1995 maintained: 'the real economic blind spot lies in the conventional treatment of families as a single harmonious economic unit, a "black box" in which the laws of supply, demand and exchange do not apply . . . families are extremely efficient markets'.
3. This being true, it follows that the structures and assumptions of those human organizations that, by definition, operate and survive in the market – i.e. large-scale business organizations – are the structures and assumptions that ought to be adopted by almost all human organizations.

Later on we shall look more closely at these structures and assumptions as they are applied to the public realm. But, briefly, they include a strong executive function, akin to a commercial directorate staffed by 'undogmatic professionals', a 'productive' legislative unit, akin to a corporate salariat and geared to 'teamwork' in the 'throughput' of laws and taxes, and a powerful, politicized judicial function, akin to a large company's non-executive directors, charged with protecting the dominant ethos from democratic challenges.

The net effect of all this for the citizen is an uneasy awareness that his own aspirations and fears have, without fanfare, been sharply demoted in a never-published league table of public goals. Just as, some years ago, householders were outraged (but perhaps not entirely surprised) to learn that domestic burglaries rated a mere handful of priority points on the scoring system employed to allocate police resources, so ordinary working people are increasingly aware not only that many of their cherished desires (security of employment, to take an obvious example) score low on the official agenda, but that they are seen as 'unhelpful attitudes', passively obstructing the full realization of that agenda ('competitiveness', for instance) and that these 'attitudes' are in need of 're-engineering'.

For anybody with a moment's spare time for reflection and reading, there is a past to be explored and perhaps remembered, a past so utterly different from our contemporary economic and social order as to provoke the obvious question: how did big-business values triumph when they appeared, so recently, to be mortally wounded?

AN HISTORICAL ROUND-TRIP

New York's New School for Social Research in 1976 may be as good a place as any to start the exploration. Here, Professor Robert Heilbroner had just published *Business Civilization in Decline*.[2] It is an interesting and pleasing read, but hardly unusual for the time. The West is reeling from inflation and the oil crisis: there is an all-pervasive distrust and contempt for large-scale indus-trial, financial and commercial operations. No economics lecture is complete without a swipe at 'multinational corporations', every bookshop boasts a shelf full of works declaring socialism the 'only answer to world crisis'. In Britain, a Conservative Prime Minister has recently decried the 'unattractive and unacceptable face of capitalism'; in the United States, his Republican opposite number has abandoned free-market rhetoric to clamp emergency controls on incomes and prices. The delicate balance of the post-war 'mixed economy' is disintegrating as inflation and unemployment blow apart the social-democratic settlement. Marxism, (un)diluted to taste, enjoys a pres-tige within Western universities unseen since the 1930s.

At every level of British society, private capitalism is suffering an 'attitude strike' by the public at large and, with particular reference to the future, by the young. It is this business-averse culture that is to prompt an alarmed sociology professor, David Marsland, to write his magisterial work *Seeds of Bankruptcy*, warning that the biases of his own discipline undermine not only its pretensions to objectivity but the entire future of the British economy. Courses at O- and A-level, he says, are saturated with a negative view of the market system: 'The free market and private enterprise are either neglected, assumed to be passé dinosaurs or treated with one-sided negativism.'[3] There is no more concise expression of the general view of business at most levels of British society during the 'fright decade' of the 1970s, for this is an anti-business culture with a vengeance, reflecting the imploding balance of the post-war years. The half-amused portrait of large-scale commercial life popular during the high noon of the mixed economy is giving way to open hostility. On page and screen, big-business executives assume a mantle of wickedness. They steal millions and bully small countries,[4] they routinely swindle their investors and are fair game to be swindled back,[5] they hire mercenaries and stage coups d'état.[6]

In such a climate, few protest (as they would today) when a professional economist, the above-mentioned Professor Heilbroner, states quite seriously that: 'Capitalism is drifting into planning. Is there anyone who would deny the fact?' He goes on to write: 'In the middle run, then, it seems plausible that the economic institutions of socialism [the Communist-bloc countries] may prove superior to those of planned capitalism.'[7]

Professor Heilbroner is far from alone. From the doyen of Keynesian economists, Professor John Galbraith (who argues that, as big business was not really competitive at all but an interlocking quasi-monopolistic 'technostructure', it ought to be treated as such by law makers), to the father of the Green movement, Fritz Schumacher (to whom big business is literally and metaphorically pulling the planet out of shape), large-scale private enterprise is taking sustained and direct hits.

For Professor Marsland, the danger is that business bashing could create such hostility as to destroy industrial society altogether. His book names others who share his fears; thus N. H. Stacey writes in 1981: 'Silicon Valley had to be established in California, not in Cumbria. Why? – because the educated layers of British society have no wish to be entrepreneurial. Combativeness has gone out of fashion.'[8]

Another commentator from the time, quoted by Professor Marsland, is Graham Dawson, writing for the Social Affairs Unit. He

proposes an even tougher version of my assumptions. He argues that the state welfare sector is of its nature anti-entrepreneurial, and that academics responsible for its training are ipso facto propagandists against business. Their role in life is specifically the dissemination of anti-entrepreneurial values. . . . Anti-business academics actually believe that commercial pressures in the private sector 'induce a materialistic outlook which inhibits the growth of such values as "concern for the individual" and respect for human life'.[9]

Mr Dawson, says Professor Marsland, 'construes the state education system as a species of advertising agency for state welfare, selling post-materialistic culture'.

But how much selling does the anti-business culture of the 1970s actually need? Mr Dawson is quoted as identifying an underlying rejection of realistic economics and 'the unrealistic belief that modern affluence in the hands of public officials can achieve the impossible'. Such a view was not limited to the educated classes, or even to those with a minimum of formal education. As we note above, it soaked through the whole of popular culture. Professor Ian Angell, of the London School of Economics, has even fingered the era's most popular fictional secret agent as a flag-bearer of anti-commercial hostility: '[The] James Bond myth, that the state is good and global corporations . . . are bad, is blatant propaganda on behalf of the nation-state; a morality-tale told by tax collectors.'[10]

Professor Angell notes that big-business figures had never been especially popular during the post-war years. But they became even more beleaguered during the economic crisis of the mid-1970s; collapsing self-confidence struck even the most buccaneering of the breed: 'The social justification of a company like Slater Walker at this particular time [1973–74] was not readily apparent. We were liquidating investments simply to survive. To find a social justification in the longer term would have required a stable period during which the company would have had to establish a real identity and role in the business and investment community.'[11]

Meanwhile, the sterner brand of leftist, never really at home in the permissive consumer society, linked the crisis in industry with the bursting of the brightly coloured bubbles of swinging London: 'Saturday 14 July [1975]

Went shopping with Melissa and we walked up Kensington High Street. We went into Biba's store which really is the end of a dream. You can see why it failed really because it was the final fling for the excrescences of Sixties' fashion, now all gone bust.'[12]

Twenty years later, the position has swivelled 180 degrees. Big-business executives – give or take the odd 'fat cat' – are at least figures of respect who have 'hacked it' in 'the real world' (i.e. the market). In newspapers and magazines, business journalists, once described by playwright Arnold Wesker as 'an army of very bright urban saboteurs',[13] have degenerated, in many cases, into the fawning authors of a stream of spectacularly non-investigative 'profiles' of 'business leaders', in which the subject's 'piercing blue eyes', firm handshake, fanatical pursuit of squash (or something similarly masochistic) and devotion to opera and/or one of the more fashionable association-football clubs will be lovingly described.

More to the point, even were 'business leaders' themselves among the least popular figures in society, it is their ethos, the 'real-world' market ethos, that dominates human activity. Large-scale private enterprise has swapped the status of problem for that of solution. Twenty years ago, it seemed possible that the crises of the 1970s would trigger stage two of the post-war social revolution, bringing public ownership ('accountability', in the buzzword of the time) to those sectors of the economy still in private hands, chiefly the newer industries such as medicines, chemicals, light engineering and financial services. Emasculated after 1945, private enterprise, on any significant scale, would soon be finished off. By 1997, the worm had not only turned but developed sabre teeth, and now the 'bankrupt' welfare states of Western Europe and North America looked the likelier candidates for termination.

Objectors may suggest that the contrast between the two periods is exaggerated, pleading different reasons why this is so. First, they may claim that new-style capitalists such as Richard Branson or Bill Gates may be heroes, but this is because they represent new, sexy technology and a fresh, casual business style. Big business, they will say, has reinvented itself, away from smoke-belching heavy industry with its up-tight buttoned-down executives. Even if this were true, it would be beside the point. Attitudes to big business have been transformed to such an extent that business values are now the dominant values in society. This is an extraordinary change, whatever the 'image' issues involved. But it is not true. The corporate 'villains' of the 1970s featured prominently, among others, Distillers (producers of the Thalidomide drug prescribed for morning sickness), ITT (allegedly involved in the anti-socialist coup in Chile), Lockheed (allegedly involved in grand-scale bribery), all operating in new industries, respectively pharmaceuticals, telecommunications and aerospace. None was in pig-iron or similar sweat-breaking activities.

A second objection may be that Professor Heilbroner was, quite simply, proved wrong: the Communist-bloc countries proved not to enjoy superior economic institutions and, once this fact became established beyond question, the Lazarus performance of capitalist values was inevitable. There is, in short, nothing astonishing about the triumph of capitalism: the other side lost. But this is not quite right either. In contrast to the 1930s, the critique of capitalism holding sway in the early 1970s was largely unconnected with any alleged superiority in the living standards delivered by non-capitalistic systems. Quite the opposite: the fruits of capitalism were routinely condemned as being as rotten as the tree itself, and the juicier they appeared, the more they confirmed the canker within the tree. Thus Dr Schumacher: 'The modern economy is propelled by a frenzy of greed and indulges in an orgy of envy, and these are not accidental features but the very causes of its expansionist success'.[14]

The steady rise in unemployment certainly brought forth more traditional attacks on big-business operations. Tony Benn declared: 'The capitalist world economy is in very serious difficulty. . . . The most dramatic event of the whole of the last decade has been the collapse of confidence of those who espouse the system. . . . Unemployment could be the catalyst. If unemployment continues to rise . . . there will be great pressure for structural change.'[15]

Jimmy Reid, Britain's best-known Communist, spoke movingly of the plight of industrial workers told they were now surplus to requirements. But even he was exercised by the spiritual, rather than material, impoverishment he saw in a society dominated by commercial interests. In the same speech he declared: 'A rat race is for rats. We're not rats. We're human beings.'[16]

The traditional critique of capitalism as a material failure was not incompatible with the newer critique of capitalism as a material success. On the contrary, the 'energy crisis' – the worldwide panic at shortages of oil and other fossil fuels — was the hinge that linked the two apparently contradictory critiques into one 'fusion bomb'. It was precisely because capitalism was so successful in its own 'rotten' terms that it was bound to loot the Earth's resources and usher in a new age of scarcity that would make socialistic, non-market solutions much more than one dish on the democratic menu. There would be no other dishes because no other food could grow in the post-capitalist desert.

Thus Dr Schumacher's book poured scorn on the idea that the Keynesian, social-democratic system had solved the problem of production: 'A businessman would not consider a firm to have solved its problems of production and to have achieved viability if he saw that it was rapidly consuming its capital.'[17] In other words, apparently successful consumer capitalism was actually burning up the fuel supplies of Spaceship Earth at a terrifying rate. According to Schumacher, it had no real answers to future problems beyond more of the same: better-armed police to deal with the spiritual victims of capitalist alienation and ultra-dangerous nuclear power to make good the exhausted fuel supply. No more promising background could have been conceived for the triumph of those forces to the left of post-war social democracy. The oil shortages even threatened that bastion of the workers' 'false consciousness', the individualistic motor car. Without petrol, there would be no more bunking off on roadside picnics for the working classes, no more snubbing of the public transport system by Ford Anglia drivers.

Overall, the left could not lose. Any recovery from the turbulence of the mid-1970s would simply underline the system's desperate attempts to prop up a 'sick', polluting society. Should the system not recover — cue the 1930s critique of big business as a force for impoverishment.

The tune could be played mod or trad, depending on circumstances. But, whatever the tune it played, the left was in as weak a position as big business itself. Contrary to its hopes and (occasional) fantasies, the left was witnessing not the 'final crisis of capitalism' but the final crisis of the post-war mixed economy. Big capital and big business were certainly major players in that economy. But so were other entities, including two traditionally associated with the left: the social-democratic state and its trade unions.

First, the state. It is hard to exaggerate the backwash from the great waves of supposed political duplicity and misfeasance on both sides of the Atlantic that broke during the crises involving Rhodesia, Biafra, Vietnam and, of course, Watergate. Much of this reaction was itself part of the break-up at the end of the 1960s of the cultural alliance between blue-collar workers and middle-class intellectuals. With regard particularly to Watergate, an enraged left-inclined bourgeoisie was desperately seeking scandal and demanding collective nationwide trauma counselling when routine presidential 'hardball' was uncovered. On a (suitably) lesser scale, it is difficult today to claim that the British government could have done anything significant to shut down the Ian Smith regime in Rhodesia, given that the colony had been self-governing since the 1920s and Britain by the mid-1960s was coming to the end of dismantling any sort of imperial strike capability (a process heartily approved by the left, except where Rhodesia was concerned).

In the early 1960s, John and Robert Kennedy seemed to epitomize the alliance between the blue-collar working class and the left-leaning intelligentsia. John's murder, in November 1963, cemented the concordat; Robert's in 1968 sounded its death knell, with the intellectual wing subsequently turning decisively against government in all its conventional forms. And this hostility was already being reflected in popular culture, as we have seen. Post-war governmental and security structures had always been fair game for scriptwriters and novelists seeking 'sinister' backdrops for their works. One has only to think of the mysterious 'government facilities', complete with domes and silos, that featured in the *Quatermass* programmes (BBC TV, 1953–58) or the cynicism and double-dealing shown by British intelligence in *The Spy Who Came in from the Cold* (1965) or *The Ipcress File* (1965). The difference was that now there were no 'good chaps' in high places to whom the hero could turn for help. Government itself had developed an enormous (fictional) capacity for evil; in the new mood of big-screen ultra-cynicism, governments killed their own employees (*Three Days of the Condor*, 1975), tortured defenceless aliens (*The Man Who Fell to Earth*, 1976), faked their own space missions (*Capricorn One*, 1978) and turned a blind eye to the slaughter of their own citizens (*Sweeney!*, 1976). It was all a long way from the days when the arrival of a G-man or Scotland Yard detective spelled nemesis for the bad-hats. In the new screenplay, these were the bad-hats.

Behind it all was the fear that governments, or at least certain arms of goverment (notably police and security operations), were drifting loose not only from the sort of ethical moorings of which left-thinking people approved, but from any sort of moorings at all and floating into the chilly waters of amorality and ultra-relativism. Anthony Burgess, in the non-fiction 'discussion' sections that wrap around *1985*, his 1970s novel set in a future trade-union dictatorship, reprints a dialogue with an unnamed friend. They have talked themselves hoarse about war, democracy, the decline of the West and so forth. Suddenly, the conversation takes an alarming turn:

Friend: You're under arrest.
Burgess: I beg your pardon?
Friend: You're under arrest.
Burgess: You're joking. Yes, joking. I knew somehow you were joking.
Friend: But for a moment you thought I was serious.
Burgess: Yes, I did.[18]

Much of the fire directed from across the political spectrum at 'the state machine' or governments was contradictory, simultaneously accusing the Western power structure of pitiable weakness (in the face of terrorists or militant trade unions) and overweening arrogance (with regard to its attempts to set prices and incomes or to second-guess the car market or the demand for housing). But, as the 1970s progressed, these apparent contradictions were fused into a new synthesis: the state was weak where it ought to be strong and vice versa. Horribly distended, it tried to run shipyards and coal mines while cravenly negotiating with aeroplane hijackers. In a phrase that was to gain currency much later, the state needed to be 'right-sized'.

Leftists, naturally, protested that their own attacks on the government apparatus had referred only to the Nixon White House and its imperialistic tentacles in Downing Street, the Elysée Palace and elsewhere. Bashing Western governments and their spies, soldiers and 'political police' in no way invalidated the socialist state of the future, which would be under 'accountable democratic control'. Tony Benn was a key figure in attempts to rebalance the left away from the state: not only did he take to quoting Lao-Tzu ('when the best leader's work is done the people say, "We did it ourselves"'), but he tried to back it up in office, putting taxpayers' money where his mouth was and supporting co-operatives at Meriden (motor-cycles), Kirby (manufacturing and engineering) and the *Scottish Daily News* newspaper. '[W]hy were these the ones where something happened? Let's be quite clear, it was not because of the Secretary of State for Industry. It had nothing whatever to do with me . . . the experiments selected themselves.'[19]

Some were willing to give Benn's state-free socialism a sporting chance. The popular columnist and essayist Keith Waterhouse declared in the *Daily Mirror*: 'They are not wild ideas. They are not revolutionary ideas. They are not even very new ideas. They are simply that those who do the donkey-work should have a say in how their factories are run.'

But even if the state could be elbowed out of the picture, it would be much harder to brush aside another estate of the post-war realm, one whose public-relations problems made those of the state appear trivial by comparison: the trade unions.

Earlier we examined in more detail the cultural shift against organized labour at this time. Suffice for the moment to identify two factors repelling previously sympathetic middle-class opinion formers: picket-line violence and the extension of the closed shop to middle-class occupations. These factors were linked: violence was a tool in the enforcement of union-only shops and, conversely, strikes in 100 per cent unionized plants were characterized by a low level of picket-line trouble, the enforcement function being unnecessary. The white-collar/intellectual left had been happy to turn a blind eye to the rougher side of industrial relations, provided it could be disguised by euphemisms such as 'argy-bargy', 'pushing and shoving', 'all-ticket job' (union bosses, never at a loss for either euphemism or turgid jargon about 'the consultative machinery', cheerfully obliged).

But the euphemistic wall was cracking. The 1970s saw explosive growth in white-collar trade unionism, ranging from teaching and lecturing through computer programming and bank clerking to journalism and even literary and creative occupations. Paul Johnson warned in the *New Statesman* in September 1977:

There is . . . a grisly little plot to form a closed shop of writers for the state theatres. Successful playwrights whose work is not exclusively determined by the sectarian politics of the extreme Left are vigorously opposed to it. One of our leading playwrights told me: 'If the scheme goes through I will never write another word. I would rather earn my living as an unskilled labourer than submit to those bastards.'

Some of the most ferocious unions of the time were directly involved in what would come to be known as the 'creative' industries: ACTT (film), Equity (the acting profession), NGA, SOGAT and NATSOPA (printing). More alarming still was the development of the trade unions' 'long-arm doctrine', whereby the closed shop could be enforced on offices and factories hundreds of miles from the union plants, against the wishes of staff and management, by the simple expedient of blacking any supplies from the non-union to the union plant, threatening the non-union plant with bankruptcy. In a notorious case, the print union SLADE was found to be an enthusiastic prosecutor of 'secondary blacking', in which small artwork companies were threatened with bankruptcy unless they agreed to unionize their employees.

That such techniques may be turned on playwrights or artists was intolerable. It is no coincidence that three of the grandest figures in the left–liberal intellectual aristocracy – director Sir Peter Hall, playwright Harold Pinter and editor of the *Sunday Times* Harold Evans – broke the habit of many years and all voted Conservative in 1979.

In all, then, the position of big business was not as grim as it may have appeared. True, it was out in the cultural cold. But so were the other two actors in the 'tripartite' post-war system, government and labour. As Andrew Swarbrick writes of Philip Larkin's 1974 collection of poems, *High Windows*:

Forces which in *The Whitsun Weddings* [Larkin's 1964 volume] were held delicately in tension can be seen disintegrating in *High Windows* . . . Stan Smith has argued . . . that in *The Whitsun Weddings*, Larkin's attitude to 'welfare-state social democracy, where mass values prevail' was usually 'to maintain an equivocal balance to such a world, poised between annoyance and deference. In more recent work . . . this balance has gone, and the mood is a more tight-lipped one, of disdain sharpening to odium'.[20]

Swarbrick adds of *High Windows*: 'the fury in these poems is the fury of disillusionment'. It is an apt summary of the forces blowing apart cultural consensus in the mid-1970s. But, contrary to all expectations, this disintegration cleared the path for a triumphant return of the one philosophy widely assumed to be safely interred for all time: laissez-faire capitalism. Before that could happen, though, the cultural and political breakdown had to experience its final climax.

JUDGEMENT DAY: THE ENERGY CRISIS AND HYPERINFLATION

For those of a moralistic bent, the cataclysm that overtook Western societies in the latter part of 1973 could not have been better timed had it been

scripted. The long post-war upswing burned out as shortages of commodities – mainly oil, but also sugar and other foodstuffs – combined with roaring
inflation and widespread industrial unrest to induce a state of near-hysteria
across Europe and North America. '[T]he machine stops', declared journalist Christopher Booker, who summed up the feeling of many when he
declared the energy crisis to be the end not only of the post-war boom but also
of the entire materialistic and rationalist experiment of the post-Renaissance
period.[21] Even fervent supporters of the post-war system bent to the new
realities: 'The party's over', declared Labour's Environment Secretary Tony
Crosland in 1975, and he did not mean only local government spending.

Nobel laureate and former Oxford professor Sir John Hicks, in an article
entitled 'The Permissive Economy', read the last rites over the Keynesian
system, with its commitment to full employment, with no pain: 'there is nothing in the system which prevents wages rising faster than productivity . . . the
primary product crisis . . . that has come upon us since 1972–73 . . . marked
a sharp fall in the real earning-power of British labour . . . now that the veil of
money has been so largely stripped off, we have to face it in terms of traditional
economics, waking up from the sweet Keynesian dreams that have been with us
for so long.'[22] Sir John made it clear that he himself was a bit of a swinger: 'the
Permissive Economy . . . was, after all, to give us about 20 years of fair prosperity; and that is not a bad showing.' But the energy and inflation crisis
combined with a cultural shift away from big technology, economic growth and
ever-rising living standards. Environmentalism led the rebellion against a future
many no longer believed would be worth having and, in a clatter of cancella-
tions, politicians responded by scrapping or curtailing the multi-million-pound
schemes (now dismissed as 'prestige projects') that had once symbolized that
future: the Channel Tunnel, the Hovertrain, the multiple-site Third London
Airport, the Black Arrow space programme, the fast-breeder reactor scheme
and, eventually, the Advanced Passenger Train.

The collapse of the permissive economy rapidly realigned social groups and
schools of thought: in an extraordinary and fascinating book *The Protest Virus*,
Peter Evans claimed the revolt against the 'throw-away' society united, *inter alia*,
rebellious Sussex students, Enoch Powell, the campaigners against Covent
Garden redevelopment, Sir Alec Douglas Home, US black militants, assorted
strikers and preservationists.[23] Suddenly everyone seemed to be – as Randolph
Churchill once said of Harold Macmillan – 'tremendously on our side'. It is easy

to smile now. But Mr Evans had a point. For the first time since the war, it was hip to hate the future. At a stroke, people who had always detested motorways, keg beer, housing estates and loud music found themselves at the cutting edge of social change. Nobody was out – other than the despised, crumpled social-democratic politicians still desperately trying to shore up confidence in the system, mouthing platitudes about a 'better tomorrow' as the lights went out .

Out of this social realignment emerged three distinct interwoven strands, each representing a facet of the newly emerging 'coalition against the future' that came out of the energy and inflation crises.

Authenticity

From real-ale and breastfeeding, herbal medicines and wooden furniture through to the 'come home to a real fire' slogan, the search was on for a 'bedrock', genuine article in many, perhaps most, areas of life. Record collectors, who only recently had bragged of their stereo equipment and its unrivalled sound quality, now outdid each other in the unlistenability of the 'original' blues or jazz records they had unearthed on some rubbish dump or junk stall. Their classical brethren developed a taste for recordings played with instruments of the time when the music was written. Elsewhere, 'original' texts of works such as *Lady Chatterley's Lover* were in huge demand. Women shunned painkilling drugs and experimented with pools, stools and sitting positions in search of the 'natural' way to deliver a baby. Indeed, 'natural', 'genuine' and 'original' were three keywords in what amounted to a rejection of the entire Victorian notion of 'improvement': the authenticity revolution. It was hardly surprising that this search for the 'real' spread to that most basic of human commodities: money. An inflating currency was no more acceptable than chemical beer; the yearning for a unit of account correctly related to effort and achievement was closely linked to the yearning for a cask-conditioned pint of proper beer. The latter led to the Campaign for Real Ale, the former to the campaign for real money: monetarism.

Ruralism

Closely allied to the search for the authentic, the pastoral urge gathered pace at all levels of society. Pop stars had led the way, with hit records since the late 1960s dwelling rather less on bright lights and big cities and rather more on the joys of open country roads. And if one thing beat the country, it was 'Western' — cod American pioneer ruralism in which the simple virtues and vices (a good woman, a jar of whisky) were addressed *ad nauseam*. By the middle of the decade, some of the most unlikely superstars were filling whole albums with material evocative of a time and place of which they could have minimal knowledge. Tony Christie conjured up an execution yard somewhere hot and dusty and Radio Two listeners sang along to the grisly chorus: 'Take an eye for an eye/And a life for a life'. Elton John hammered his way enthusiastically through a stack of numbers praising Greyhound buses, elderberry wine, record machines, his daddy's farm and other phenomena far removed from his native Middlesex.

In Britain, diaries of long-departed country rectors and rural gentlewomen sold like hot cakes; the reminiscences of a Yorkshire vet, James Herriot, ballooned into a best-selling run of books, a film, a TV series and a multi-million-pound tourist industry so large as seriously to threaten the environment of the Yorkshire Dales. By the early 1980s, it seemed as if every retired village bobby or rural stationmaster was determined to 'do a Herriot': bookshelves were packed with titles along the lines of *It Shouldn't Happen to a Storekeeper/Sheep Farmer/Country Doctor/Tree Surgeon*.

Elsewhere on television, man's four-legged friend was a guaranteed audience-grabber, from the horse sanctuary of *Follyfoot* (ITV, 1971–73) to *The Adventures of Black Beauty* (ITV, 1972–74). Smallholding and 'smallternatives' became fashionable for the more Bohemian-minded, while the suburban snob was suckered by glossy magazine advertisements promoting cars or sherry against backdrops of roaring log fires, Norfolk jackets and hand-crafted shotguns.

Small business / self-employment virtues

Perhaps the most obviously 'political' of the three strands, the rediscovery of the 'little man' is also the strand most obviously linked to the eventual triumph of business values. For once the small businessman was declared a cultural hero, it was the easiest thing in the world for larger operators to claim his virtues for themselves. By the end of the 1970s, the small businessman had merged into the 'entrepreneur', a tag which could be claimed

by the likes of Freddie Laker, Lord Hanson and Rupert Murdoch. The rehabilitation of the small-scale economic operator in the middle 1970s was
dramatic: just a few years earlier, during the spate of state-inspired mergers
of the late 1960s, the small businessman had been stigmatized as hidebound
and reactionary, as much an enemy of economic progress as he was of social
progress. On 10 May 1965, a Labour minister of state at the Department of
Economic Affairs had responded to Tory opposition claims that government
policies would cause the break-up of family companies by declaring: 'And
about time'. The future lay with the 'go-ahead boys' such as Arnold
Weinstock (GEC), Jim Slater (Slater Walker), Lord Stokes (British Leyland)
and other chieftains running giant companies and imbued with 'modern'
ideas such as the need to 'get into Europe' and be more 'efficient'.
Discredited utterly by the economic collapse of the mid-1970s, these
Olympians shuffled off, leaving only the honest, dowdy small businessman
still standing: solvent, requiring no government handouts and never on
strike, the small businessman represented not only all that was best in Britain,
but perhaps all that was left that was best in Britain.

In this new mood, the BBC achieved the seemingly impossible, keeping
millions of television viewers gripped week after week with a serial describing the trials and tribulations of a small haulage company. *The Brothers*
(1972–76), although spiced with adultery and backstabbing, was a world
away from the big-business dramas with their cigar-chomping power-mad villains. The fictional managing director Edward Hammond (Glyn Owen)
epitomized the small-business virtues: he could drive every lorry in the yard,
had come up the hard way, was a clean fighter and played fair by his men. A
physical man, he would prefer to thump miscreants than either sack them or
engage bureaucratic British Leyland-style 'grievance procedures'. Trade
unions exist in *The Brothers* only as obstacles to the fruitful partnership
between straight-talking Edward and his workforce. Merchant bankers and
big-business competitors fulfil similar black-hat roles. Edward, on one occasion, enrages shareholders by insisting on putting his drivers first.

The new small-business paragon was no Captain Mainwaring-type petty
snob, but an open-handed democrat. The ethos was Washington State, rather
than Warmington-on-Sea. Hired hand and master could look one another in
the eye in mutual respect. Hard work, comradeship, fair pay and the occasional 'bollocking' were to be the ingredients of this idealized workplace. It

was a world away from the working style of, for example, poetry-loving railway chairman Sir Peter Parker and other 'tasteful' nationalized-industry grandees. This new paradigm was to play a part in establishing the 'democracy of taste' that was to have far-reaching cultural implications in the 1990s.

Back in the 1970s, the homespun wisdom of the shop counter was much in demand: asked at this time for her favourite saying, the Cabinet minister Shirley Williams responded not with some impeccably left–liberal aphorism of, for example, George Bernard Shaw, but with the old peasant proverb: 'Take what you like – and pay for it.' (By coincidence, the same proverb was selected by Sir Keith Joseph, economic policy guru in the Tory opposition.) Her boss, the Prime Minister James Callaghan, was homelier still, interspersing his sentences with 'bless my soul' and similar phrases. The contrast between the rock-steady former naval officer and tax inspectors' union delegate (he had even once represented the Police Federation in Parliament) and the 'brightest and best' metropolitan Oxford juntas headed by Harold Wilson and Edward Heath was stark. But in an age demanding the bedrock good sense of the corner shop, even Callaghan could not compete with someone who had actually grown up in one: Margaret Thatcher.

GOOD HOUSEKEEPING: THE DEATH OF COMPLEXITY

This new cultural force, the 'authenticity revolution', took its first scalp with the slaying of the notion of economic policy as a complex, pseudo-scientific process that, in the hands of technicians, could deliver pain-free growth and the limitless expansion of living standards. According to the new thinking, governments had to balance their books, just as everybody else did. Some failed to notice the changing tide. Lord Lever, Harold Wilson's economic adviser and Chancellor of the Duchy of Lancaster, assured one and all that the slump could be cured by the simple expedient of borrowing from the Arab OPEC countries all the money they had sucked out of the West through higher oil prices. In the *Sunday Times* on 5 March 1978, he summarized his view of the events of 1973–74: 'A remarkable period of advance in prosperity and world trade, which marked the first decade of the post-war system, has clearly ended . . . deficit countries must recognise that deficit represents a receipt of resources over and above national production. . . . Any period of deficit is not a time for the infliction of self-injury. It is a period of opportunity.' But such permissiveness was becoming deeply unfashionable. A few short years after the oil crisis, Mrs Thatcher rounded on those 'eminent economists' urging her to 'borrow' (she almost spat the word) and declared: 'The lady's not for turning.'

Bridging these two periods were the (for the time) novel accountancy tools of 'kitty bargaining' and 'cash limits'. No longer would the bill for pay rises and recruitment simply be tacked on to the 'volume' costs of industries and services. Now, more pay would equal fewer staff. A key figure in this imposition of business values on the national economy was the South African-born businessman Sir Michael Edwardes. Taking the helm at British Leyland, the car maker, in 1977, he relished the opportunity to spell out the facts of life to BL's turbulent workforce. In an early encounter, the unions learned these facts the hard way:

A watershed came in the autumn of 1978 . . . [at] Bathgate, near Edinburgh . . . when I went on the ITV and BBC lunch-time news programmes . . . I was very angry . . . I added: 'If we say we will not meet the demands of the strikers because we cannot, and should not, we mean it. Furthermore, I tell you now that investment at Bathgate will be reduced by the amount of cash flow we have lost due to the strike. We simply can't pay twice. I mean what I say. We will not cry wolf.'[24]

Sir Michael was the prototype for the high-flying business heroes of the 1980s. Squash-playing, meritocratic, executive-minded and impatient with bureaucracy, Sir Michael also boasted impeccable small-business credentials: he declared his first business to have been 'Lucy', a 1938 Chevrolet lorry in which he had carried oil drums into Port Elizabeth when a young man. His success in bringing the British Leyland workforce to heel cleared the path for a string of key victories against organized labour and their 'corporatist' business sponsors: steel (1980), civil service employees (1981), the railways (1982), health workers (1982) and, famously, the miners (1985). More surprising than these defeats was the generally lukewarm public support accorded the strikers, especially when there was any suggestion of picket-line violence, in a country traditionally pro-underdog and anti-big boss. Here was another facet of the New Authenticity. Artificial jobs were no more acceptable than artificial bread. Measures to 'stimulate' the economy lost favour as rapidly as did substances to 'stimulate' the individual: decaffeinated coffee and dealcoholized wine showed explosive sales growth. In the neighbourhood doctor's surgery, the 'pill for every ill' philosophy of the post-war period gave way to 'emollient', 'non-invasive' treatments. And the pill itself, that symbol of post-war personal freedom, was hit by scare after scare; that it survived at all is some sort of tribute to the original architects.

We believe, from the vantage point of the late 1990s, that it was this New Authenticity, rather than any mysterious outbreak of 'greed' or 'selfishness', that propelled the business market transformation of cultural attitudes of the past two decades. The profundity of this transformation was illustrated in the spring of 1997, when France elected a Socialist government committed to an historically modest programme to create about half a million jobs. France, Britain's news media and politicians declared, had 'opted out of the real world'. A nation determined to maintain jobs and living standards by pumping up demand cut as dated a figure as the lounge lizard determined to dance all night by pumping himself full of gin, phenobarbitone and cigarettes. Defying 'the market' had become as grave a crime as defying nature. Paying heed to the market was the economic equivalent of 'listening to your body'. Both represented the only safe and certain way to health, economic and personal.

The two recessions merely confirmed this analysis. The 1979–83 slump was sworn into court as prima-facie evidence of the unhealthy state of the system; the recession of the 1990s was cited as proof that the revolution of the 1980s had to be 'completed'.

IN CASTERBRIDGE MARKET: THE DAY OF WORKER, INC.

The year 1967, which saw the film version of Thomas Hardy's novel *Far from the Madding Crowd*, also, by coincidence, saw the last bastion of casual industrial labour, the docks, join the modern world and offer permanent employment. Newly permanent dockers could, with a light heart, watch Peter Finch play the part of Farmer Boldwood, strolling around Casterbridge market-place, taking his pick of the forlorn shepherds and labourers offering themselves for hire. Should any of the would-be employees ask for more than a pittance, Boldwood and his fellow squires would march down the line to the next man.

But thirty years later, Farmer Boldwood was having the last laugh. The 'internal market', with its 'contracting out', 'compulsory tendering' and 'market testing', takes the concept of the market as judge to the ultimate conclusion. Not only companies but departments within companies and, critically, individual workers must permanently present themselves for validation by external market conditions. At the centre of the new economic system in the Age of Insecurity is the rotating worker, forever in danger of being revolved out into the market to be replaced by cheaper labour from outside. The internal market, the process whereby employees live in a state of constant competition against each other and against external contractors, is the final development in the transformation of work from a sort of quasi-tenancy from which the employee could be evicted only on payment of redundancy money into a fleeting, transitory experience, infused with terror at the prospect of its ending, akin to a teenage love-affair.

Contracting out labour completes the smashing-up of the career path and its replacement by a series of random 'work packages' for different employers. By fading the distinction between employee and outside 'bidder', the former is in permanent danger of replacement by the latter. The endgame is for each worker to become, in his own right, a 'company', shifting him from employee to supplier. Ultimately, the employer becomes the customer and the employee the purchaser. This is the *reductio ad absurdum* of the triumph of business values: everyone is now a business.

INSIDE THE CONTROL ROOM

The executive hook

Mr John Prescott, deputy prime minister, said the mayor [of London] would be 'akin to a dynamic chief executive – a mover and shaker who would forge partnerships with others and get things done'.

Financial Times, 30 July 1997

Presiding over the Age of Insecurity is a series of political institutions based explicitly on the large-scale business organization. And a striking feature of the 'marketized' society is the 'powerful' political executive, modelled quite openly – as the above quotation displays – on the corporate board of directors. An obvious example would be the 'operationally independent' Bank of England, to which has been hived off the formerly political judgement on the correct level of interest rates. There are many others, ranging from the adjudicator of parliamentary standards through to the 'tough' food-standards agency with, at the heart of the machine, the tightly controlled executive of executives, the Cabinet. But the independent Bank is a useful example to bear in mind as we tick off the distinguishing features of these bodies.

- Professionalism. Executive members, whether Cabinet ministers or political appointees, are expected to be 'undogmatic' and to prize technique and 'results' above all else. Management-school theory is in, conflict is out. Unprofessional behaviour includes the serious crime of going 'off message'. Ideology is as welcome as smallpox.
- Unfettered discretion. This phrase, borrowed from the police service, aptly describes the operational goal of the political executive. Given that it is composed of 'undogmatic professionals', there can be no legitimate reason for constraining the actions of its members. Impatient with restraints, the executive likes to act swiftly, with legal and constitutional niceties tied up later.
- The deal ideal. As with its business mentors, the political executive likes to close deals. Due process is not a concern for the executive; it prefers to 'call in' key actors in the economy and strike a bargain. Tony Blair's pre-election agreement with British Telecom, whereby the company would 'wire' all schools free of charge in return for greater commercial freedom, was an early example.
- The reluctance to rule out any position. Never say never is a useful piece of advice for any businessman, but its translation to the public realm is dubious, to say the least. It shifts an essentially private mode of behaviour – that of rubbing along with others and letting drop unimportant issues – to what ought to be the realm of high principle, the public realm. This is intimately bound up with the final distinguishing feature.
- The abandonment of 'reversibility'. That no Parliament can bind its successors is a cornerstone of British democracy. But, with the

electorate transformed into 'shareholders' by executive politics, 'reversibility' ceases to operate. Provided the 'exit price' is right, any permanent 'sale' of British interests – including the ultimate sale of the nation's independence – can be judged 'in the interests of shareholders'.

The legislative line

While the executive moves and shakes, the legislature toils and quakes. Far from checking the executive, today's legislature is its workforce, albeit of a rather superior, white-collar type. The key features of the 'productive' legislature are as follows.

- Team-work. In an extraordinary constitutional upheaval, today's MP or regional assembly member has been squeezed into a new, corporate format. Codes of conduct and – in the case of the Conservative Party – management-style 'bonding weekends' help ram home the message that the legislator is now a 'team member' rather than an individual representative with an individual conscience. Displays of this conscience are met with mutterings about 'bringing the party into disrepute' and the invocation of 'tough disciplinary measures'.
- Salesmanship. The legislator is expected, as a matter of priority, to act in a 'sales' role for the executive. 'Progress' in this area is closely monitored.
- Throughput. Laws have lost their majesty in the Age of Insecurity and have come to resemble a stream of corporate memos, issuing instructions to the workforce. This process is the responsibility of the legislature, whose 'productivity' is closely monitored.

The judicial sinker

Fulfilling the function of 'non-executive director' is the newly beefed-up judiciary, an arm of the state whose importance is likely to grow as instruments for judicial control such as the European Convention on Human Rights are incorporated into domestic law, permitting the judicial review of the High Court of Parliament (hitherto expressly forbidden). These non-executive directors fulfil three important functions in the new economic order.

- Protective. The senior judiciary protects the initiatives of the executive from future democratic challenges by 'irresponsible' or 'populist' elements.
- Supervisory. The judiciary supervises the legislature and its less 'responsible' elements, and urges upon the executive the prosecution of the agreed agenda of the ruling group of the new economic order.
- Palliative. The judiciary mitigates the worst effects of the Age of Insecurity with National Lottery-style payments to individual victims of peculiar circumstances.

SECURITY AND SAFETY: THE ENFORCEMENT ARM

Economic policy in the new, 'business' order may have been contracted out to 'market-driven' organizations but, as with any commercial organization, there is still plenty for the 'management' to do in terms of 'personnel development'. If nineteenth-century laissez-faire was characterized by the minimalist 'night-watchman state', it is only fitting that capitalism, 1990s-style, has given rise to a political organization modelled on the night-watchman's latter-day incarnation, the 'security and safety officer'. These pestiferous individuals are among the few corporate employees whose employment prospects have improved out of all recognition since the 1970s; today, they loom large in every worker's daily round, issuing identity cards, promulgating 'safety policies', monitoring the workforce via closed-circuit cameras and, in concert with their colleagues in 'human resources', planning alcohol and drug testing, lifestyle surveys and other intrusions. Similarly, in the nation as a whole, the state direction of habits, diet and 'attitudes' becomes ever more visible. In the new capitalist order, laissez-faire is strictly for big business, not for the proles. A feature of the new order is that it has surrounded itself with enemies: money launderers, drug barons, 'international organized crime' (this week the Triads, next week the Russian Mafia), and, above all, the 'outdated' and 'inflexible' attitudes inside the heads of the population at large. Front-line troops in the battle against these enemies are 'professionalized' police forces, headed by executive-minded chiefs. Fittingly enough, given their remoteness and fondness for paramilitary equipment and uniforms, some of the expanded force areas take their names from ancient Saxon kingdoms such as Mercia and Northumbria.

But this is more than old-fashioned heavy-handedness on the part of the authorities or the meddling of the 'nanny state' with which we have become familiar since the war. It is a project for the creation of what may be described as compulsory tranquillity. As detailed principles are banished from the public realm, and replaced by the rubbing-along, consensual approach, so the proper arena for such pragmatism – the private world – is subject to increasingly detailed blueprints with the force of law. The family kitchen, the private company boardroom, even the bachelor-girl pad are no longer to be left to regulate themselves.

As with the 'executivized' public realm, the object of the exercise is the elimination of conflict. No more will parents and children argue over homework and bedtimes: there will be national norms covering these conflict points. No more will female workers suffer 'inappropriate' comments, as a 'code of conduct' will specify 'appropriate' sexual behaviour. Diet, smoking, alcohol and exercise will all be regulated; conflict at home, in bed and at work will be replaced by an eerie silence.

THE TECHNOLOGY FIX

Hopes that scientific advance would somehow take the tough choices and the conflict out of public life are at least as old as the century. Technology, married to rational planning, has been touted as the key to unlock a future of boundless prosperity and public harmony. After all, if conflict is, at root, a fight over available resources, then limitless resources in a new age of plenty would soothe all trouble and strife.

More recently, the huge post-war strides in 'big technology' – space exploration, jet travel, atomic power – gave the search for a technology fix a moral dimension: if we could put a man on the moon, the argument ran, why could we not turn that ingenuity to negotiating an end to the Cold War? But this fairly reasonable proposition spawned a sub-argument that is far more dangerous, to wit that precisely because we can put a man on the moon, we will find an end to the Cold War. This is an attempt to substitute human technics for human values. It equates 'can do' in the objective, physical field with the handling of relationships in the mercurial world of principles, politics, religion and ideology.

Worse, it implies that technological advance somehow makes redundant all value judgements. To give a crude example, it would lead to the suggestion that schism in the Christian Church, or the partition of Cyprus, are 'irrelevances' left behind by the triumphant march of technology. As with everything else in the new economic order, this attitude is lifted straight from the world of business and imposed, unaltered, on the public realm. Technical advance may well render boardroom arguments of a year or so previously as stale as old directorial cigar smoke. It is the function of the businessman to adapt and survive. This principle does not translate to the public world. No piece of machinery, however impressive, can offer a short cut past the clashes of principle that are at the heart of politics. Yet, although the illusion of boundless plenty was laid to rest by the events of the late twentieth century, a parallel illusion – what may be described as the high-tech multiple-dogma by-pass – is being assiduously fostered.

Hence, during the 1997 election campaign, Tony Blair quite lost himself as he told one audience of his children's proficiency in computer skills. The point of his story was, it emerged, that the Conservative Party's concentration on educational structure and content was woefully out of date in the age of information technology. The implication of this line of thinking is that our primary duty to our children is to ensure they have access to computer equipment, with thought given much later (if at all) to the content of their lessons.

As it happens, computerization and the Internet are already showing signs of having been as seriously over-sold as was civil nuclear power in the 1950s. Just as 'atoms for peace' was touted as the source of 'electricity too cheap to meter', so the net was touted as a tool of liberation, allowing high-flyers to work from anywhere, connected to the outside world via a super-efficient 'information superhighway'. By mid-1997, the majority of homeworkers seemed isolated and exploited low-status employees, and the majority of high-flyers stayed close to where the action was: in the big banks, embassies, fashionable restaurants and clubs, and corporate headquarters. But even were the information revolution to fulfil all its promises to the (electronic) letter, it would make not the slightest difference to the invalidity of the technology fix. Political conflict does not arise from a shortage of information, or from a dearth of computer screens.

THE WONDERFUL SECONDARY-REALITY MACHINE: ADVERTISING, PUBLIC RELATIONS AND DESIGN

In the middle of the last decade, Fleet Street veteran Tom Baistow wrote a book taking apart the many failings of the British press and predicting worse to come. One chapter – 'PR: The Fifth Estate Makes News' – warned that the public relations industry was posing a threat to honest reporting. The ratio of PR officers to journalists was close to one to three, he said.[25] A few short years later, the PR machine described by Baistow seems laughably amateurish, full of dolly-birds called Mandy proffering white wine and press kits. Of all the aspects of commercial operations lifted wholesale by government, the importation of advertising and publicity on a grand scale is among the most striking. Blending seamlessly into the propaganda practices of private industry, the state PR machine is concerned with the manufacture of what the journalist Martin Pawsey called 'secondary reality'.[26] And this is one area where British manufacturing leads the world.

In February 1997, the assurance and insurance giant Prudential announced that its famous door-to-door salesman, the 'man from the Pru', was to make a welcome comeback. The neutral observer may be forgiven for assuming that this statement bore some relation to the re-employment of actual Prudential sales agents. But the man from the Pru's 'return' was a prime slice of secondary reality. The 'return' was strictly limited to an advertising slogan; real-life Pru agents were being phased out, from October 1994.

Another example, again from financial services, comes from the early 1990s. National Westminster Bank, as it then was, ran a series of advertisements set in a fictitious branch. One spot concluded with a male clerk holding hands with a female colleague as they enjoyed an evening date after a tough day in the service of the bank's customers. A suspicious newspaper inquired as to NatWest policy on relationships between staff members. The bank confirmed that romances of this type were actively discouraged.

More recently, advertisements for the coffee company Kenco have featured its 'managing director', supposedly the boss's daughter and effective inheritor of the company, as she tangles with male-chauvinist coffee growers in suitably warm locations. Inquiries to Kenco confirmed that there is no such figure in the company, that it does not have a woman in such a senior position and that the image created is entirely fictitious.

What is remarkable about these examples is not that the companies were found out, but that none showed any great embarrassment after exposure. This is the difference between the old hucksterism and secondary reality: the first was flim-flam, the second has developed its own internal reality.

FOREIGN POLICY: BIG TAIL, VANISHING DOG

Nowhere is the commercial paradigm more clearly in view than in the conduct of foreign policy. 'I am off', declares the minister at the airport press conference, 'to do business with our partners in Europe.' That 'doing business' may not be an appropriate description for the legitimate activity of government is never considered. As with a multinational company, the directorate of the new economic state is interested only in a vague notion of 'the best interests of the shareholders', not in matters of immutable principle, such as the independence of the nation. As a result, negotiations in Europe, in particular, tend to involve cashing in permanent British rights in return for sometime-never hopes that British companies may one day be able to compete for telecommunications contracts in Italy or airline routes in Spain.

This confusion of political and commercial objectives is a striking by-product of the triumph of business ethics. It has led to the pursuit of an external affairs strategy that elevates 'British influence' and 'vital British interests' at the expense of self-government. On inspection, 'British influence' translates as the ability of figures from the British political and diplomatic classes to play on a large stage and to attempt to exert leverage over other countries, and 'vital British interests' translate as important contracts and market openings sought by joint-stock companies notionally based here but with an international shareholder register.

This endangers the future existence not only of the British state, but also of the Welfare State which, in its broadest sense, presupposes a self-governing society. Only the controls and accountability provided by a (reasonably) culturally and politically homogenous national unit present the framework of trust within which the 'mild and provident care' promised by the Welfare

State can be delivered. The priority given to foreign policy over domestic welfare not only jeopardizes the welfare and economic security of the public, but pulls the entire policy-making structure out of shape. What ought to be issues of principle (such as the single currency) are subjected to a sort of hale and hearty sleeves-rolled-up pragmatism more appropriate to private arenas. Meanwhile, these very arenas where the commonsense, rubbing-along mentality ought to hold sway are, as mentioned above, subject to ever more detailed prescriptions.

We accept that, from the traditional Tory/British Conservative standpoint, the exercise of British influence in the world and the securing for Britain of a 'seat at the top table' is, almost of itself, a beneficial activity. This is a school of thought with a long history, stretching back through Europe, the special relationship, the Empire right back to the Concert of Europe after the Napoleonic Wars. From this viewpoint, the ability of Britain (or rather, of a foreign service elite drawn from Britain and assisted by big-hitting British-based industrialists) to engage in balance-of-power diplomacy and realpolitik is of vital importance. That the territorial entity from which they spring may have ceased to exist in its own right is of little consequence, provided 'influence' is maintained.

But there is a second tradition, stretching back to Bright and beyond, the tradition that deprecates imperialism, balance-of-power diplomacy and the construction of big, powerful political units. This tradition – one which may, for shorthand purposes, be described as the 'Little England' tradition – represents, we believe, the appropriate and moral foreign policy stance of a left-of-centre government. In other words, we believe that neither the British people nor the world at large benefit in any way from Britain 'boxing above her weight' (who is being punched in this scenario is never made clear). We believe this because the government is then free to make foreign policy once more the servant and not the master of domestic welfare. It is moral because it is based on the principle that Britain is no more important (except to its own inhabitants) than any other country, that it does not have any special 'civilizing mission' and that the world can manage quite well without the exercise of British 'influence'.

The good society, in our view, is a self-governing, self-regulating Welfare State, one in which the elected authorities retain control of all the tools needed to manage the economy in the interests of all the people. It is not a fortress state, but a modern trading nation with a secure base for its citizens. No householder who let his family go hungry while he squandered both his money and the title-deeds to the house in an attempt to gang up with others in order to gain 'influence' over the neighbourhood would be accounted a good householder. The same rules ought to be applied to nations.

CHAPTER THREE

SYSTEM FAILURE: THE FREE MARKET UNDER BATTLE CONDITIONS

That he had form'd a Kind of Corporation of Thieves, of which he was
the Head or Director
from the warrant of detainer issued against Jonathan Wilde, 1725
(Gerald Howson, *It Takes a thief*, The Cresset Library, 1987)

money goes to money heaven
bodies go to body hell
i can't read (David Bowie/Reeves Gabrels, 1989)

'All industry and commerce will end in a single huge bazaar, where a
man will provide himself with everything.'
Emile Zola, *Money*, 1891 (Alan Sutton edition, 1991)

The late Richard Crossman, it is said, during his brief editorship of the *New Statesman*, called in one of the paper's journalists and briefed him on a tip he had received concerning newsworthy goings-on inside the Conservative Party. The journalist checked the item and it failed, as they say in the trade, to stand up. Tackled by Crossman as to why the story had not appeared, the journalist protested that it had proved to be untrue. Never said it was true, Crossman is said to have responded in a huff, said it was interesting.

Few would doubt that the promises made on behalf of the free market economy in the mid-1970s were interesting. To political anoraks and economic policy wonks, they were absolutely fascinating. But have they been proved true? Nothing could be easier than to criticize the market order for failing to deliver on the goals of those hostile to the market: social equality, for example, or an end to the consumer society. It is more worthwhile to judge the new market economy on its own implied promises.

Quantifying those promises is no simple task. As discussed in the last chapter, the cultural counter-revolution that brought the new market economy into being was powered far more by vaguely defined feelings and intuitions – towards 'authenticity' and small-business values – than by detailed proposals for privatization, the public debt, or trade-union reform. Nevertheless, big themes, each connected with the others, emerge from the mêlée of ideas that swirled in the turbulence of the mid-1970s. And, at the risk of distortion through over-simplification, we believe these themes – these implied promises – can be conflated into one apparent oxymoron: dynamic stability. The dynamism would be supplied by the unleashing (a favourite word of the new market economists) of the energies of the private sector; the stability would follow as naturally from the new emphasis on free enterprise as night follows day. By shifting responsibility from the state to the individual, the market revolution would, it was suggested, restore the small-town/suburban virtues as a matter of course. Just as the market was itself the 'authentic' form of economic organization, so family and community represented the 'authentic' form of social organization. The post-war system's original sin, in this version of events, was to switch the dynamism and the stability from their rightful places, thus creating lethargic industry coupled with a hyperactive 'swinging' society.

Henceforth, the workplace was to be the appropriate forum for dynamism, the family home that for stability. Were one to put this strong cultural current into words, it would run something like this: 'We used to believe you could buck human nature and nature in general, that plausible "experts" could do anything, from abolishing morning sickness to suspending the laws of supply and demand. But the results of all this are dismal: sawdust bread, tower blocks, crime, vandalism, drug addiction, strikes and inflation. So we are not going to do that any more. Instead, we are going to return to basic values, within the family, the firm and the community, in our cooking and our drinking, in architecture, in crime and punishment, in education and, above all, in economics.'

Opening out from this simple theme are many facets: the empowerment of the individual, the elimination of 'moral hazard' (the process by which favoured groups and activities receive largesse at the expense of ill-favoured groups and activities), a newly vibrant cultural life (brought about by restoring the proper link between artist and audience and removing funding from the dreary state culture represented by subsidized avant-garde painting and theatre and the drab outpourings of writers-in-residence), the restoration of the age-old, neutral judgement and discipline of the market in place of political favouritism and 'expert' tinkering, and the restoration, *pari passu*, of the middle class, without whose virtues and values the nation was as unstable as an aeroplane robbed of its gyroscope, its pilot and its cabin crew.

As the Conservative Party put it in its 1976 statement of aims *The Right Approach*: 'The society that in the end will be the most prosperous and the most contented is that in which there is the least possible conflict between the economic incentives, the ethos of accepted morality, and the laws which regulate behaviour and activity.' How did this big idea and its different strands perform under battle conditions? Had they represented, as their promoters claimed, 'common sense' (one of the subheadings in *The Right Approach* is 'Practical common sense'; others are 'Individual enterprise', 'A long haul' and 'Rights and duties') in opposition to Keynesian mumbo-jumbo and its priesthood of head-in-the-clouds social engineers, then the result ought to have been impressive.

THE X-RAY'D MAN: RE-REGULATING THE 'SOVEREIGN' INDIVIDUAL

Classic laissez-faire capitalism was derided by critics as the freedom of the poor man to sleep beneath Waterloo Bridge. The post-war system, with its strict controls on finance and permissive attitude to the individual, may be said to have delivered the freedom to squat in a free-love commune on social security but not to own a steelworks. Our new economic order has changed the rules once again, and may be said to offer the freedom to own a steelworks but not to forgo the use of seat-belts or crash helmets. The individual of the 1990s has been 'empowered' in the narrowly financial sense: no more exchange controls or wage freezes, no more mortgage rationing. Pensions, shares and other items once closely supervised by the state have become portable pieces of personal property. A person can dabble on the Thai Stock

Exchange via his high-street broker without so much as a by-your-leave from the authorities. He can pay his mortgage in German marks, his insurance premiums in drachmas and draw his salary in Swiss francs. Truly, the citizen-capitalist has arrived.

Or perhaps not: our mini-George Soros may be free as a bird when acting as a financial entity, but stepping outside this role puts his relationship with the state in an entirely different light. Video-taped by closed-circuit television (by spring 1997 government grants had paid for 4,500 such cameras in public places, with official hopes that 11,000 would be in operation by 1999), his house liable under 1997 legal changes to search without warrant, his childrearing scrutinized by an army of public employees, tested at work for drugs and alcohol, psychoanalysed by dubious 'counsellors' on corporate 'team-building' weekends, hounded by national 'days/weeks of action' against smoking and drinking, our share-owning citizen may justly feel far more tightly circumscribed in his non-financial actions than he would have done in the 1970s. And even the apparently generous manoeuvring space afforded him in his financial life is not all it seems. Retreating to the calm of his broker's office, he is required to meet stiff tests in order to prove his identity before being issued with a unique code number allowing all his share dealings to be monitored by IMAS, the London Stock Exchange's artificial-intelligence system. At his bank, he faces similar demands to prove his identity: the Briton's long-established right to open a bank account under any name he chose was swept away in the early 1990s by legislation designed to combat 'money laundering'. Calling on his accountant, he learns that changes to the tax system now make him solely responsible not only for supplying all relevant information to the Inland Revenue but for keeping all paperwork that may prove of any possible relevance to the taxman. He learns also that moves are afoot to allow police to require him to account for the source of all his wealth (a power already in force in Northern Ireland). Just to make his day, he hears of renewed calls for financial offences to be tried not by jurors but by a judge sitting with two 'lay assessors'. Not only is he under strict control outside the financial realm, but also within it. And at this point the ghastly truth may dawn: it is not he who has been set free, but his money. It is controls on capital that have been reduced, and controls on people that have multiplied. The unimpeded movement of the citizen's money is a hallowed principle of the new economic order; no such principle exists in relation to individuals. On the contrary, individuals, cosseted by decades of misguided welfare policies and lax law enforcement, are deemed to be in urgent need of 'tough love' and 'personal re-engineering', American euphemisms for the effective nationalization of the surplus labour force (and, given the 'rotational' nature of modern employment, that means a very substantial proportion of the total labour force) and its subjection to state-directed 're-education' (or retraining, as its proponents would have it).

This development – the simultaneous freeing of capital and control of people – marks the extraordinary outcome of a debate that began in earnest in 1976, a debate that focused on the possibility or otherwise of preserving individual freedom alongside state control of capital. At a speech in Anglesey in January 1976, the Labour Home Secretary Roy Jenkins warned: 'I do not think you can push public expenditure significantly above 60 per cent [of national income] and maintain the values of a plural society and freedom of choice. We are here close to one of the frontiers of social democracy.'

At issue was the link between individual and economic freedom. Some denied it existed: Labour's Deputy Prime Minister and future leader Michael Foot was among the most prominent of the 'libertarian socialists', to whom Mr (now Lord) Jenkins's 60 per cent could comfortably inflate to nearly 100 per cent with no unpleasant side-effects for the liberty of the individual. Further to the right, Mr Foot's Cabinet colleague Tony Crosland led an influential school of thought that saw very high levels of public expenditure, combined with 'liberal' legislation, as an emancipating force, a powerful motor for social change. This, roughly, was the position adopted under the post-war system: the Jenkins speech was one indicator among many that this system was now coming to an end.

As it did so, new voices were raised, alleging that no one in their right mind could seriously imagine that the liberty of the individual and that of his money could be separated, the former a free spirit cheerfully walking on the wild side while the latter was clapped in government irons. Friedrich von Hayek expressed this view in its purest form: giant corporations such as ITT and General Motors were, he said, entitled to the same rights as any other economic individual. His fellow free-marketeer Milton Friedman sounded the alarm:

The experience of recent years . . . raises a doubt whether private ingenuity can continue to overcome the deadening effects of government control if we continue to grant ever more power to government, to authorise a 'new class' of civil servants to spend ever larger fractions of our income supposedly on our behalf. Sooner or later — and perhaps sooner than many of us expect — an ever bigger government would destroy both the prosperity that we owe to the free market and the human freedom proclaimed so eloquently in the Declaration of Independence.

We have not yet reached the point of no return. We are still free as a people to choose whether we shall continue speeding down the 'road to serfdom', as Friedrich Hayek entitled his profound and influential book, or whether we shall set tighter limits on government and rely more heavily on voluntary co-operation among free individuals to achieve our several objectives.[1]

Thrashing around in the turbulence of the mid-1970s, defenders of the existing order — among them the intransigent Social Services Secretary Barbara (now Lady) Castle — squared the circle by insisting that the 'social wage', the entire package of benefits and services for which taxation was raised, was itself a form of disposable personal property, a liberating asset placed in the hands of the individual by the community. A concrete example of this philosophy was the Public Service Obligation (PSO) grant arranged with the British Railways Board, whereby the state paid as a 'customer' for 'social' (i.e. loss-making) services to be maintained on a basis broadly comparable (or comparably awful, as a cynic put it) to that existing on 1 January 1975. The hope seemed to be that the state could be realigned alongside the individual as a fellow consumer, a friend and a sort of neighbourly bulk-buyer, a chap with a large estate car happy to run down to the cash and carry. An initiative of the 1974–76 Wilson government called 'Little Things Mean a Lot' involved, *inter alia*, a scheme to leaflet all citizens with information showing precisely where their taxes went. Interestingly, at the same time, the Labour Party was working on a scheme called 'Life-lease', a rearguard action against the Tories' new (and wildly popular) policy of selling council houses to their tenants at a big discount. Life-lease effectively proposed selling council houses to their tenants only for the tenant's life-span. Whether it would have worked will never be known: Labour abandoned the scheme and the Tories swept into power in 1979.

Another circle-squaring attempt was the vogue for 'participation'. Social democrats grudgingly admitted that government may seem huge and remote; these defects could be cured by giving people 'input' into decisions. The

Skeffington Committee report of 1969 examined ways and means of increasing participation, with particular reference to planning decisions. The committee found the concept easier to talk around than to implement.

By the early 1980s, 'participation' had mutated within the large metropolitan authorities, most notably the Greater London Council from 1981 to 1986, into a sort of right-on grantsmanship, under which elected officials disbursed large sums to 'community' organizations of which they approved. This sort of kiddie-kit money-politics was hard enough to operate within its natural home, the student union. It had little chance of achieving much within a metropolis of eight million people, beyond irritating many of those who formed the tax base. Powerful voices began to argue that participation neither equalled freedom nor compensated for its loss. Colin Welch declared in the *Spectator* on 11 September 1982:

Only very intermittently seems he [David Owen, former Labour Cabinet minister, later founder-member of the Social Democratic Party] aware of the fact that many people find participation a frightful bore and would rather cultivate their own gardens than argue ceaselessly with hordes of busybodies. He favours participation for our own good. . . . But democratic participation is not freedom; nor can eager participators alone be regarded as 'wholly human'. Gardeners are human too.

In this view, the only true form of participation was the restoration of the individual as the fundamental decision-making unit.

In their different ways, Life-lease, the PSO grant, participation and the 'social wage' all suffered from the same defect: they were too little, too late. After three decades of insisting that the man in Whitehall knew best, it was a little late in the day for the social-democratic establishment to reinvent him as the citizen's best buddy. And anyway, few of social democracy's elite were seriously prepared to offer the individual much more than observer status in the running of society. It may have been a decade since Anthony Crosland had informed his wife: 'If it's the last thing I do, I'm going to destroy every fucking grammar school in England . . . and Wales. And Northern Ireland.'[2] But the urge remained; in 1976, the government was soundly thrashed before senior judges over its attempts to force the Tameside education authority in Greater Manchester to introduce comprehensive education. Its humiliation was linked in the public mind with two other defeats in the higher courts, that meted out by Freddie Laker, who went to law to get his bargain Skytrain airborne against government/nationalized industry opposition, and the victory of Australian entrepreneur Kerry Packer against the MCC and Cricket Council (later the Test and County Cricket Board). Strictly speaking, Mr Packer had not bested an organ of the state, but the song remained much the same: plucky, gutsy, energetic loner against a lethargic behemoth that stirred itself into action only in defence of its own monopoly position.

Robert Moss, writing in 1975, declared: 'Without economic pluralism, political pluralism cannot survive for long. We have seen already that the survival of a free society depends on the dispersal of power. . . . This is as clear in economic life as in politics. If the State is the sole employer, then anyone who objects to its policies risks going hungry.' Mr Moss's chapter heading was evocative: 'The necessity of property'.[3]

To the horror of traditional social democrats, Roy Jenkins's question was answering itself. No, the reply seemed to be, it is not possible to combine personal manoeuvrability with an ever increasing public-sector 'bite'. The robust yeomanry that was to be conjured into existence by the new market order would demand maximum financial and fiscal freedom, not as an end in itself but as the *sine qua non* of personal freedom.

Several thousand new criminal offences and several billion pounds of new police equipment and weaponry later, Jenkins's question has been turned on its head: no longer need we ask if the ordinary person can be free when his money is in chains, rather can his money be free when he is in chains? The answer given by developments since the late 1980s is yes. Indeed, it could be the very freedom of money to roam the world, causing untold havoc as it does so, that necessitates increasing clamps on individual behaviour. The robust yeoman conjured up by Mrs Thatcher and others at the end of the 1970s is the cowed vassal of a new 'securiocracy' whose senior members, in their public addresses, no longer bother to conceal their long-term policy goals: nationwide DNA fingerprinting, compulsory identity cards, 'unfettered' search and seizure powers, an end to the right to silence and jury trials, and near-total TV surveillance of all urban public spaces and major highways.

In May 1997, South Yorkshire Police – responsible for the maintenance of law in one of the most crime-infested of Britain's conurbations – devoted considerable resources to a campaign against car windows tinted more darkly than the regulations allowed. The ability of the state to 'look through' the private life of the citizen, to X-ray him, has become the over-riding priority of security policy. Just as nationalized industries of old were at their least lethargic in the enforcement of their monopoly privileges (the BBC in TV licence collection, British Rail in objecting to bus routes and car-sharing arrangements), so the new security establishment is at its most energetic in enforcing its powers over the citizen. On this, the first test of the new order's promises, we grade the market system F for Fail.

LES JEUX SONT FAITS: MORAL HAZARD IN THE NEW MARKET ECONOMY

Marking the new system's performance on individual freedom is fairly straightforward. But a second, closely linked, virtue claimed for the market system was the elimination of 'moral hazard', and this is a concept easier to recognize than to describe. Put simply, an arrangement is at moral hazard when it means the good are subsidizing or otherwise supporting the bad. For example, a motor-insurance system that charged one premium for all drivers, regardless of their conduct on the road, age, experience and so forth, would generate moral hazard. Moral hazard can be broadened to include any situation in which one group is unfairly subventing another. On a trivial level, the 'full English breakfast' served by hoteliers may be objected to on similar grounds: if all pay the same £7.50, or whatever the figure, then he who eats several rashers and sausages, a couple of eggs and a rack of toast is in receipt of a subsidy from he who is content with a little scrambled egg and a glass of orange juice.

Packaged transactions of this type are said to be 'in the black box', economic slang for any hard-to-unpick bundle of payments, benefits, goods and services. In the eyes of market proponents, large parts of the British economy had, by the end of the 1970s, passed into just such a black box. Great gouts of money flowed around the system in various forms: wages, transfer payments, dividends, subsidies, tax breaks, compensation for loss of tax breaks, surcharges, food subsidies, farm support. No one player seemed to know exactly what was going where or whence it came. Such a cat's cradle of payments and repayments, handouts and give-backs could only 'distort' the market and, in doing so, distort rational decision making. In 1989, the businessman and writer Rodney Atkinson declared in his work *The Failure of the State*: 'Government has overturned the natural laws of personal responsibility. It has rewarded those that make foolish decisions, subsidised those who fail, heavily taxed those who succeed [and] financed the birth of children to those who cannot even take care of themselves.'[4] Incentives were in the wrong places, which meant goods, services and people followed suit. Costing anything in such a climate – thus assessing its 'real' market worth – was well-nigh impossible.

Sir Michael Edwardes recalled his efforts to find out the cost of each vehicle: 'I knew from my NEB [National Enterprise Board] involvement, that there was no breakdown of cost information model by model . . . imagine trying to manage a business without knowing the cost of the individual products – it seemed unbelievable.'[5]

One important subdivision of the supposed moral hazard of the time was the 'responsibility without power' imposed on Britain's managers. Unable to hire and fire, they were forced to maintain large payrolls of often rebellious workers in defiance of the 'real' economic facts. Here was a set-piece case of moral hazard: for an unsackable worker to strike for higher pay was seen as a one-way bet. All the hazard was displaced onto people unconnected with the strike, either the company's shareholders or (worse), in the case of public services, the innocent public.

'Unbundling' – a phrase beloved of corporate takeover specialists keen to sniff out buried assets – was used to describe a much broader drive throughout society to apportion cost and responsibility correctly. By breaking open the black box, the new market order would make the opera-goer pay for his ticket, the train traveller pay for the railway and the striker pay (with his job, if necessary) for the damage he had done his employer. The poll tax was an attempt to make those who voted for big-spending councillors pay for the big spending. Unbundling, by pricing out each item correctly, would clear the distortions resulting from political, economic and personal action.

Free-market think tanks envisaged unbundling the ultimate black box: the Welfare State. They continue to do so, with increasing conviction. In July 1997, the European Policy Forum, a London- and Brussels-based think tank, produced a report suggesting eighteen million families could switch from welfare to private insurance. 'Millions of people are already comfortable with the habit of insurance solutions in their daily lives', said the report. 'There is now an opportunity for the insurance industry to reach out to them.' Among the claimed advantages was the reduction in moral hazard.

Just as the more extreme leftists of the 1960s and 1970s scoured the world for locations where 'real' socialism was alive and well, so do the free-marketeers hunt down jurisdictions alleged to have successfully privatized welfare. As with the workers' paradises of yesteryear (Cuba, Tanzania, Communist China), the new model Welfare States are suitably remote. Malaysia and Singapore were popular in the early 1990s, and Chile became the shining example of our radiant private future at the end of the decade.

Ironically, it was Singapore that provided the setting for a drama proving beyond doubt that moral hazard – far from having been eliminated or at least reduced by the new economic order – was flourishing in new and more virulent forms. In February 1995, Barings – one of the oldest banks in London – learned the ghastly truth about its Far East-based star trader, Nick Leeson. Rather than winning the bank millions with inspired gambles on high-risk 'derivatives' business, Leeson, based in Singapore, had bankrupted his employer, running up debts of nearly £1 billion. Had Leeson been merely potty or malicious, the episode would have been one of simple failure to control an unstable employee. But the 'profits' hallucinated by Leeson were the platform upon which huge bonuses were calculated. By 1997, Britain's financial regulators were in a state of ill-concealed panic over the structure of bonus systems, which seemed predominantly designed to encourage traders to gamble for their own profit with their banks' money. Losses fell not on the traders but on the banks' shareholders (including pension funds and unit trusts held by ordinary people) and the banking system as a whole.

In August 1997, Howard Davies, chairman of the new financial regulator, told London Weekend Television: 'We are certainly going to have to take an interest in remuneration. . . . The bigger the risks they take . . . the bigger the pay-off at the end of the day.' Shortly before, Richard Farrant, chief executive of the stockbroking regulator Securities and Futures Authority, conceded it was 'devilish difficult' to do anything about 'moral hazard' bonus systems, especially when firms were being 'sucked along by the market'.

Even the Barings affair was dwarfed by the slow-motion eruption in the early 1990s of the scandal of the mis-sold pensions. This blew apart one of the centrepieces of the market order, the 'New Beveridge' package of welfare reforms unveiled in the mid-1980s. Employees had been given the freedom to opt out of state or company pensions and purchase their own schemes direct from assurance giants and other financial combines. City rules supposedly ensured salesmen gave 'best advice' to their clients, but the juicy commissions on offer – like the bonuses available to City traders – proved too tempting. By 1997, it was calculated that a total of perhaps £4 billion worth of personal pensions had been 'mis-sold', i.e. sold to people against their own best interests by salesmen in search of commission and other earnings.

The pension scandal was, in truth, part of a much larger scandal of mis-sold financial products stretching back to the early 1980s. Most notable were endowment mortgages – savings vehicles designed to pay back a home loan – which had been forced on millions of people whose circumstances made them better suited to a traditional 'repayment' mortgage. Other than for doctors, vets and other professionals traditionally combining home and professional premises, and certain categories of people moving house more often than the average, the endowments – having been stripped of their tax breaks in the mid-1980s – were the best choice for almost nobody. But their popularity with salesmen was easy to understand: endowments paid big commissions, repayment mortgages did not.

Moral hazard on this scale was not confined to financial services. Low pay, widespread in Britain by the 1990s and touted as evidence of 'competitiveness', effectively meant that the burden of keeping workers and their families at something approaching a twentieth-century standard of living was shifted from the sweatshop employers to the taxpayer, who receives the bill for family income supplement and other schemes designed to top up low pay.

Linked to this has been big business's persistent, and largely successful, bid to unload the cost of training its workers onto the state. As thousands of apprenticeships disappeared in the early 1980s, the first Thatcher government lavished £1 billion a year, a huge sum at that time, on training young people to fit them for British industry. Effectively, business and industry had shrugged off the inventory cost of apprentices, trainees and 'office juniors', and passed it to the state. Any hope that a Labour government would restore the 'skill bill' to its rightful place – with the beneficiaries – has been cruelly disappointed. Not only has the Blair government shouldered the burden with enthusiasm, but seems to regard it as the chief legitimate economic activity of the state.

Were this ballooning example of moral hazard not bad enough, the late 1980s and the 1990s have seen insult added to injury as giant corporations have demanded – and received – colossal sweeteners in return for either opening plants or agreeing not to close them. The sums are staggering. In the 1990s, the British government paid Ford £71 million to modernize the Jaguar plant at Coventry and about £15 million to renovate the Halewood factory on Merseyside. South Korean manufacturer LG accepted £200 million for investing in Wales, a record total of £30,000 per job. Siemens picked up about £16,000 per job for a new plant near Newcastle. To pile further insult on the insult already added to the injury, many of the sweeteners are never fully disclosed to the taxpayers from whom they are extracted. The *Financial Times* reported on 24 July 1997: 'Precise figures are difficult to obtain because they are kept secret by the government, and because they come from different sources, including local and regional authorities and the DTI [Department of Trade and Industry].' As a final insult, these companies make much in public of their support for good-quality education yet they know – they have to know – that their bribes will be paid, *inter alia*, from the education budget.

The problem is worldwide. In 1993, that great 'stakeholding' company Mercedes-Benz invited US states to bid for a new car factory. Alabama, one of the poorest states, 'won', at a cost of nearly $300 million. It has since tried to raid its education budget to maintain payments to Mercedes. Over in South Carolina, BMW – another supposed German stakeholder – received $100 million. And it is not as if these sweeteners can be justified on the grounds that much of it came from the big companies in the first place and, even if it didn't, the tax 'take' generated by the installations would more than compensate. In a final example of the moral hazard inherent in the new market system, corporate tax avoidance and evasion is now so widespread that former Fraud Squad officer Rowan Bosworth-Davies warned a conference in Lisbon in June 1997: 'It is the inability of our chosen governments to collect the lawfully-levied taxes on which mandate they were elected that determines the new agenda for concern for the 21st Century.'

Nobody is suggesting that any of the above companies have evaded tax, although their duty to their shareholders will necessarily involve taking advantage of legal avoidance measures. By their own lights and those of our time, they are good corporate citizens. But it is unrealistic to imagine that no beneficiaries of public largesse have been involved in either 'borderline' avoidance or outright tax evasion. In May 1996, it emerged that accountants Deloitte & Touche had calculated that taxes out of which the Crown had been swindled in the previous two decades totalled £2 trillion, or £2,000 billion, at current prices. This colossal figure counts in tax evasion only, and takes no account of lawful tax avoidance, practised on a huge scale by the biggest corporations. The removal of exchange controls, one of the first actions of Mrs Thatcher's 1979–83 government, has cleared the way for a tax revolution. While billions disappear offshore, frantic governments tax to the hilt anything that can be nailed down: buildings, retail goods, food, fuel, cars, land and, of course, the income of the great mass of ordinary 'immobile' working people. Then, in a final twist, much of the money raised is offered in sweeteners to tempt the sort of giant companies whose tax avoidance left the public coffers bare in the first place.

This relatively new development sits alongside aspects of moral hazard inherent in any private enterprise system but exacerbated in the 1990s, the most obvious of which are limited liability and insolvency. Limited liability is an unusual concept in that it was rumbled as a huge fraud on society more or less on day one; as the legislation ground through Parliament in 1862, critics claimed commerce had become 'paganized'. The years since then have more than confirmed their fears, as 'phoenix' companies (entities that bankrupt themselves to avoid debt, then re-emerge with a 'clean sheet') have flitted across the landscape. In any insolvency, corporate or individual, that part of the cost unrecovered from the debtor falls elsewhere – a classic example of moral hazard. The difference today is one of scale and of official attitude. Insolvency has become an instrument for displacing hazard, a transmission system for absorbing risk that was once shouldered by the business and financial interest.

Individual bankruptcies in England and Wales in 1996 totalled 26,271, eight times the figure for 1960. Behind this huge upward rise is the story of job insecurity, short-term contracts, self-employment and all the other factors that have made working life so precarious. This, in reverse, was the position of a Department of Trade and Industry spokesman in early 1997, who explained that higher levels of personal insolvency reflected a more entrepreneurial society and were thus nothing to worry about.

Both government and large-scale banking and finance can afford to be relaxed: when a person or small business goes 'belly up', both taxes and 'secured' debts (i.e. bank mortgages secured on hard assets) are first in the queue for repayment. The real victims of bankruptcy are other individuals and small traders, many of whom, in turn, go bankrupt.

This aspect of moral hazard leads to another. As formal credit has been extended further and further down the income scale (with a commensurate drying-up of the informal credit systems, such as the shop 'slate', that used to support poorer people), so the platform for interest rates has been steadily raised, to cover the higher risk now facing the lenders. This in turn is just one piece of wiring dangling from the great 'black box' that is the modern credit business. Far from 'unbundling' goods and services, the new market order has seen the biggest bundlers of all – the finance houses – flourish as never before. The package of services included in today's credit card – ranging from overseas medical assistance to cash-machine access, legal advice, debit and credit functions and insurance – is almost impossible to unbundle and price individually, putting the consumer at precisely the sort of 'information dis-advantage' that the new economic order was supposed to eliminate. The opportunities to 'clip' the customer – above and beyond the standard usurious rates of interest charged – are enormous; to take one example, an unscrupulous operator charges not only a transaction fee on foreign-exchange payments, but clips the customer again with an unfavourable exchange rate and – potentially – a third time on the rate of interest.

Unscrupulous financial operators can, of course, be pursued through the law. A major selling point of the new market order was that it would restore the rule of law – battered and bashed about by over-mighty bureaucrats and trade-union militants – as the legal framework within which the market would flourish. But which law and whose courtroom would be reinstated? A feature of the new system is the hiving-off of economic crime into a self-regulatory labyrinth of 'disciplinary tribunals': effectively private courts. Nor do these courts try only 'regulatory' offences. They increasingly hear theft charges. In February 1997, the Securities and Futures Authority announced it had dealt with the case of a merchant-bank trader who had stolen a large sum of money. He was expelled from the SFA register. The case went nowhere near a criminal court. In April 1995, in a similar case, a man was expelled from the SFA for stealing securities.

Mr Bosworth-Davies, speaking in Blakeney, Norfolk, in October 1996 warned: '[B]ehaviour which would be criminal to any ordinary person, if committed outside the City environment, is being allowed to be called something else and increasingly dealt with in a different, quasi-civil, regulatory manner.'

Of course, the existence of these 'private courts', which allow the financial elite to avoid the indignity of trial in the criminal courts, may simply be regarded as evidence that the beneficiaries of the new economic order do not intend the strictures on unbundling and moral hazard to apply to them, evidence of good old-fashioned hypocrisy, in other words. This is the world of the 'Alex' strip cartoon in *The Independent* and, later, the *Daily Telegraph*, in which striped-shirted high-flyers sit poker-faced for the first few frames mouthing the verities of the new market order (competitiveness, flexibility and so forth) only to be exposed in the final frame as plotting to ensure that their own air miles, boxes at Wimbledon and other perks are spared the ruthless 'downsizing'. Indeed, the businessman's beloved first-class/business-class air ticket may be seen as the epitome of the 'bundled' black-box product, providing entitlement to a great grab-bag of uncosted and unordered goods and services, from champagne to in-flight films to witty little Japanese snackettes and copies of the *Financial Times*. So far, it seems to have survived the great unbundling as, of course, has the whole world of 'corporate hospitality'. But the moral hazard thrown up by the new economic system amounts to far more than the ancient vice of hypocrisy. It is intrinsic to the system, not some flaw that can be designed out with a few more laws and 'codes of conduct'.

In March 1994, traders in gilts marked down sharply the price of British government securities. They were responding to official data for January showing a rise in annual UK average earnings growth from 3 per cent, the first such rise in almost two years. Here was the new system working as it should: free-flowing capital has created a 'market' in government policies. When those policies show signs of laxity – such as the signal given by the earnings increase – then markets respond, shifting funds to 'sounder' investments, whether other governments' stocks and currencies or corporate securities, punishing the lax government and its electorate, both of whom will now have to tighten their belts, usually through higher interest rates. But all was not quite as it seemed. Statisticians believed the rise was almost entirely due to the enormous bonus payments made to City partners and traders in the 1993–94 period; in one celebrated case, top people at Goldman Sachs had shared money equivalent to the national income of Tanzania. Ordinary workers had seen little or nothing in the way of increases, but among the biggest bonus earners had been gilts traders, the very people now taking punitive action as the largesse they had enjoyed showed up in national data.

In other words, millions of people at a time of very great austerity in the United Kingdom faced higher interest payments as their government sought to make its own paper more attractive to the group of people responsible for the problem in the first place. This is not to say the gilts dealers had made a mistake. On the contrary, they were running the system as it is supposed to be run. Indeed, it can be run in no other way. No amount of 'transparency', 'greater disclosure' or the other panaceas suggested for the gaping flaws in the market order can change that.

Of course, there was one way to avoid the unpleasantness of higher interest rates for all as a result of the 'earnings blip', and that was for some other groups of workers to experience what people in the City would no doubt sanitize as a 'negative blip' – a cut in wages – to cancel out the overall effect of the City traders' good fortune. But the likelihood of such a wage cut depended critically on the success or otherwise of that major subdivision of the marketeers' plans for the elimination of moral hazard, the reform of the labour market.

On the face of it, the success has been dramatic. The trade unions, chief pillar of the old 'one-way-bet' full-employment system, have been tamed and sidelined. The 'rotational' labour market we discussed earlier is the fulfilment of the new-capitalist dream: it maintains competitive pressure on wages and thus prevents 'distortions', chief among them the 'job for life'. The very title of this book expresses the outcome: the Age of Insecurity.

Yet one apparent contradiction would seem to mar the moment of triumph. As unions have retreated along with the other one-time social partners – the governments that kept demand at full tilt and the employers who implicitly accepted a duty to employ – so the law would seem to have stepped into the breach. It is quite possible, sometimes on the same radio bulletin, to hear of several thousand workers losing their jobs at one plant while, from the High Court, Court of Appeal or House of Lords, a group of lollipop ladies/policewomen/cleaners/dustmen is reported emerging blinking into the sunlight, 'delighted' with their 'historic' victory over low pay/wage cuts/unequal pay/unfair dismissal. Where the men in cloth caps have been beaten off, it would seem, the men in wigs are proving far tougher opposition in the long run for the new market economy. And the shrunken trade unions have themselves been transformed to a great extent into middle-men for the legal profession, packaging up possible cases involving their members and bringing them to the lawyers. These days a union official is more likely to be found warming himself by the fire in a barrister's chambers in the Temple than rubbing his hands over a picket-line brazier.

Furthermore, to the optimist, the two phenomena – the brutal 'down-sizing' and the 'historic' courtroom win – can surely not coexist permanently within the same economic and legal system. Is it not the case that, step by step, judges are building a plinth of rights upon which employees will regain the position they enjoyed under the post-war system and even improve upon it? This is a nice idea, but let us look back to the 1970s. Unfair dismissal law was in its infancy, the finer points of sex discrimination, stress, workplace trauma and the prohibition of Irish jokes were a mere gleam in a trainee solic-itor's eye. Employers confronted few legal – as opposed to trade-union-negotiated – constraints upon hiring and firing. Small businesses faced none (with the exception of racial discrimination), nor did domestic employers. Should a small company wish to insist on female tea ladies or male foremen, that was its own affair. In short, the social aspects of employment were con-strained by a minimum of controls.

By contrast, the economic aspects of employment were clapped in a polit-ical and legal straitjacket. Firing someone for falling pregnant or 'coming out' may have been fairly easy, but firing someone on the sole ground that the employer would be able to make more money without him was a very dif-ferent business. Closing a chronically loss-making plant was difficult enough: government, committed to full employment, would turn the full panoply of state planning onto the hapless company that declined to subsidize the factory in question. Even when government itself decided to pull the plug on 'lame ducks', as with the Upper Clyde shipbuilders in 1971, outraged public opin-ion forced an about-face.

When Chrysler pulled out of Britain in the mid-1970s, the government – having failed to persuade the company to stay – bent its efforts to finding a new owner. Sure enough, the Linwood and Ryton plants switched from

Chrysler to Talbot with barely a break in their step. As for closing or radically downsizing a plant simply because it was not making sufficient return on capital, the idea would not have registered in the public thinking of the time. Nobody who wished to continue to do business in the world's fifth-largest economy would have contemplated such a 'nineteenth-century' (as it would have been described) manoeuvre. True, there was no actual single law against pulling the blinds on a poor profit centre. But apart from anything else, the peer-group pressure from within the 'tripartite' system would have killed the idea stone dead.

In some industries, it was more than peer-group pressure that preserved jobs in the face of what now would be seen as overwhelming economic facts. The most obvious example was the legal framework encasing Britain's main ports, the 1947 National Dock Labour Scheme, jointly administered by the port employers and the Transport and General Workers Union. The scheme defined dock work, reserved it for registered (i.e. union) dockers and listed the eighty-four ports to which the scheme applied. By the early 1970s, a combination of new technology (the widespread use of containers unloaded at terminals) and the chronic inefficiency of the registered ports had begun to threaten employment there. The (Conservative) government responded with the 1972 Aldington–Jones agreement (named respectively after the responsible minister and the general secretary of the TGWU), which compelled employers to keep on basic pay any docker for whom work could not be found and to take on board any docker made redundant as a result of the closure of dock companies. Registered dockers were, quite literally, unsackable. Should their work practices force their employer to the wall, a competitor would be obliged to employ them. Only when a docker volunteered for redundancy could he finally be let go. The huge costs of this scheme provided a competitive bonus for operators of the inland container ports. But not for long. In 1976, the (Labour) government passed the Dock Work Regulation Act, extending registered dock work to cold-storage depots and warehouses five miles away from any waterfront. We dwell on the dock scheme simply to illustrate how deeply the post-war cultural climate deplored any attempt to sack employees on economic grounds. In the (admittedly extreme) case of the dockers, they could not be sacked even if their employer went out of business – the ultimate in job security.

Today, the one sure and certain, legally unassailable way of sacking a group of people is to announce that they are generating insufficient profits. The social aspects of employment now merge with social relationships generally, and are thus ripe for governmental and legal direction and intervention. The employer who discriminates on the grounds of age, or sex or disability is quite simply a morally flawed human being and in need of correction. But the employer who responds, automatically, like a thermostat, to the 'internal rate of return' or 'economic value added' or whatever is the latest tool for measuring profitability, faces no sanction, legal or social. Even the much-vaunted European 'social model' is falling victim to this development. In March 1997, Renault announced it was to close its plant at Vilvoorde in Belgium. The move stunned the Belgian nation, and politicians – including the Prime Minister Jean-Luc Dehaene, whose constituency included the plant – responded in a robust manner. One official described the closure as an act of terrorism against the economy of Flanders. Demonstrators denounced the new Europe as a 'social cemetery'.

Help was at hand, however. A few weeks later, France elected Lionel Jospin's Socialist Party to government; among its pledges was a reprieve for Vilvoorde. Some saw this as the dawn of a new era of transfrontier social solidarity in Europe. Mr Jospin promptly ordered Renault to reconsider the closure. Renault obliged, and concluded that its original decision had been entirely correct. And that was more or less that. Renault, according to the new market order, is responding to the real world, whereas Mr Jospin is a decent enough cove, a sort of Gallic Michael Foot, who ought to confine his ideas of 'social inclusion' to the election meeting and not try to 'distort' reality by actually implementing them.

A very different case in this country in July 1995 underlined the parallel, never-touching relationship between the new social controls and the complete absence of economic controls. Three school dinner ladies won a House of Lords hearing against North Yorkshire County Council's decision to cut their pay in order to allow its direct-labour organization to compete with cheaper tenders being offered by outside contractors. The council was obliged to accept competitive tenders and was unable simply to continue employing its own staff. The women won their claim not because competitive tendering was unlawful (it was a legal obligation), but because the cuts infringed an equal-pay assessment of 1987 that had graded the women as comparable to dustmen, gardeners, cleaners and other mainly male council employees. As the women and their union, Unison, celebrated, the council pointed out the 'victory' would not only mean that the dinner ladies and their 1,297-odd colleagues in the county would now almost certainly lose their jobs to cheaper tenders, but could also mean that all council direct-labour operations around the country – now effectively prohibited from competing for tenders – would have to be disbanded. Unison had little or nothing to say on this point and seemed to regard the council's mentioning it as a breach of the etiquette observed on the occasion of 'landmark victories' such as this.

From Belgium and Paris to Northallerton, employers are almost entirely free to fire at will, provided they are doing so in response to 'real' market factors. To do so in response to mere prejudice is unacceptable and (usually) unlawful behaviour. That the 'real' market is itself a prejudice is, of course, one of the contentions of this book. In other words, the employer is unhindered as long as he is acting as the embodiment of capital and money values. To act in a human (i.e. 'distorted') way is to expose himself to sanction. As with the 'sovereign' individual, the sovereign employer is confined to the narrow corridor of 'financially sound' practice. And this 'soundness' is, in fact, honeycombed with moral hazard and conflicts of interest.

On this issue, we grade the new market system with the lowest mark available to examiners of the old O-level system: U for Unclassified.

FAHRENHEIT 45.1 FM (STEREO): CULTURAL MELTDOWN IN THE NEW ECONOMIC ORDER

The new market system was just as much a cultural as an economic project, its promises of vitality in place of sterility applicable to the arts, media and literature as well as to manufacturing industry or the balance of payments. In both commercial and cultural life, the problems diagnosed were similar: the state, by interposing itself between consumer and producer (or artist and audience), had created 'distortions' that, as with the progressive inaccuracy of the Julian calendar, compounded themselves as time went by. Value was lost, or destroyed, in both cases, and a catastrophe point was reached at which rethinking was urgently required: 30 per cent inflation in Britain in

1975 in the economic case, and the 'Tate bricks' affair of the following year in the cultural case.

By a neat coincidence, both state-managed economics and state-managed art had been invented by the same man, Lord Keynes. The rewriter of the economic rulebook had, in his spare time, founded the Arts Council. His rejection in the economic field ought surely to lead to his rejection in the cultural field. Furthermore, the state's handmaidens in its woefully misguided attempts to steer both economic and cultural life were similar: corporate-minded big businessmen/arts bureaucrats and their trade-union allies. The former mouthed platitudes ('export or die'/'artistic excellence') while the latter insisted on labour costs that deadened competitiveness/creativity. (For every anecdote about sleeping car makers and 'two men in the cab' there was a tale of mob-handed camera crews and grossly overmanned printing presses.)

The net result, according to market arguments, was that, by the end of the 1970s, both industry and the arts were becalmed.

Britain's National Theatre does not have to be 'national' to survive. It survives because it is an ornament of the capital. Our political centre contains both opera-loving City financiers and theatre-loving administrators. The National Theatre puts on 'difficult' plays for left-wing bureaucrats or explores the long tail of the European avant-garde . . . The 'public' is out there somewhere, indistinct, like a patient ignored by the health service.[6]

Alongside the supposedly bloated arts establishment, with its heavy public subsidies for VIP entertainment, sat the broadcasters, no longer hailed as guardians of the best television and radio services in the world but increasingly attacked as complacent quasi-monopolists, serving meagre helpings of unrelenting mediocrity from their privileged legal positions.

In 1982, Andrew Neil, later to edit the *Sunday Times* and head the Sky satellite-television company, edited a booklet entitled 'The cable revolution'. The publication heralded a future of dozens of TV channels and 'interactive' cable services, and Mr Neil's own article tackled head on the standard objection to such a state of affairs: 'The result will not be an endless diet of junk. . . . It may hurt British pride to hear it, but the average American cable viewer now has a far wider choice of quality programming to choose from than the average British viewer.' To prove the point, Mr Neil reprinted two television schedules for 9 p.m. on the same night, 7 June 1982. The first showed the choice available to Manhattan Cable viewers: twenty-seven channels displayed wares ranging from sport and mainstream films through news and Chinese cooking to ballet, opera and a seminar on nuclear weapons. The second described the choice available to viewers in London: *The 9 O'Clock News* on BBC 1, a repeat of *Hitch-hiker's Guide to the Galaxy* on BBC 2 and a repeat of *Minder* on ITV (Channel Four had yet to launch).

Mr Neil conceded there would be much junk on cable. But thanks to the wonders of 'narrowcasting', the discerning subscriber would enjoy a feast of cultural riches. No more would the viewer and listener need to trust BBC and IBA mandarins to maintain standards. Henceforth, the consumer himself would be the guarantor, just as he was already in the newsagent or bookshop. Or was he? Even the humble bookstore had a role to play in the market revolution. Since 1901, book prices had been controlled by the Net Book Agreement, a form of retail price maintenance that prohibited big shops and chains from undercutting the 'net' price. The NBA was a measure designed to keep in business a diversity of small shops that would otherwise be swept away by cut-throat price competition. By the end of the 1980s, big retailing interests, including supermarkets and the Dillons book chain, were demanding an end to this 'distortion'. Cheaper books, they declared, meant more and better, not fewer and worse. Sympathetic press articles detailed the glories of the (uncontrolled) American book market, with its all-night bookshops boasting coffee-shops and attentive staffs. A net book agreement, declared the campaigners, was no more valid than a net wallpaper agreement.

Alongside the bookshops stood the newsagents, purveying the products of an industry considered in dire need of market reform: the press. By the end of the 1970s, the excesses of Fleet Street had become legendary. As executives and journalists reportedly caroused on fat expense accounts and 'freebies', the industrial bowels of the national newspaper industry ran alive with print workers enjoying double and treble manning, wildly inflated pay packets, 'ghost' working and effective powers of censorship over the contents of their titles. In one case, that of the News International group, later events were to prove that the company was forced to employ ten times the necessary level of printers and kindred workers. So overmanned was the Express group that in 1978 it actually launched a new title, the *Manchester Daily Star* (later the *Daily Star*), simply to soak up some of the surplus labour.

Three deleterious cultural consequences were said to flow from the reckless extravagance and waste of Fleet Street. First, feeding the ravenous cost base meant cost saving in once-sacrosanct editorial fields. Foreign bureaux were closed, staffs pruned. Second, the appetite for cash exerted pressures that militated against truly 'highbrow' newspapers. Intellectual standards were compromised in the search for 'sale' and thus advertising revenue. Third, the huge cost base of national newspapers provided an effective barrier to new entrants, stifling diversity and creativity. Across arts and media, the charge was the same: regulation plus subsidy plus union power equals sterility. Take the state out of the equation, reunite audience and artist, patron and genius, remove union obstacles to new technology, sweep away barriers to entry, and sit back in expectation of a New Renaissance.

How has it worked out? First, the good news: British theatre – its reduced public grants made up in part by more generous business sponsorship – continues to flourish, although few would be so bold as to declare the 1990s has brought forth new writers to compare with those produced by the age of 'sterility': Harold Pinter, Tom Stoppard, David Hare, David Edgar. And the semi-permanent atmosphere of crisis pervading the performing arts (programme cuts, the partial withdrawal of the Royal Shakespeare Company from London, the huge question mark over the future of the Royal Opera House) is no doubt a useful antidote to complacency, bureaucracy and the other alleged wrongs of public-sector culture.

Elsewhere, the results of applying market values to cultural life have been quite the reverse of what was suggested. The combination of technology and private money that was to have allowed the brightest and the best to conquer a new intellectual high ground has instead flattened the cultural landscape. Applying business values to cultural life has proved similar to Ray Bradbury's vision of applying a fireman's hose to a pile of books. By the late 1990s, cultural values were in collapse, toppled by market values.

Cable television, for example, has not allowed a hundred cultural flowers to bloom. There are no channels specializing in ballet or the opera. Instead, there are stations such as the notorious Live TV, possibly the worst television channel in the world, with its topless darts players, 'news bunny' and shoestring budget. At one point, Live TV – born in 1994 – filled one evening a week with a transmission of a party held at its own offices. Live TV is owned by the Mirror newspaper group, whose chief executive David Montgomery was able to claim with a straight face that it represented 'a unique brand of national television'.

The late 1980s and 1990s did produce some superb television drama: shows like *Taggart*, *Prime Suspect* and *Inspector Morse* reached worldwide audiences totalling perhaps one billion people, with a second wave coming up behind: *Cracker* reached New York in 1994, to a rave reception. None of these programmes emerged from pay-TV, but from the supposedly clapped-out and bureaucratic mainstream channels.

Cable's big sister, satellite television, rarely touches the depths plumbed by Live TV, but here too there is little sign of a cultural renaissance. Aside from beaming into Britain hard-core pornography such as the Red Hot Dutch channel, satellite's chief contribution to our shared cultural life has been to buy up major sporting events, thus restricting enjoyment of them to its own customers. This has, if nothing else, revived both pub going (as fans crowd bars fitted with satellite television) and the forgotten pleasures of listening to sports commentary on the radio (the one corner of public-service broadcasting still able to cover such events).

The deregulation of commercial radio in the 1990s has certainly brought dozens of new stations onto the air. And at least two of them – the self-explanatory Jazz FM and Classic FM – have undoubtedly enriched cultural choice. But in the latter case the effect has been, again, the opposite of that suggested. A popular, middlebrow, commercial classical music station ought, according to market thinking, to have liberated the highbrow BBC Radio 3 to take an uncompromising stand at the very highest end of the cultural spectrum. This, after all, was what 'niche' marketing and narrowcasting was supposed to be about. Nothing of the sort took place. Panicked by the success of Classic FM, Radio 3 hurried in the mid-1990s to embrace sugary presentation, 'drive-time' programmes and a more 'accessible' format.

The proliferation of new stations in the 1990s has made inevitable some decline in the audience share of established services. People running those services ought to accept such a decline with equanimity, recognizing it as part of the 'narrowcasting' process implicit in the new market order. They have not. While Radio 3 tiptoed downmarket with as much dignity as it could muster, Radio 4, the speech channel, took a header in the same direction. In

July 1997, the BBC announced a wholesale restructuring of its flagship radio station, to take effect the following year. Among the most conspicuous casualties was the full-length radio play; henceforth, no drama lasting more than forty-five minutes would be transmitted. This comprehensive redevelopment exposed the deep penetration of business values into the heart of the BBC. 'Grow or die' is a market imperative, as is the injunction that 'the status quo is not an option'. In the fevered atmosphere generated by such a value system, 'standards' represent just one more 'distortion' or 'overhead cost'. The objective is to 'deliver market share'.

In market-think, Radio 4's frequency is an 'asset' and the station itself is a 'brand'. Assets must be made to 'sweat' and brands have to be 'developed'. In such a situation, Radio 4's existing, famously conservative, audience is the equivalent of a group of rent-controlled tenants who have to be persuaded to leave a property so that its underlying value can be 'unlocked'. Radio 4's travails form just one part of the transformation of the BBC into one vast facsimile market-place. The system of 'producer choice' attempted to mimic open-market conditions by setting internal service providers in competition with outside commercial operations. By mid-decade it had become clear that producer choice, just like the very similar National Health Service 'internal market', required a huge bureaucracy to simulate the artificial market-place. Paying for this vast secretariat required funds that could only come, and duly did come, from sweeping redundancies elsewhere in the corporation and cuts in programme-making money.

The verve and conviction with which the BBC was 'marketized' contrasted strongly with a widespread collapse of nerve in terms of cultural standards. But this is not surprising. The standards stood in the way of the market, so priority went to the latter, not the former. While Radios 3 and 4 pursued the mirage of bigger, younger audiences, and the flagship television current affairs programme *Newsnight* was given a lighter, frothier formula, BBC mandarins fell over themselves (in vain, as it turned out) to retain the services of Radio 1's foul-mouthed disc jockey Chris Evans. In keeping with the new economic order, Mr Evans was hired not as a person but as a company. He took to the air in April 1995 and provoked a flood of complaints from listeners who objected to his language and his habit of humiliating studio employees on air. The corporation's top brass insisted Mr Evans was, in truth, a broadcasting genius and flatly refused to contemplate the dismissal that would surely have faced him ten years earlier. The line was that, for all his faults, he represented a great improvement on the superannuated mid-Atlantic presenters who had gone before, men for whom everything was amazing, fantastic and simply great. It was hard to see how. At least Mr Evans's predecessors had faithfully reflected the long Saturday morning that had been the post-war years. What Mr Evans reflected was difficult to guess. In summer 1996, Matthew Bannister, who, as head of Radio 1 had been responsible for the employment of Mr Evans and who was to remain his defender and 'handler' for the remainder of his time with the BBC, was promoted to chief of all BBC radio. He and his protégé had, as the *Guardian* pointed out on 17 June 1996, delivered 'more or less what corporate strategy demanded'; in other words, more listeners.

But holding BBC management to account for the many assaults upon the corporation's core values was far from easy, because watchdogs in the print media had contracted a similar disease to the one they would have been called upon to diagnose at Broadcasting House. Fleet Street, liberated from its high-cost structure by the defeat at Wapping of the print unions, ought, according to plan, to have witnessed a flowering of diversity, with special emphasis on the now economically viable upper end of the market. For a while, this seemed to be happening, with the successful launch in 1986 of *The Independent*, a newspaper whose cool grey type and air of authority gave the impression it had been around for at least a century. The upper-middlebrow renaissance, however, proved a false dawn. In September 1996, the distinguished journalist and commentator Anthony Sampson complained in the *British Journalism Review* that the frontier between serious and popular newspapers had 'virtually disappeared', not because all the tabloid papers now resembled *The Times* of old, but because popular press values had been adopted wholesale by the broadsheet titles. Foreign news, parliamentary reporting and investigative journalism had been eased out, he said, to be replaced by hordes of columnists anxious to tell readers what had happened to them on the way to Sainsbury's.

He was not the only critic of the 'thinning-out' of serious newspaper content. But, in keeping with the new system of business values, the response of the editors concerned was, in many cases, to resort to packaging changes. Margarining over the lightweight intellectual content of their papers, some took to plastering their pages with quill-pen emblems and other 'quality' symbols above pieces with portentous titles such as 'The Saturday Essay', all intended to convey the impression that the reader was entering a Hazlittian treasure-house of wisdom. But all the cod-Enlightenment symbolism in the world couldn't hide the acres of space devoted to *Baywatch* actresses, the Spice Girls and the aforementioned solipsistic columnists.

This retreat into packaging is typical of all arts and media in the new economic order. Playwright David Mamet has complained of filmgoers' recently acquired habit of praising a picture for 'fantastic cinematography': 'Yeah, but so what? Hitler had fantastic cinematography. The question we have ceased to ask is, "What was the fantastic or brilliant cinematography in aid of?"' He goes on to list 'production' or 'production values' as the theatre equivalent of 'fantastic cinematography'. Were he exposed to the workings of the British press, he may well add the oft-heard phrase on the lips of senior executives – 'Our pages looked good today' – to his hit-list. Not: 'Our pages read well today', but 'looked good'.

If matters are any healthier in the world of publishing, it says more for the persistence of writers determined to reach a public, however small, than for any pastoral, nurturing role on the part of either big publishers or major bookshop chains. In a frenzy of greed and aggrandisement, the industry was convulsed by merger mania in the mid-1980s, with the entirely predictable result that the new combines, driven by business rather than literary ethics, promptly 'downsized' their lists of modest-selling authors and threw their energies into a series of mega-bids for the work of top-name writers such as Salman Rushdie and Martin Amis. Advances that could never be 'earned out' became commonplace, topped only by the absurd prices paid by some publishers for the privilege of swallowing up their smaller brethren. In 1988, the most notorious publisher of all, Robert Maxwell, paid $1 billion too much for America's Macmillan group. This was the deal he had to do to achieve his aim of becoming a 'world-class' publisher; the total consideration of $2.6 billion went a long way to explaining the staggering $3 billion debt total discovered within his empire after his death in November 1991. Robert Maxwell's greed was merely an extreme example of a disease that had the entire industry in its grip. The new combines had little time for the old author–editor relationship; their editors were now middle-status employees whose every book-buying decision required approval from marketing people. By the mid-1990s, second-line authors were learning that such people could 'see no way of selling' their latest works.

Following the destruction of the Net Book Agreement – finally accomplished in law in March 1997 after years of skirmishing – the price of books had raced ahead at twice the rate of inflation during 1996, the first full year in which the NBA had effectively ceased to operate. This is the opposite of what had been predicted, and may be explained by publishers increasing the cover price so that booksellers could then be seen to be offering generous discounts (packaging again). Nor did it do a lot for the industry: Hodder Headline issued a profits warning and HarperCollins reported a dramatic revenue slide.

To say that deregulation of prices brought no obvious improvement in the quality of those works the marketing departments did feel able to sell would be an understatement. Once-reputable publishers were, in the new market era, prepared to put their imprints upon books that could most kindly be described as a waste of good trees. In 1996–97, some of the most heavily promoted non-fiction (supposedly) books on sale included one suggesting that the Holy Bible contained elaborate codes that could be cracked by computers, one claiming to have located Jesus Christ's tomb in France, the usual slew of flying saucer/conspiracy theory junk and a book whose claims of a British government 'death squad' in Northern Ireland were so ludicrous as to be rejected not only by the security forces but by the IRA as well. Unfazed by the demolition of the book's claims, the publisher plastered London with posters brandishing the official denials as proof positive that the book's claims had to be true. As the century draws to a close, a publishing industry that had once taken pride in its role as educator and promoter of enlightenment seems to be degenerating into a gargantuan pre-eighteenth-century rumour and superstition machine, hawking fables and tall tales to a gullible populace.

Mirroring the rapacity and chaos of book publishing, the classical record industry entered 1997 in a state of crisis after years of similar takeover mania and uncontrolled spending. Many of the top labels were up for sale, holed below the waterline by cheap-priced discs offering reasonable recordings by non-name orchestras. The big labels, lavishing money on stars such as Nigel Kennedy and Vanessa Mae, looted the glories of Western music for anything that could be packaged into easy-to-listen-to collections of the 'great music for lovers' variety.

Art itself was, by the mid-1990s, being held up as a fantastic British success story. We do not intend here to wade into the controversy over dead sheep, concrete house-sculptures and 'naked shit'. Instead, we merely quote from the recantation of George Soros, the billionaire speculator, first published in *Atlantic Monthly* and reproduced in the *Guardian* of 18 January 1997: '[A]s the market mechanism has extended its sway, the fiction that people act on the basis of a given set of non-market values has become progressively more difficult to maintain. . . . Unsure what they stand for, people increasingly rely on money as the criterion of value. What is more expensive is considered better. The value of a work of art can be judged by the price it fetches.' Money values corrupted not only new art, but the masterpiece collections of the great galleries. Thomas Hoving, former director of the Metropolitan Museum of Art in New York, claimed in 1997 that fakes or fraudulently restored work accounted for more than a third of the art hanging in the world's great galleries. Tintoretto, Dürer, Rubens, Corot, Renoir . . . the list continues. And the biggest buyers of fakes, said Mr Hoving, are not gullible billionaires but so-called professionals: collectors and curators. How were they fooled, again and again? 'Three words tell the whole story: *need, speed* and *greed*.'[7]

The guardian and guarantor of a healthy culture is a healthy education system, and – since the last century – the governing wheel of the education system has been the open, competitive, anonymously marked examination. Here, too, it had been hoped that market thinking would drive standards upwards. The 1988 great Education Reform Act allowed schools to 'opt out' of local authority control and enshrined the principle of funding following pupils rather than institutions, in order to force poor schools to 'raise their game' or close down. How well this has actually worked is difficult to judge, because the same market principles, applied to examination boards and universities, have worked in completely the opposite direction. Keen to attract new 'business' – i.e. schools – the boards lowered standards so far that the proportion of pupils receiving A or B grade at A-level rose 30 per cent between 1989 and 1997. Giving the lie to any idea of a sudden outbreak of genius among sixth-formers was the increasing practice of universities of offering 'remedial' courses in basic skills for students newly arrived from their A-level 'triumphs'. The boards' behaviour, wrote Stephen Glover in the *Daily Telegraph* on 15 August 1997, was: 'A nice example of competition driving standards down rather than up.'

The ruination wreaked by money values on the cultural landscape did at least spare those who ought to have known better the need to make any hard judgements. Not only were too many critics and commentators in awe of the colossal sums of money involved in arts and media, but both the Conservative government's Department of National Heritage (until mid-1997) and its Labour successor, the Department of Culture, Media and Sport, touted the dollar-earning capacities of 'Brit-pop', 'Brit-Art', advertising, TV and film as all the evidence needed for the rude vitality of British culture. Government's task was to jolly along this bustling, neo-Elizabethan age with tax breaks, grants, National Lottery funding and parties for the glitterati at 10 Downing Street.

In such an atmosphere, few were prepared to blurt out the ghastly truth that what appeared to be the bloom of cultural health on the nation's cheeks was, in fact, the symptom of a raging fever. One with the courage to do so was Stuart Jeffries, who lamented the collapse of critical standards in the *Guardian* on 6 September 1997:

there is a trend to reduce the work of art to a commodity, to make aesthetic appreciation just another form of shopping. No wonder, then, that in some papers restaurants are assessed next to ballet performances. . . . The presumption . . . is that what readers really want to know is whether something is worth paying to see, hear, digest or own. Aesthetics is just a minor branch of economics, great art just another spending opportunity.

Another fail on the new economic system's report sheet.

'A UNIVERSAL WOLF': THE MARKET JUNKIES SEEK THE ULTIMATE HIGH

Early in 1997, Britain's Co-operative Movement learned, to its considerable surprise, that it was 'in play', City slang suggesting it was the target of a takeover bid. The Co-op, a rag-bag of funeral parlours, supermarkets, an insurance company, a bank and other businesses – all with a nice little political party attached – was surely takeover-proof? There were no shares and no market of any sort in its corporate equity. Indeed, it was scarcely 'corporate' in any meaningful sense whatsoever. But in the spirit of 1997, roughly Year 21 of the market era, anything, any entity, any institution, was considered fair game for a spot of looting and ransacking. Hot on the heels of the Co-op bid rumour, press reports lined up a series of fresh lambs for the slaughter: the Automobile Association, Royal Automobile Club and Interflora were high on the lists. None was a 'company' in the accepted sense; all were membership-based organizations. It was doubtful if the constitutions of some or all of them even permitted them to be taken over. But that posed no fundamental problem for the bid merchants. Slavering for fresh meat (or, as its proponents would have it, seeking dormant assets to liberate), the financial interest was becoming less and less fussy about the who, whys, wherefores.

The Co-op bid failed shortly before the 1 May election that swept several Co-op MPs into Parliament under the Labour banner. Optimists wrote off the whole sorry affair as the last fling of the 'years of greed' before the new era of communitarian harmony. These optimists may have failed to notice that, rolling through 1996 and 1997 like the Severn bore, the wholesale ransacking of mutual building societies and insurance companies to the tune of £35 billion in payoffs to policy holders and other customers was effectively closing down the mutual financial sector in Britain. In vain were voices of protest raised from within the shrunken mutual sector claiming that morally and, quite possibly, legally the mutuals had no right to squander reserves built up by generations of members. In typically British fashion, the big picture was ignored while the media concentrated their fire on 'carpet-baggers' – people who had opened accounts solely in the hope of qualifying for payouts on de-mutualization.

A decade earlier, the privatization of the Trustee Savings Bank, against the non-binding advice of the Law Lords suggesting the government did not own TSB and had therefore a dubious claim to be able to sell it, cleared the path for the 'liberation of value' across the mutual sector. On 2 September 1997, the *Financial Times* reported that the 'de-mutualization' hurricane was far from blown out, according to a report by banking giant HSBC (owner of the Midland). The article concluded: 'HSBC also believes a raft of other mutuals may change status, including the Co-op, Bupa [the medical insurance group], the AA and RAC. It describes the church as the ultimate mutual organization, but stops short of predicting a stock exchange listing for it.'

The 'dynamic stability' promised by the new market system was instead turning to chronic instability as the financial interest sought deal after deal, asset after asset. One way to give the City its 'fix' was to churn the same assets round and round, merging, de-merging, downsizing and expanding, each time with a similar cast of merchant bankers, brokers, public-relations men, accountants, lawyers, headhunters and the rest of the mercenary army taking a cut of the action. Another was to seek Co-op-style situations, looting assets previously thought locked up in co-operative or non-commercial structures. It can only be a matter of time before the National Trust is declared a 'property play' or the National Farmers Union a 'valuable brand'.

This manic hunt for 'value' took other forms. A notable feature of the 1990s was the packaging of items or features of commercial services previously provided gratis and making them saleable commodities. A small example is the seating on overnight ferries: where once decks would have been well provided with sofas on which steerage passengers could sleep, now there were special lounges where those without a cabin paid a supplement for an easy chair for the night. The decks themselves contained hard plastic seating. Another, more substantial, example is the range of services once provided at a bank manager's discretion, from storage of wills to financial advice. All are now decreed potential 'profit centres', required to 'hack it' in the market-place. Just as the new management-think declared all problems to be opportunities, so it insisted every cost centre was potentially a profit centre. Charges proliferated as any number of actions were packaged for sale; at times it seemed as if the whole of life were becoming like the old joke about the solicitor's bill ('Crossing the road to say hello to you: 6/-. Recrossing the road when I realized it was not you: 6/-'). Among the items ripest for such packaging was 'intellectual property', a concept once thought to apply to piano concertos, novels, industrial patents, trademarks and not a lot else. In the new era, teams of lawyers attempted with considerable success to enforce copyright almost without limit; in the most notorious sequence of cases, McDonald's, the snack-bar chain, sued anybody or anything using for business purposes the celebrated Gaelic prefix. In 1990, the Law Lords ruled, albeit with some reluctance, that the Jif plastic lemon (used as a container for lemon juice) was the intellectual property of its owner Reckitt & Colman, the food and household products group, and that an American competitor was not permitted to use the design. The days have passed when the 'design' of the humble lemon would have been attributed to an authority greater than Reckitt & Colman, greater even than the Lords of Appeal in Ordinary.

Elsewhere, the less intellectual the property, the more ferociously was it defended. Owners of the children's television programme *Star Trek* registered its illiterate catchphrase 'to boldly go', while the Disney organization took steps to prevent garage owners from announcing, without permission, the geographical fact that their garages were situated *x* miles from a Disney theme park.

Meanwhile in the real world, rogue capitalists embarked upon an orgy of counterfeiting and forgery. In 1990, it was estimated that up to 9 per cent of world GDP consisted of counterfeit goods, with engineering components and medicine among the most heavily faked products. Forged financial instruments presented an even more alarming problem; by the mid-1990s, the Commercial Crime Bureau, part of the International Chamber of Commerce, estimated investors around the world were at risk from up to $5 billion worth of forgeries described variously as 'prime guarantee notes' or 'standby letters of credit', supposedly inter-bank instruments but worthless fakes. Among the victims of this racket were the Salvation Army and the Chicago Housing Authority. In a final surreal twist, experts doubted whether a conviction could be obtained against the racketeers: given their claim that the 'instruments' were a well-kept secret among the big banks, would any jury decide beyond reasonable doubt that this financial UFO story was untrue? Far from providing a clean market-place with properly priced investments available for all, the market order had conjured into being a free-fire zone in which honest securities slugged it out with criminal forgeries. No activity on the 'rogue' side of the fence was without its counterpart in the legitimate market. Straightforward counterfeiting was mirrored by legal copying by big retailers of a range of products developed and marketed by smaller outfits, from the natural cosmetics sold by the Body Shop to electrical goods and clothing.

A linked development of the 'virtual-reality economy' was the trend towards 'brand accounting' and 'brand valuation', the attempt to write into company accounts the intangible worth of a name or a design. Symbols, words and colour arrangements became the subjects of vast lawsuits; 'brand development' became a spurious subdiscipline in its own right, alongside 'active brand management'. Image consultants charged millions for dreaming up new corporate logos. By 1997, it seemed that the 'virtual' company of the future need amount to little more than a logo and a board of directors:

in that year, British Airways announced it was 're-branding' its aeroplanes and contracting out many of its in-house operations. Bolder voices suggested BA would one day have to lose the aircraft as well and shrink to a core seat-booking system. The slavering beast – having eaten everything in sight – was now eating itself.

Indeed, the hunger for ever greater 'return on capital' led some to cut the final link with the real world and plunge into the oldest form of non-productive money circulation known to man: gambling. Respectable banks sank billions in the 'derivatives' markets, buying and selling futures and options on a scale that dwarfed their own capital bases. Gambling proper boomed on a scale unseen in living memory: in Britain, the National Lottery, launched in 1994, was the most conspicuous example of the rehabilitation of gaming, the one vice to have ended the 'permissive' 1960s more tightly con-trolled than it had been at the beginning. The lottery proved the thin end of the wedge: in its wake came deregulation of pool betting, bingo and the hardest of hard gaming, the casino industry, this latter measure promoted by the supposedly tough Home Secretary Michael Howard. Nor were these merely benign measures promoting a live-and-let-live attitude to simple pleasures. Gaming fever infected all aspects of the new market economy; chain letters and pyramid schemes abounded, most notably in the former Communist countries now experiencing 'shock therapy' to convert them to market practice (Albania came to the brink of civil war after a number of pyramid schemes, amounting to perhaps a third of GDP, collapsed) but also in Western countries including Britain. During 1996 and 1997, the Department of Trade and Industry struggled to get on top of a contagion of such schemes, including one claiming affiliation to a church and another promising to disclose the secrets of Ancient Egyptian money making in return for an appropriate fee. The new supposedly 'rational' attitude to gaming epitomized by the launch of the National Lottery – that it was a 'bit of fun' that raised funds for good causes – in reality hid a huge upsurge in a quasi-mystical belief that fortunes could be made by a mixture of random luck, bogus odds-based mathematics and possession of the right pieces of paper (whether share options for top executives or the worthless 'bank paper' or chain letters promoted by the swindlers).

Such developments were inevitable once the ethic of gambling was allowed to move from the margins to the centre of the economic system.

Gaming is quite different from legitimate commerce: the latter is bound up with the concept of a balance of interests between buyer and seller, the deal being struck when the scales sit level at (from the buyer's point of view) six apples and (from the seller's point of view) 1lb in weight. Gaming is fundamentally about one side getting an 'edge', about coming to the deal armed with a hidden advantage over the other actor. Nothing could have been further removed from the just rewards for hard work implicit in propaganda for the new market order. The lurid carnival of the new system seemed at times to be lurching into a late twentieth-century parody of Trollope or Zola. In spring 1997, the 'world's biggest gold deposit', at Busang, in Indonesia, was discovered – after the 'suicide' of the company's chief geologist – to be a hole in the ground. Investors had been rooked by fake ore samples. At the same time, Britain was reeling from a parliamentary corruption scandal without parallel in modern times; one of the key MPs fingered in the bribery affair insisted on his total innocence even after an investigation found him guilty, while the man who had bribed him declared no one had done more than he to clean up public life. For the ordinary citizen, the new economic order must have resembled a garishly lit upside-down version of the 'random walk theory', the thinking suggesting that perfect information meant investment analysis amounting to little more than throwing darts blindfold at a list of shares. So imperfect were information flows proving in the market order that wealth or poverty, promotion or 'downsizing' seemed to depend on little more than crazy chance. The lottery winner and the former water-services manager now picking up vast 'share options' after privatization appeared interchangeable. All that mattered was to remain 'ahead of the curve' as assets were looted, whether in terms of 'cashing out' of securities before a shares plunge or of ensuring your name was top of the chain letter.

The new market system has not delivered the broad-based commercial and social stability promised. The absolute priority given to finance has created what George Soros has described as 'far-from-equilibrium' conditions, as hot money has scoured the globe in search of an ever greater 'fix' in terms of rates of return. In its wake it leaves the wreckage of yesterday's 'tiger' economy (now abandoned for another tiger in another time-zone), yesterday's high-yield investment (UK property, the escudo, Australian brewers), yesterday's workforce (South Korean, Czech, Welsh).

From the twisted social wreck, we must, with all the stoicism of a veteran driving examiner, inform the new economic system, with regret, that it has not passed the test.

CUI BONO? ('WHOSE BREAD IS IN YOUR GRAVY?')

It was a central tenet of the new economic system that it was not really a 'system' at all, in the sense of being a man-made construct; it was simply the natural order of things, an objective reality with which government and social engineers tinkered at their peril. Ayn Rand, high priestess of unfettered individualism (she described capitalism as 'the unknown ideal'), named her philosophy 'objectivism'. *The Right Approach* declared: 'The facts of life invariably do turn out to be Tory.' Hayek disputed the use of the word 'economy' in relation to the national economic operating environment: economies, he said, had ends and objectives, thus the word ought to apply strictly only to firms and households. The 'national economy' was ends-independent, a 'catallaxy', the way things were. To impose ends and aims was to begin the long march down the 'road to serfdom'. We know what works, declared George Bush in 1989. Free markets work. Week after week, *The Economist* magazine lays policies and governments alongside the market yardstick to see how they measure up. The International Monetary Fund does much the same, behind closed doors. Those countries defying 'the real world' may qualify for an IMF 'structural-adjustment facility', provided they promise to mend their ways; the loan is viewed as a sort of financial methadone supplied to an economic heroin addict on condition he promises to 'stay clean'.

Following from this, the new market economy is claimed to be, in a curious way, impartial: impartial not in the sense that its rewards are evenly distributed, but in the sense that the weather is impartial. It can play no favourites, because it is blind. When the market shuts down Cornwall's last tin mine, as it did in August 1997, or plunges the Thai economy into chaos, as it did a little earlier in the year, it is passing no judgement other than a market judgement. Such happenings are, as former Chancellor Lord Lawson said of monetary policy, the 'routine and unceasing' operations of the market. Or, in the renowned Mafia phrase, this is business, not personal.

One may as well abuse a thermostat for responding to changes in temperature. Because the market is impersonal and impartial, the market system (which is not really a system at all, merely the natural way of things) can have no vested interests, no 'in' groups. Of course, some profit more than others from the ever changing swirl of market conditions, but they form no permanent class of beneficiaries. Indeed, the market is claimed to be unique in that it is the only socio-economic system not to give rise to a dominant beneficiary class. How different from post-war social democracy, with its squadrons of bureaucrats, planners, meddlers and hangers-on.

To return to our beginning, this is all very interesting. Unfortunately, it is not true. The new economic order is a cultural construct that has taken one part of the human experience – the interaction between buyer and seller – and made it the narrow and fragile base for a rickety and unstable Theory of Everything. The social order brought about in conformity with this theory is no more 'natural' than the mixed economy, the Israeli kibbutz, Scandinavian social democracy, President Johnson's 'Great Society' or any other socio-economic system arrived at under constitutional democratic political conditions. Indeed, one may have thought the proponents of the new market order may have learned something from the complacency of their social-democratic opponents. They in their day had claimed to be in conformity to some higher, natural order: to take a small example, they had assumed railways, posts, telecommunications, power and water to be 'natural monopolies' with which only a maniac would wish to tamper. Given that it is a social construct, the new order – in which unfettered financial activity reduces political activity to a non-dogmatic 'management' of the population in a sanitized zone free of ideological conflict – has its own beneficiary class, and the system's pretensions to deliver 'fairness, not favours' is largely bogus. So: *cui bono?* We ask you to add one and one and reach two.

One: unemployment across Europe is at chronic levels, job insecurity in Britain and the USA barely below its peak despite the recent recovery, all parties demand an end to the Welfare State, top salaries have never been higher, social inequality has returned to the levels of a hundred years ago, trade-union organization is weak and famine sweeps the Third World.

One: which entity in society most closely mirrors the new, executive, 'independent', conflict-free model of government, in which 'doing business' is more important than abstract principles, in which there is no one who cannot be 'brought on side' and in which there is no such word as 'can't'? Is it not the boardroom of the large, international corporation or bank? The dirty little secret of the new 'independent' political structure is that it is nothing of the sort. Not only is any 'independent', non-conflictual entity automatically predisposed towards the status quo, but this particular political and social model is explicitly designed with the needs, interests and demands of big business in mind.

Our market system has accordingly its own 'new class' of interchangeable political and financial chieftains. Labour and Democrat politicians prefer to hang out with bond gurus and investment analysts than with unemployed people; Lord Simon moves effortlessly from chairmanship of British Petroleum to a Labour government ministership; President Clinton urges American workers to 'compete not retreat'; Tony Blair exhorts European socialist leaders to wake up to the rough, tough competitive world out there. Not only does this new class promote the interests and objectives of international finance, but its non-financial values and beliefs are no more 'neutral' or 'plain commonsensical' than their financial ones. The late Christopher Lasch pinned down exactly the strangely rootless nature of the new class's values: 'The new elites are at home only in transit, en route to a high-level conference, to the grand opening of a new franchise, to an international film festival, or to an undiscovered resort. Theirs is essentially a tourist's view of the world – not a perspective likely to encourage a passionate devotion to democracy.'[8]

But Mr Lasch may have been over-eager to tie the new class's beliefs to its interests and aspirations. While what he calls the elites doubtless tailor what he labels their 'political rectitude' to their material perspectives, it is notable that this rectitude, social as well as political, is remarkable for its apparent lack of relation to anything outside itself or indeed to elements within itself. President Clinton's Democrats appear, for example, simultaneously to support prosecutions for 'foetus abuse' of women who drink during pregnancy and the 'scissors abortion' procedure, under which a baby is partially born only to have its brains removed. In Britain, the Labour Party is proposing a straight 'swap' of two civil rights, with the lowering of the age of homosexual consent to sixteen and the raising of the age at which a person can be sold cigarettes to eighteen (the two age limits are currently the other way round). Nor is this the end of the matter; Labour's frontbencher Ann Taylor (later

President of the Council in the first Blair government) suggested in early 1997 the raising of the age of heterosexual consent to eighteen, echoing a similar call in the United States from Mrs Clinton. In California, the net result of various changes is that the only socially correct (and soon, perhaps, legally correct) method of smoking tobacco will be to mix it with cannabis. Above all, as Mr Lasch wrote, the new class mounts crusades 'to sanitise . . . society: to create a "smoke-free environment", to censor everything from pornography to "hate speech" and at the same time, incongruously, to extend the range of personal choice in matters where most people feel the need of solid moral guidelines'.[9] In Britain, *Financial Times* columnists thunder all week about the need for economic discipline and ruminate in the weekend edition about vegetarianism and the environment.

All the above positions may be admirable, or they may not. They may even (arguably) be said to be consistent with one another. But what they are not are 'impartial' truths, derived from the operation of the 'objective' social and economic order. They are the values of a ruling group, as impenetrable to outsiders as the etiquette at Versailles. They are the taboos of the new order's in-class and are as fallible and open to challenge as the new order itself.

Jonathan Cohn has noted the class bias of 'objective' US media reporters. In an article 'Perrier in the Newsroom', he chronicled the effects that journalism's new-found respectability has had on the profile of editorial staffs, chiefly 'the creation of an elite class of reporters with a conspicuously upper-middle-class sympathy. Sometimes this instinct manifests itself as a sympathy for liberal causes such as abortion rights, gay rights and the like. But the same bias also expresses itself as an uncritical faith in conservative doctrines about inflation, trade, taxes, and government spending.'[10]

Cui bono? To ask the question, as Enoch Powell once said in a different context, is to answer it. The market system has failed to meet a primary objective: it has failed to be objective.

AT THE STILL CENTRE: ELY PLACE, HOLBORN

Liberal democracy decisively broke the link between property and sovereignty. It had to do so, by its very nature; democratic government had to apply across the sovereign territory without fear or favour, and, similarly, exercise of political authority had to be divorced from ownership of the territory over which that authority was exercised. In democracies born of sudden revolution, the divorce was swift and final. In Britain, with its evolutionary tradition, the odd link survived here and there well into living memory: the landowner who, acting as magistrate, effectively 'ruled' his patch, the local government curios swept away (largely) by the 1972 reforms, the rights of Cornish tinners to convene their own parliament. Some oddities still survive: the lordships of manors (some of which allow minute 'taxes' to be levied on pieces of land) form one example. And this tiny street, Ely Place, is another. Step past the car barrier at its entrance and leave the London Borough of Camden for the jurisdiction of the Bishops of Ely. Note the men guarding the barrier, not car-park attendants but beadles, private police employed to patrol what has to be the country's smallest local authority. Note also the lockable gate that can block access through the pedestrian passageway from Hatton Garden. Ely Place, a possible inspiration for the Ealing comedy *Passport to Pimlico*, is a charming curiosity, proof that bureaucratic standardization doesn't always have its way.

Then look straight across Holborn Circus at the huge demolition job under way on the south side in 1997–98. There, workmen are tearing down not only the old *Daily Mirror* building but the heart of what has been described as virtually a rogue state: the Robert Maxwell empire. Former *Mirror* editor Roy Greenslade describes this power-unto-itself as 'Maxwellia', a one-man tyranny with branches around the world.[11] It had even its own 'currency', as jurors heard during the 1995–96 trial of four former Maxwell aides, including two of his sons (all were found not guilty): an entry on the group's 'inter-company account' was considered a form of 'payment' for valuable securities.

Maxwell died at the end of 1991, but developments since suggest he may have been something of an amateur on the subject of DIY statehood. Four years later, in a fascinating exposé, Joshua Wolf Shenk detailed how the Walt Disney organization was able 'to act with the power of a government', thanks to its arrangements governing relationships between the state of Florida and the 27,400-acre state within a state that is Disney World and its environs. The Disney zone is an 'autonomous civic unit, providing its own energy, water, police and fire protection. It . . . [sets] its own building codes and its own zoning authority'. It taxes and issues tax-exempt bonds. Mr Shenk warned the Disney Way was spreading:

variations on the same blueprint abound not only in entertainment complexes but also in shopping malls and urban development districts where special tax arrangements and exemptions are increasingly popular means for extricating property from government oversight. In suburbs across the country, perhaps one-third of new developments are gated, with security, utilities, and other traditionally public services delegated to private authorities.[12]

Property does not have to take the form of real estate, however. In May 1994, British Airways, claiming to exercise its legal rights under French and European law, proposed to fly aeroplanes into Orly Airport in defiance of a French government ban, despite a statement from the French authorities couched thus: 'the most express warnings about the consequences which illegal flight attempts could have'. Taking civilian airliners into national air-space in such circumstances would have been simply unthinkable twenty years earlier. But BA, like Maxwell, like Disney, clearly considered a national government to be merely one negotiating partner among many, one power in the world roughly analogous to itself.

Proponents of the free-market system claimed as one of its advantages that it would clarify the lines between powerful economic agents and the state; legal reform would topple the trade-union 'barons' who behaved as the 'fifth estate' of the realm while privatization would get government out of business, restoring each to its rightful sphere. Instead, big business and wealthy individuals are effectively setting themselves up as pre-eighteenth-century mini-sovereignties, claiming rights and freedoms more fitting to medieval principalities than to conventional private operators, corporate or individual. The trade-union barons may be long gone, but the Bishops of Ely are having the last laugh.

ZERO HOUR: THE DESTRUCTION OF WORK AND THE ARITHMETIC OF FEAR

Central to the new order was the resuscitation of the traditional middle class, the backbone of society that had taken a severe kicking during the last, crisis-prone years of the post-war system. The mid-1970s air was thick with howls of pain from suburbs and market towns; any programme for national revival, it was said, would have to involve – indeed, have to start with – the revival of the middle class. Financial journalist Patrick Hutber caught the mood with his book *The Decline and Fall of the Middle Class and How It Can Fight Back* (1976). The Tory MP John Gorst founded the Middle Class Association. The historian Paul Johnson declared in 1977 in his magisterial work *Enemies of Society* that: 'Throughout history, all intelligent observers of society have welcomed the emergence of a flourishing middle class, which they have rightly associated with economic prosperity, political stability, the growth of individual freedom and the raising of moral and cultural standards.'[13] Without the middle class, 'dynamic stability' could not be delivered, for dynamism in the workplace and stability at home were quintessential middle-class virtues.

In a later chapter we examine the recessions and other crises to which the new system is prone. Here, we restrict ourselves to the last and perhaps most important broken promise of the market order: the destruction of the middle class and its central economic tenet, the career path.

By the middle 1990s, any notion that the 'rotating worker' we examined in the previous chapter was strictly a blue-collar phenomenon was well and truly exploded. Not only was the middle-class 'salariat' experiencing the full force of 'downsizing' – a well-documented phenomenon – but the two pillars of the bourgeois professional's world view, career ladder and status, were systematically demolished. Of course there are and always have been two middle classes: commercial and professional. The former ran small businesses, shops and farms, the latter staffed banks, solicitors' offices, libraries, schools, medical practices and the higher reaches of local government. As we saw earlier, it was the former branch that played the more important ideological role in the cultural currents of the 1970s, although the professional branch had its part to play, whether in the guise of Herriot-style local vet or lovable Horace Rumpole-type lawyer.

So savage has been the destructive whirlwind unleashed on both wings of the middle class that an outsider may be forgiven for imagining the country has been under the tutelage of a fundamentalist-Marxist junta determined to 'smash the kulaks'. The commercial branch has lost its businesses, its shops, sometimes its homes. The professional class has lost not only money, but also all those things money cannot buy: pride, status, respect and a clear path for promotion. Surveying the wreckage in the late 1990s, we draw one conclusion immediately: middle-class life, whether commercial or professional, was far better nurtured and protected under the post-war mixed economy than it has been under the market order, however much the latter system was supposedly an expression of middle-class values. Both the small business and the professional practice were, in the strictest sense, non-market institutions, in that neither (as has been proved) was compatible with hurricane-force laissez-faire capitalism.

The trouble with crooks, New York county assistant district attorney John Moscow commented in April 1997, is that they're crooks. He was referring to the impossibility of organized crime ever truly 'going legit' in an ordinary market-place. The crook, unlike the businessman, destroys the competition; he does not compete with it. In a similar way, the giants of the new market era flatten all opposition. Of course, they deny this. The supermarket-hypermarket chain insists there is plenty of room for the small shop, the financial services combine foreswears the destruction of the independent broker, the conveyancing group chuckles at the very idea that the family solicitor could be endangered. The figures give the lie to all this expensive public relations. Every day during the decade 1986–96, eight independent shops went out of business. Butchers, bakers and fishmongers have disappeared from large stretches of urban areas. The number of corner-shop grocers has halved. In 1988, independent shops still held 43.5 per cent of the market; this dropped, according to retail research group Management Horizons, to 32.2 per cent by 1995 and will stand at just 18 per cent by 2010. In 1945, small bakers produced 83 per cent of Britain's bread. By 1995, they produced 8 per cent. Just 3,500 family bakeries remained open in 1995, a drop of 1,500 on 1990. Between 1985 and 1995, local butchers' share of the meat market plunged from 45 per cent to 29 per cent.

With this sort of dominance, one might have thought that the giants would ease off, but not a bit of it. A successful campaign of lawbreaking led in the early 1990s to the legalization of limited Sunday trading by the big chains, removing one of the last selling points of the small stores. In 1995, the supermarkets prepared to destroy the small chemist, with a call to end resale price maintenance on over-the-counter medicines. The small independent garage was already well on the way into the history books, thanks to the cut-price petrol operations of the supermarkets. And, in September 1996, energy giant BP joined forces with Safeway to open a 100-strong shopping chain on garage forecourts, a move reported thus in the *Mail on Sunday*: 'The little corner shops of Britain came a step closer to extinction last week.'

The trouble with crooks is that they're crooks. And the trouble with big business is similarly circuitous. It has to dominate. It has to devour and destroy. There can be no peaceful coexistence between, for example, the cigarette counter at Tesco and the local tobacconist. Somebody has to go under, and it will be the latter. By 1997, having destroyed half the high street with their 'edge-of-town' superstores, the giants lumbered back into centres of population with their own-brand convenience stores, presumably with the intention of destroying the other half.

Meanwhile, the professional arm of the middle class was faring little better. The bank manager, once all-powerful behind his frosted glass, lost much of his status as his discretion in matters of loans and charges diminished. Indeed, as head offices have transformed him from counsellor and financial GP to front-line salesman for a range of 'packaged products' (pensions, life assurance, unit trusts), it is doubtful whether he counts as a 'professional' at all in any meaningful sense. Solicitors, buffeted by cut-price conveyancers and battered by the collapse of the housing market, fared a little better, although doctors – burdened with the paperwork required to make the 'internal health market' work – found themselves lumbered with the gruesomely prosaic labels of 'producer' or 'purchaser', depending on whether they worked in hospitals or general practice.

For those outside the main professions but still working in definably middle-class, 'responsible' jobs, the picture was even worse. From local and national government through teaching, estate agency/auctioneering, publishing and media even to the army and Church, career paths were deliberately broken up as the new order insisted upon 'flat' command structures. Their two great crimes in this new order were offering either a 'job for life' or promotion based on 'Buggins's turn'. In 1977, a young local government officer or Anglican curate would have been able, with some confidence, to plot the next two decades of his working life. The only contingency was his own conduct, both in terms of reasonably hard work and keeping his nose clean. Twenty years later, he would have been foolhardy even to plot the next five years.

In the new order, not only was it declared not possible to offer a job for life, it was declared not desirable either. The emphasis in professional advancement had ceased to be upon character and conduct, shifting instead to a mixture of the 'random walk' we examined earlier and 'attitude', the ability to mouth the credo of the new order with conviction. Of course, market apologists insisted it was 'performance' that mattered in the new era. But, as management seminars and 'team-building' weekends proliferated, the sneaking suspicion grew that 'performance' was measured largely in terms of obeisance to consultant-speak and the other pieties of the market system.

At the heart of the crisis facing the professions was the new system's inability to recognize what Jane Jacobs has called, with a nod to Plato, 'guardian values'. In her 1992 book *Systems of Survival*, Miss Jacobs compiles two lists of values, one applicable to 'traders' – openness to others, initiative, enterprise, efficiency – and the other to the public service class (the 'guardians') – obedience, loyalty, discipline, respect for tradition, fatalism and fortitude.[14] Neither moral character is superior to the other, and a healthy society requires both groups of people to thrive. Interestingly, she lists farming as one occupation whose values straddle both characters and farming is, of course, the original small business.

The market system cannot recognize guardian values. Its software is faulty in this regard: thus it promotes the 'structural adjustment' that involves imposing market values where they have no application. Seen in this light, the destruction of the middle class – both its professional wing and the small-town small-business wing that, like agriculture, borrowed some guardian values – makes perfect sense. It is not merely that the middle class itself, with its peculiar working habits, is a market distortion, although it is. Rather, the problem with the middle class is one of values. It is these values that distort. The smashing-up of the middle-class way of life is therefore not an incidental part of the process, but an integral one. Putting the professional and small-business classes on effective 'zero-hour' contracts – the notorious work arrangement whereby employees are paid only during 'live' working time and can be stood down at a moment's notice – is a key tool for the subordination of 'guardian' to 'trader' values. In October 1995, Will Hutton declared in the *Guardian*: 'The British are increasingly at risk.' The net effect of the market revolution, he said, was to shrink to just 40 per cent of the population those who could be said to be secure in their work and homes. A further 30 per cent were unemployed or economically inactive and a middle

30 per cent were in 'structurally insecure' employment. Critics declared his maths was all wrong, that rich men's wives were in the wrong category and so forth. That those identifiably winning from the system had dipped below 50 per cent was, for some, an idea too dreadful to contemplate.

In conclusion, the new market order's pledges have proved to be worthless rubber kites. Instead of personal liberty we have a top-heavy, super-intrusive police and security structure. Instead of clearly established personal responsibility we have moral hazard run riot. Culture has been looted by money values, as has the economy at large. A new class of beneficiaries grows fat on the profits of the market system; the middle class is dismantled. Hucksterism and fraud run riot – the values of the new order are less Milton Friedman and more Sergeant Bilko. And, in a final act of autophagia, the system that has ransacked everything else begins to ransack itself, shrinking the 'two-thirds/one-third' society upon which it rested to the more precarious (from the system's point of view) 40–30–30 society. Devouring itself may, in the long run, prove the market system's one unalloyed contribution to social progress.

CHAPTER FOUR

A LONGING LOOK ABROAD (1): THE BRITISH LEFT AND THE UNITED STATES

Clinton and Gore had appropriated the lingo of Recovery and group
therapy for their campaign pitch; they had gone in soft, dramatising
'concern' and 'healing'.

Robert Hughes, *The Culture of Complaint*

In 1948, Harry Truman desegregated the armed forces – a much bigger
step at the time than permitting gays to remain in the military in 1993.
Yet the white working class voted Democrat because Roosevelt and
Truman were seen as being on the workers' side in the struggle over
economic security.

Mark Levinson, writing in *Dissent*, Fall 1996, p. 52

Gutman turned the bird upside-down and scraped an edge of its base
with his knife. Black enamel came off in tiny curls, exposing blackened
metal beneath. . . . His face became turgid with hot blood . . . 'It's a
fake,' he said hoarsely.

Dashiell Hammett, *The Maltese Falcon* (Cassell edition, 1974)

Le Pont de la Tour is one of London's swankiest restaurants. The rich and the
famous troop across the Thames from the City for the riverside setting, the
view upstream of Tower Bridge and the studiously trendy food. The *Good Food
Guide* describes it as offering contemporary marriages of French and Italian
dishes, but suggests that it has a tendency to lapse into occasional blandness.
It was to this 'smart but not stuffy' restaurant that Tony Blair and his wife
Cherie Booth brought Bill Clinton and his wife Hillary Roddam Clinton one

spring evening in May 1997, less than a month after Labour's landslide election victory. Earlier that day, Clinton had become the first American president to address the Cabinet, an honour that even Margaret Thatcher had not bestowed on her friend and soul-mate Ronald Reagan. However, it was the dinner date that grabbed the headlines in the tabloid press, with the *Sun* inviting the food critic, Egon Ronay, to run an eye over the dishes chosen by each of the quartet. Here, said the leader writers still bewitched by the crushing of the Conservative Party, was the symbol of the new world order; the takeover of power by the 1960s generation, a breed of pragmatic politicians who were redefining what it meant to be on the centre-left for the twenty-first century. The Downing Street and White House spin doctors could hardly have bettered the *Guide*'s assessment. 'Smart but not stuffy' was Tony and Bill to a T.

LOOKING WESTWARD: LABOUR AND THE AMERICAN WAY

More than half a century earlier, George Orwell said that Britain's intelligentsia took their cooking from Paris and their opinions from Moscow. As the millennium approached there was some debate as to whether Paris or Tuscany was the source of culinary inspiration for Britain's political elite, but no doubt that they turned to Washington for their ideas and their policies. Talk of Britain being Greece to America's Rome, a description of the special relationship that may have had some validity when the Beatles held the top five positions in the US charts in February 1964, was risible in an age when President Clinton's basic philosophy was to export the American way of life to the rest of the world. Britain's subservient role in the transatlantic compact quickly became clear.

On the day after the election, and within hours of accepting his seals of office from the Queen, the new Chancellor, Gordon Brown, used what was expected to be a familiarization meeting at the Treasury to tell his senior civil servant, Sir Terence Burns, that the government intended to hand over operational control of monetary policy to the Bank of England. Brown produced plans, drafted by his adviser, Edward Balls, which would reshape the Bank along the lines of the Federal Reserve, America's central bank. Just as the

Fed's twelve-strong Open Market committee was charged with setting short-term interest rates in the USA, so the Bank would have a nine-strong monetary policy committee that would meet once a month to fix British interest rates. The Chancellor would set a target for inflation, and the Bank would have the job of setting base rates to comply with it. Brown stipulated that five of the nine members of the committee would be full-time Bank offi-cials, while the other four would be appointed from outside by the Chancellor of the day. The news, when it was announced on Tuesday, 5 May, less than four days after Blair had moved into Downing Street, came as a shock. When Labour had enjoyed its only other landslide victory, almost the first act of the Attlee government had been to nationalize the Bank of England to ensure that the politicians held sway over the bankers. Its aim was to ensure that an independent-minded governor, such as Montague Norman in the 1920s and 1930s, could no longer impose deflationary policies on Britain. Now here was a Labour administration doing the exact opposite, handing over one of the main economic levers to a group of central bankers, acade-mics, economists and – for political correctness's sake – a businesswoman. The City loved it, as did the free-marketeers and the dwindling band of hard-line monetarists. Central Bank independence meant the bias would be towards curbing inflation; moreover, it meant that experts rather than politi-cians would be in control. Defending the move, Brown said that the Labour Party election manifesto had foreshadowed the change, although it had clearly said that any move would be contingent on the Old Lady building up a suit-able track record. To some, four days hardly qualified as a long track record, but Brown said that the need to provide long-term macro-economic stability meant that the time was right to depoliticize interest rate decisions. This, of course, begged the question of how handing control of monetary policy to a central bank, with a particular world view, could be anything other than a political decision. But such criticisms were shrugged aside. Brown and Balls, it transpired, had taken the decision two months before the election on a visit to Washington, where they had met senior members of Clinton's economic team and the chairman of the Fed, Alan Greenspan. Brown had been impressed by the steady non-inflationary growth that Greenspan had deliv-ered for Clinton and made up his mind on the flight back to London that he would act as soon as Labour was in power.

If independence for the Bank of England was the most egregious example of stealing policies from across the Atlantic, it was far from the only one. Ever since the 1986 Financial Services Act had fragmented regulation over the post-Big Bang City, the need had been felt for one unified body that would wield more clout. Faith in the system had been undermined by three factors: the widespread pension mis-selling that followed the Conservative government's championing of private pensions, the failure of the authorities to spot what Robert Maxwell was up to, and the spectacular collapse of two banks, BCCI and Barings. Nevertheless, the Bank of England, which regulated the City's multiplicity of domestic and foreign-owned banks and kept a watchful eye on the entire financial sector, thought the system worked tolerably well. It argued, with some justification, that it had not been at fault with either BCCI or Barings, the former being outside its jurisdiction in Luxembourg, the latter ruined by the disastrous speculative activities of the trader, Nick Leeson. It also made the point that Maxwell would have evaded detection under any known system of financial policing and that pension mis-selling was more the consequence of executive error than of supervisory neglect. But the case made by the Bank's governor, Eddie George, made little impression on Labour. It wanted Britain to have an all-embracing financial regulator that would be more in tune with the multi-function global financial institutions in London. The old system, like the mechanism for setting interest rates, was both inefficient and parochial. Brown announced that the Bank was losing its powers of banking supervision to the Securities and Investment Board, which would have greatly enhanced scope, and powers to bring it into line with the Securities and Exchange Commission, which since the 1930s had been the guardian of American financial stability. The man chosen to run the so-called super-SIB was Howard Davies, the technocrat's technocrat. Davies, who had started life as a diplomat, had been a management consultant with the US firm McKinsey's, head of the Audit Commission and director-general of the Confederation of British Industry before joining the Bank as deputy governor in 1995.

Brown was not alone in his enthusiasm for all things American. The Home Secretary, Jack Straw, had visited New York City and expressed interest in the zero-tolerance policing methods – a tough line on even the most minor of indiscretions – favoured by the city's mayor, Rudolph Giuliani, and police chief, William Bratten. Crime was a big issue for Labour, in the light of advice from the focus groups (another American innovation) set up for consultation and accorded absolute trust. Echoing Clinton's 'three strikes and you're out', a policy that guaranteed mandatory life sentences for a third violent offence, Straw had, while in opposition, declared war on offensive beggars and the 'squeegee merchants' who used a form of inertia selling to persuade motorists stuck at traffic lights to pay to have their windscreens washed. Once in power, Straw announced plans for mandatory life sentences for certain types of crime, took immediate steps to fulfil Labour's election pledge of processing young offenders through the criminal justice system more quickly, and announced an extension of the pilot schemes for electronic tagging of criminals let out on parole. The message Blair had learnt from Clinton was clear; the trendy image could go only so far. The one might keep his Fender guitar in Downing Street, the other might play his sax on Arsenio Hall's late-night chat show, but these were not liberals when it came to law and order. Clinton had deliberately taken time off from campaigning in 1992 to return to his governor's mansion in Little Rock so that he could personally oversee the execution of a mentally defective murderer. Blair, while shadow Home Secretary, had developed the policy – heavy with Clintonesque rhetoric – of 'tough on crime, tough on the causes of crime'. This was intended to rid Labour of its image of being friendlier to criminals than to the police, and Blair's initiative was taken further by Straw, who seemed more interested in the first half of his leader's soundbite than the second. The extension of the prison-building programme announced by the Conservatives was upheld, while Straw had an answer to youth crime in his proposal for curfews for the under-tens.

By the end of Blair's first hundred days in office, the Americanization of British politics was pretty much complete. Advertisements had been run in the press for a drugs czar, an idea that was first tried by Ronald Reagan in the late 1980s and was notably unsuccessful in persuading teenagers in America's ghettos to give up crack cocaine and homicide in favour of a low-paid job working as a domestic servant for a member of the technocratic elite. There were plans for elected mayors, for home–school contracts between parents and teachers, proposals to send hit squads into failing schools. Above all, Labour took the Clinton buzzword 'opportunity' and applied it to the Welfare State. Welfare was to be recast to provide a 'springboard' back into work and, as in the USA, there was to be a clear distinction between the deserving and the undeserving poor. The deserving poor were to receive help through the tax system; Clinton's earned income tax credit was much admired by Brown as a way of boosting the take-home pay of the in-work poor. But there was to be no mercy for the undeserving, those who refused to take advantage of any of the options under the Chancellor's Welfare to Work programme – subsidized employment, education, training or participation in an environmental task force. There was to be no fifth option of doing nothing for those people who wanted to keep their benefits. After three months in which he had fulfilled his promise to 'hit the ground running', the Chancellor went on holiday . . . to Cape Cod in Massachusetts, presumably to find out from the assembled policy gurus and think-tankers gathered in Martha's Vineyard whether there were any Clinton ideas that Labour had yet to transplant to Britain. It was hard to believe that there were.

THE IVY LEFT: LABOUR, THE DEMOCRATS AND THE TRANSATLANTIC TIE

There were a number of reasons for this symbiotic relationship. First, the Democrats in Washington and the Blair modernizers in London formed an interchangeable and mobile global governing elite. They shared the same values, had the same world view and, in many cases, had been to the same schools and colleges. Clinton had been a Rhodes scholar at Oxford, and so had one of his closest aides George Stephanopolous, Ira Magaziner who advised on the health care reform, the head of the CIA R. James Woolsey and the Labour Secretary in the first term, Robert Reich. But the intellectual traffic had also been in the other direction. Brown used to boast that he spurned the glens of Scotland to spend his holidays rummaging in the Harvard University library. David Miliband, a Blair policy adviser, did a Master's at the Massachusetts Institute of Technology, while Balls and his partner Yvette Cooper, elected as Labour MP for Castleford and Pontefract in 1997, studied at Harvard. Marjorie Mowlam, the Northern Ireland secretary, did a PhD at the University of Iowa in the 1970s, while the Heritage Secretary Chris Smith was a Kennedy scholar. The transatlantic links went beyond Westminster. Howard Davies studied at Stanford, while his successor at the CBI, Adair Turner, was another McKinsey alumnus.

The second reason for the umbilical cord tying London to Washington was the cultural homogeneity. In the late 1970s, a British visitor to America would have noticed the difference between the two countries immediately. While the language, the movies and the music were the same, America's freeways, shopping malls, strip developments, drive-through McDonald's branches, and armies of beggars huddling beneath towers of steel and glass jarred with the shabby, small-town feel of Britain. As the millennium approached, this was no longer true. Britain had become thoroughly Americanized, with almost every provincial town of note boasting its own leisure complex complete with multiplex cinema, ten-pin bowling alley, a hypermarket, a couple of fast-food joints and acres of car parking spaces. In the Britain of the late 1970s, amusement rides meant Dreamland at Margate or the Golden Mile in Blackpool. By 1997, it meant Alton Towers, Thorpe Park, or even a trip through the Channel Tunnel to EuroDisney. High culture in Britain was still influenced by François Truffaut, Paul Bocuse and Pavarotti, but mass culture was American through and through. British TV had been profoundly affected by both the style (satellite TV, game shows, chat shows) and the content (sit-coms like *Friends*, crime drama like *Miami Vice*) of American TV. Most people in Britain could talk about the latest Quentin Tarantino movie and had an opinion about Madonna; little general interest has ever been shown in French films, however sexually charged, or any European rock stars with the exception of Abba.

These cultural similarities have been mirrored in the shape of politics and economics. There has traditionally been interest in Britain about the race for the White House, and, unlike the result of a French or German election, the choice of Republican or Democrat is seen as having a bearing on what might happen in Britain. Hillary Clinton is a known face in the UK, as were Barbara Bush, Nancy Reagan and first ladies going back to Jackie Kennedy. It is unlikely that one person in a hundred could name the wife of Jacques Chirac, let alone recognize her photograph.

Over the years, Britain's trade has become more European, but the structure of the economy has not. The economic cycle tends to run in tandem with America rather than with Germany and France; the pound tends to rise and fall in line with the US dollar, Britain has tended to be good at the things America is good at, and suffer from similar problems. Traditionally, this has been seen as a source of weakness, with the suggestion that Britain would be better advised to turn its back on the Anglo-Saxon variant of capitalism and embrace the more consensual, firm-based industrial structure of Germany. However, America's economic performance in the 1990s has led to something of a change of heart. It has been noted that America has been in the vanguard of the so-called sunrise industries of biotechnology, microprocessing, multimedia, areas in which Britain is also strong and where a number of small, innovative firms form networks for the interchange of people and ideas. According to one commentator: 'The UK is second only to the US in its present competence in network-based industry. It is very strong in pharmaceuticals and reasonably so in information and communications technologies and in advanced chemicals. It is a leader in entertainment, music publishing and many international service industries.'[1]

Moreover, America's dynamism compared to Europe is rooted in its history. The defining economic moment for the USA this century was the Great Depression, and ever since the culture has been geared to avoiding mass unemployment. In Germany, the key event was the hyperinflation of 1923, and the Bundesbank is still haunted by the image of citizens trundling wheelbarrows full of worthless banknotes through the streets. It is no coincidence that in the thirty years of American economic domination after the Second World War the emphasis was on growth and employment, while the two decades of German predominance have seen sluggish growth and deflation.

These factors would certainly not have been lost on Labour, even had the party not been intellectually and personally beguiled by America. Blair made it clear where his own sympathies lay in one of his first European Union summits, when he said Britain would only support an Employment Chapter in a treaty provided it 'encouraged flexible labour markets'. There had to be 'less obsession with ourselves and our institutions, more focus on the things that matter to people'.

THE VIEW FROM THE BRIDGE: FOUR LAWYERS SURVEY THE WORLD

Run by Labour-supporting Sir Terence Conran, Le Pont de la Tour was certainly an appropriate venue for some mutual back-slapping. It offered expensive if unthreatening cuisine, and was exactly the sort of place that four young(ish) and successful lawyers would choose for a night out. In this regular haunt of the

City's mobile technocrats, Blair and Clinton would be among their own people, rather than being hemmed in by the formality of a state dinner at Downing Street or Buckingham Palace. The Prime Minister had already announced his intention of making his administration less formal. He had asked his (reluctant) officials to call him Tony rather than Prime Minister; now here was another example of Labour announcing, after eighteen years of uninterrupted Conservative rule, that times had changed. John Major and Margaret Thatcher would never have dreamt of hosting a dinner for a visiting head of state anywhere except Downing Street, but Blair wanted to get away from the chandeliers and the flunkeys to a place more in keeping with a man at ease with life in the late 1990s. Just as Harold Wilson had burnished his man-of-the-people image by smoking a pipe and letting it be known that he dolloped HP sauce on his meat pie, so Blair was showing that he too had the populist touch.

Le Pont de la Tour was a relatively recent addition to the London scene. While not quite as new as New Labour, it had not even been a glimmer in its owner's eye when Jim Callaghan had left office in May 1979, and bore testimony to the transformation of the physical and political landscape in the intervening eighteen years. London's Docklands had fallen into decay in the 1960s and 1970s as containerization moved its business downstream to Tilbury, providing Mrs Thatcher with one of Labour's traditional strongholds to use as a test-bed for her free-market principles. The result was Canary Wharf, an eastward and low-cost extension of the City, together with up-market housing for high-flying financiers, lawyers, management consultants and accountants. It proved to be an uneasy marriage; the two London boroughs most affected by the Docklands regeneration – Tower Hamlets on the north of the Thames and Southwark on the south bank – continued to have some of the highest levels of unemployment and social deprivation of any local authorities in Britain. Like any American city Bill Clinton could have named – New York, Chicago, Los Angeles – Docklands was a microcosm of an economic revolution in the 1980s that had enriched some but at the expense of levels of inequality not seen since the nineteenth century. This was the dilemma for Blair and Clinton. They were both committed to healing the wounds left by fifteen or more years of the free market; they made all the right noises about social justice and the need for everybody to have a stake in the system. But they themselves were part of the new global elite, the class of footloose administrators who believed passionately in free trade, free movement of capital and the dynamism of business – and had done very nicely out of the years of free-market dominance.

Appropriately enough, Blair hosted an Anglo-French summit with Jacques Chirac in a Canary Wharf suite in November 1997. The rooms were made over by the best young designers Britain had to offer, with the spin doctors making the point that this was what the Prime Minister meant by 'a young country'. But not every commentator was impressed. Writing in the *Guardian* on 17 November 1997, Jonathan Glancey declared: 'Old-fashioned, mid-Atlantic and a homage to Baroness Thatcher and her money men, Canary Wharf represents the transformation of Britain from a welfare state to a neo-Victorian free-market economy.'

To the extent that they modelled themselves on anybody, Clinton and Blair were closest to businessmen like Bill Gates or Richard Branson, who were children of the 1960s but were able to succeed in the ultra-competitive global market of the 1990s. Clinton relied on Republicans to get his North American Free Trade Association bill (NAFTA) through Congress, and was quick to respond to Wall Street's pleas for a bail-out when the financial sector was left exposed by the crash in Mexico in early 1995. In Britain, it was hard to find a more vociferous supporter of Blair in the summer of 1997 than Madsen Pirie, director of the Adam Smith Institute, the most ideologically pure of the free-market think tanks. He said: 'I am very strongly in favour of the current government. I don't regard it as left wing . . . they have lowered corporation tax and are spending a lower proportion of GDP. Gordon Brown [the Labour chancellor] is definitely to the right of Kenneth Clarke [his Conservative predecessor] on markets.'[2] In contrast to America, where the most vituperative criticism of Clinton came from the religious right, the real opposition to Blair in Britain came not from the demoralized rump of the Conservative Party but from within his own ranks. Roy Hattersley, on the right of the movement in the 1980s, expressed disgust at the party's unwillingness to raise benefits for the poor by levying more tax on the rich. Tony Benn, Hattersley's old left-wing enemy, accused the Prime Minister of wanting to turn the Labour Party into a centrist party of business and a carbon copy of the Democrats.

Benn's comment was apposite. Whatever Blair and Clinton were up to, it was obvious that they felt they were in it together. They felt as though they had come through against the odds, when both their respective parties had been written off as anachronisms. The friendship had been forged in the heat of battle and, for once, was deserving of the cliché 'special relationship'. After the 1992 election, Labour had sent a team of helpers led by advertising guru Philip Gould to prevent Bill Clinton suffering the fate of Neil Kinnock. With Conservative Central Office backing Bush, Gould was able to give the Democrats invaluable advice on what to expect: the attempt to play on the fear factor, the claim that a vote for Ross Perot would allow Clinton in by the back door, the demonization of Jimmy Carter, the claim that the Democrats would mess up the economy. Clinton was suitably grateful and, after he won on his New Democrat ticket, the moderniz-ers believed that they could lay their hands on the holy grail that would enable Labour to win its first general election since 1974. Special conferences were held, the key slogan of the 1992 Clinton campaign – 'It's the economy, stupid' – was ingested, focus groups were liberally consulted so that any Labour policies that voters fond unappealing could be ditched. When Newt Gingrich appeared on the scene in 1994 to capture both houses of Congress for the Republicans, the Blair camp was almost as shaken by the mid-term swing as Clinton himself, but then watched in admiration as the President took advantage of the row over the budget to foist blame for the shut-down in the federal government on right-wing extremism. In truth, Clinton left his 1996 rival for the presidency, Bob Dole, little room to work in, tempering his support for a Republican bill that meant 'the end of welfare as we know it' with an increase in the minimum wage and some judiciously timed warm words for organized labour.

Blair finessed the same trick in Britain in 1997. The Conservatives were as riven over Europe as the Republicans were over morality. It was simple, as sleaze allegation followed tax increase, to portray the Conservatives as both incompetent and extreme, the very labels that had been hung on Labour by Mrs Thatcher in the 1980s. The Labour campaign involved taking up a series of orthodox, even right-wing, positions on issues such as tax and privatiza-tion, knowing that anybody on the left would still prefer to have Blair rather than Major in Downing Street.

FORTUNE FAVOURS THE BLAND: LADY LUCK SMILES ON THE LEFT

Blair and Clinton had repositioned their parties with some skill. But they were still blessed by good fortune. Back in 1991, when Clinton announced that he would be seeking the Democratic nomination for the White House, he was the little-known governor of a poor southern state. It was assumed that George Bush's conduct of the Gulf war would win him a second term, and that his opponent would be one of the better-known Democrats, such as New York state governor Mario Cuomo. But these calculations were upset by four factors. First, the more illustrious Democrats preferred to wait until 1996, believing that they would have a better chance against a new Republican candidate than against Bush. Second, the American public turned against their president with sudden ferocity as the recession of 1991 led to job losses and a further squeeze on real incomes. Third, the Republican Party was increasingly dominated by the religious right, culminating in the riven Houston convention in August 1992, which meant that although Clinton's centrist stance was too tepid for many traditional Democrats, they had nowhere else to go. Fourth, the appearance of a third candidate in the shape of Ross Perot leeched votes away from Bush, allowing Clinton to win the presidency with 43 per cent of the vote, the same as Michael Dukakis had achieved when losing to Bush in 1988.

Labour, too, had been lucky. Five years earlier, in May 1992, the Conservatives had been seemingly unbeatable. They had followed up their fourth successive general election victory in April with gains over a demoralized opposition in the local council polls the following month. TV coverage of the test matches and one-day internationals that summer was incomplete without a close-up of the cricket-loving John Major relaxing, glass of wine in hand, in a box provided by one of his supporters. The general election had been fought amid one of the severest recessions since the 1930s, with unemployment rising towards three million for the second time in a decade, yet Major had secured a record fourteen million votes for the Conservatives. Pessimists in the Labour Party wondered whether they would ever be able to form another administration on their own, and talked openly of a realignment on the left to include the Liberal Democrats.

Black Wednesday changed everything. Britain's recession had been prolonged and deepened by membership of the Exchange Rate Mechanism, which pegged the value of the pound against the German mark, and prevented the government from cutting interest rates to stimulate the domestic economy. Despite the mounting costs of the policy, the Prime Minister and his chancellor, Norman Lamont, insisted that there was no alternative. The financial markets had other ideas. On 16 September 1992, sterling was swept out of the ERM by wave after wave of speculative selling despite the announcement of a 50 per cent increase in base rates to 15 per cent and frantic buying of the pound by the Bank of England which used up Britain's entire stock of foreign exchange reserves. Black Wednesday was a blow to the government's reputation for economic competence from which it never recovered. However, the economy actually recovered quite quickly from the depradations of the recession as the authorities followed a blatantly Keynesian strategy of providing plenty of cheap money together with fiscal measures to boost housing and the car industry. 'A strategy for growth is what we need. A strategy for growth is what we are going to have', Major said in a series of TV interviews a month after Black Wednesday. But it was too late, particularly since the six months that followed the ERM debacle heaped disaster after disaster on the Conservatives. Colonels in Cheltenham, the very backbone of Mr Major's party, took to the streets to support the miners after the industry secretary Michael Heseltine announced that thirty thousand jobs in the pits – many of them in the coalfields that had defied Arthur Scargill and worked through the 1984–85 strike – were to go. This was followed by what came to be known as the arms-to-Iraq scandal, in which it emerged that some of the weapons used by Saddam Hussein against British troops in the Gulf war of 1991 had been supplied with the connivance of ministers despite a government embargo. Events outside the government's control also conspired against it. December saw the fire that destroyed part of Windsor Castle and it was announced that the Prince and Princess of Wales were to separate. At the end of the 1960s, John Lennon responded to the break-up of the Beatles by saying: 'The Dream is over.' The same applied to Charles and Diana. In an age when 40 per cent of marriages ended in divorce, they were supposed to be different – happy, monogamous, perfect. It transpired, as the illicit recordings of their indiscretions became public knowledge, that they were no different from any other miserable couple.

Although base rates were reduced to 6 per cent in January 1993, the New Year brought no respite. The abduction and murder of two-year-old James Bulger by two ten-year-old Liverpool schoolboys prompted national soul-searching, with the government's critics arguing that the incident was proof that, far from making Britain a more law-abiding country, four terms of Conservative rule had produced a violent, amoral society in which an underclass had been left to rot or riot. Finally, the budget of March 1993 announced large tax increases to reduce the £45 billion budget deficit accrued during the recession. Given that the government had fought the 1992 election on its claim that Labour would add £1,000 to the average tax bill, this was not good politics, even if the economic argument for tightening fiscal policy was unimpeachable. The government's poll ratings slumped to record-low levels in the spring of 1993 and stayed at rock-bottom until the election. They lost all but one shire county, Buckinghamshire, in the local elections of May 1993 and on the same day lost the Newbury by-election to the Liberal Democrats on a 28 per cent swing.

SOUND OF THE SUBURBS:
THE LEFT'S LONG REMIX

In his essay 'The Lion and the Unicorn', Orwell wrote: 'In England such concepts as justice, liberty and objective truth are still believed in. They may be illusions, but they are very powerful illusions. The belief in them influences conduct, national life is different because of them.'[3] Voters in Britain and America expected the parties of the right to be tough; the smack of firm government appealed to the upwardly mobile working classes of the London suburbs as it did to the blue-collar Democrats of the Michigan car towns wooed successfully by Ronald Reagan in the 1980s. What they did not expect was incompetence mingled with extremism, arrogance and sleaze. The affront to these bedrock values of decency and honesty gave the parties of the left a chance to make the sort of political comeback that had seemed impossible during the 1980s. But the Clinton–Blair calculus was that some of the changes had been permanent and that only by tailoring policies to the demands of the suburban middle class could a party of the left hope to challenge the hegemony of the right.

In fact, the 1980s was far less monolithic than right-wing propaganda would suggest. Certainly, many of the cultural trends that had brought Thatcher and Reagan to power in the late 1970s and early 1980s were still in evidence and, to some extent, even more powerful. But there was always dogged resistance to the sort of policies pursued by the Conservatives and the Republicans – TUC days of action against unemployment, riots in Britain's inner cities in the summer of 1981, internal opposition from the 'wets' in the Conservative Party, even the formation of a party (the Social Democrats) that had as its sole object the rescue of the post-war system from the grasp of uncaring monetarists on the one hand and Bennite socialists on the other. It was a time of open struggle: Reagan was faced with a hostile Democratic Congress and broke union power in the dispute with the air-traffic controllers just as the unions and the Greater London Council were prepared to set themselves against the Conservatives. As such, there was no instant demolition of the Keynesian–Beveridge Welfare State, merely a slow-motion collapse that took seven years to complete. By 1986, unemployment had reached a post-war peak of 3.1 million in Britain, but the government had a majority over a divided opposition of 144, and in the 1983 general election Labour had barely beaten the SDP/Liberal Alliance into third place. The Conservatives had defeated the miners in the year-long pit strike; they had overcome opposition from CND and had sited American cruise missiles on British soil; they had used the SAS to storm the Iranian embassy in Princes Gate; they had been prepared to dispatch British forces to the South Atlantic to recapture the Falkland Islands following their seizure by the military junta in Argentina in April 1982. At home, the government had been prepared to watch 25 per cent of Britain's manufacturing industry be lost in the slump of 1980–81 as the price of reducing inflation from 20 per cent in 1980 to 2.4 per cent in mid-1986. This was the new 'get a result' philosophy in practice, and it applied across the board, from the sinking of the *General Belgrano* to the corner-cutting methods used by the police to secure convictions against those suspected of terrorist or violent crimes and to government support for Eddie Shah and Rupert Murdoch in their attempts to smash the print unions. The no-holds-barred approach fitted well with the new individualism: the desire of the baby-boom generation to own their homes, to travel abroad unfettered by exchange controls, to buy a new car or video recorder. Just as the 1960s was permeated by the spirit of 'finding yourself', so the 1980s was the decade of 'achieving your own goals'. Even so, the avatars of the new order had to be careful. One of the most widely used phrases of the decade was 'greed is good', taken from the Oliver Stone film *Wall Street* and uttered by the asset-stripping anti-hero, Gordon Gecko. But Gecko had his comeuppance at the end of the film, as did Ivan Boesky, the New York financier on whom the character was based. Stone was a classic Hollywood liberal, and so was John Landis, whose *Trading Places* contained the explicit message that not only was greed bad, but that it led ultimately to ruination. Mrs Thatcher found herself in trouble when she remarked that 'there is no such thing as society', and took trouble in her memoirs to explain that the quote had been misinterpreted. The rest of the quote was: 'There are individual men and women, and there are families. And no government can do anything except through people, and people must look after themselves first. It's our duty to look after ourselves and then to look after our neighbours.'[4]

To Mrs Thatcher, this was not an invitation to people to be selfish, but a reiteration of Victorian values. But that was not a widely held view, and even one of the architects of Thatcherite economic policy, Nigel Lawson, bemoaned the 'unattractive vulgarity' associated with the height of the 'yuppie' phenomenon.[5] If this was a contradiction, then so was the disparity between the emphasis on 'quality' and the 'dumbing down' associated with tabloid newspapers and Australian soap operas. Norman Tebbit, Mrs Thatcher's employment secretary and party chairman, defended the naked women on page 3 of the *Sun* by declaring that they were the working man's equivalent of the titillation offered to the middle classes in the nation's art galleries. Naturally, this caused quite a stir. There were no fiercer critics of Thatcherism than those from Britain's artistic community, for whom the cuts in government subsidy were evidence of a new 'philistinism' in Westminster.

Meanwhile, a 'quality revolution' gained momentum as a reaction against the poor workmanship and slapdash working practices of the previous decade. Egalitarianism was no longer seen to be either desirable or achievable, and there was a drive on both sides of the Atlantic for 'excellence'. Firms were given the 'right to manage', so that they could force workers to provide goods that consumers actually wanted to buy. There was to be no protection for the weak; if people wanted to buy Japanese and German cars rather than American gas guzzlers, or Bang and Olufsen stereos made in Denmark rather than Ferguson systems made in Britain, that was not something Downing Street or the White House was unduly worried about. Quality meant that there was a new emphasis on packaging, marketing and design, not just of drink, cars and clothes, but of the political process itself. The parties started to market themselves more carefully, with Labour's shambolic performance in 1983 followed by the radical overhaul of presentation under Neil Kinnock. The red rose, the Hugh Hudson party political broad-cast that had the feel of a TV ad, and the liberal use of Brahms were never going to win Labour the election of 1987, which took place at the height of an economic boom. Kinnock, in fact, won only twenty more seats than Michael Foot had done in 1983; but the party's decline was at least arrested.

The idea of quality became all-pervasive. Firms talked of 'total quality management' and spent millions on consultancy fees, training courses and awaydays at country-house hotels in order to achieve it. The language of business invaded government, so much so that Britain was no longer Britain but Great Britain PLC. The clear suggestion was that the country could and would go to the wall unless old, bad habits were shed and change along man-agement lines enthusiastically embraced. Similarly, when it came to decisions on tax and spending, ministers intoned gravely that the 'bottom line' was that there was no money in the Treasury coffers to spend on schools and old age pensions, as if filching the phrases of a chief executive somehow proved the point.

In part, the drive for 'quality' was bound up with technology, either through innovation or by the refinement of old products. Some of these advances were rapid. One of the episodes of *Inspector Morse* from the late 1980s shows a successful lawyer using a personal telephone the size and weight of a house brick. A decade later personal phones were not only common but cheaper and much smaller, and Morse himself was sporting one of the new slimline models in the episode shown in the autumn of 1997. Similarly, the idea of transmitting documents by fax was unknown at the start of the 1980s, and taken for granted by the dawn of the 1990s. When Callaghan and Carter were defeated, not only were the e-mail and the Internet a long way in the future, but most offices and government depart-ments were based around the typewriter and the filing cabinet rather than the computer and the floppy disc.

But there were two sides to this technical advance. First, it was essentially elitist. Poor people could not afford the range of hardware on offer; many struggled to pay their telephone bills, let alone find the extra cost involved in hooking up to the worldwide web. Second, technology helped management to control the workforce. Pagers, answer-phones and faxes meant that the boss could always keep in touch with his subordinates; computerization opened up the possibility of a new range of banking and insurance services in which a member of staff would don a pair of headphones at the start of the shift and have no contact with anybody other than members of the public or a supervisor. Finally, much of the demand for the new technology was not consumer generated but stimulated by the need of capitalism to sell new products to each generation. Thus, colour TV was the big consumer product of the 1970s but once almost every home had dispensed with black and white, the industry started to push video cassette recorders, so that consumers could tape TV programmes they had missed or watch films at home that they previously would have gone to the cinema to see. An even better example of how supply could bring forth its own demand was the compact disc player. The rock 'n' roll generation had grown up with music; it had bought lavish sound systems in the 1960s and 1970s on which to play its considerable collection of LPs. But in the early 1980s, the record business came up with a marketing ploy designed to persuade people to abandon vinyl and move to CD. The top end of the market – classical music – was seen as the soft underbelly of vinyl and was attacked first. CD was promoted as the format that would eliminate surface noise, clicks and scratches – giving listeners the chance to get concert-hall sound quality in their living rooms. It was assumed, rightly, that the people who listened to classical music were generally well-heeled and would not be deterred by the cost of purchasing the new CD players and the discs to go on them. Once the CD was established as a status symbol, the next step was to move into the much bigger rock market, where the pivotal moment was the release by EMI of the Beatles back catalogue in 1987. As demand for CDs increased, the industry made vinyl less attractive by pushing up the price of LPs and making them harder to find in the shops. There were those who said that the new format was colder and lacked the range of sound offered by vinyl; still others wondered why the teenagers who had listened to the Sex Pistols in 1977 were ten years later anal retentive about owning a hiss-free version of 'God Save the Queen'. But the industry – where companies like Sony not only made both the hardware and the software, but also owned the record companies – said that there was falling demand for vinyl and that they were simply responding to consumer demand for 'quality' sound. One upshot was that by the late 1980s, rock music had fallen into its deepest trough since the period between Elvis Presley joining the US army and the rise of the Beatles. Music became safe, pompous and middle-aged, as the array of 1960s and 1970s retreads wheeled out for the 1985 Live Aid concert showed only too clearly. Not that the music industry minded; it had seized back control from the independent labels of the punk era and happily repackaged ten- and twenty-year-old albums for the yuppies tuning into radio's rash of adult-orientated rock stations. Appropriately enough, Bill Clinton's theme song for the 1992 election was Fleetwood Mac's 'Don't Stop Thinking about Tomorrow', released in 1977.

The quality revolution bored through the decade, hollowing out many of the totems of the post-war system. The surge in designer labels destroyed the idea of the 'denim uniform', the car of the decade was the Golf GTI, favoured by the affluent young Sloane Rangers. Then there was quality money. One man's quid was no longer as good as the next – the accent now was on the quality of earnings and the quality of the loan book. It was also the age of the celebrity chef, who emerged in response to the almost sexual obsession with good food. In the 1970s, TV cookery shows had been the preserve of Fanny Cradock, and the furthest reaches of the avant-garde came in the shape of the Galloping Gourmet, Graham Kerr. This all looked pretty tame by the mid-1980s; indeed, the food that Basil Fawlty proposed to serve up on his gourmet night – tournedos Rossini, duck à l'orange – was seen as hopelessly outdated by the devotees of the Roux Brothers, Anton Mossiman and Raymond Blanc.

For those who could not afford to wear Armani on their visits to Le Manoir aux Quat' Saisons, there was always a £99 Next suit or a Marks and Spencer chicken with tarragon ready to pop in the microwave.

This emphasis on quality swamped the countervailing trend towards catering for the less refined tastes of the mass market. There was the growth in low-budget holidays which offered the young sun, sea and sex, the rapid proliferation in fast-food restaurants, the need for the political class to take seriously the opinions of the *Sun* and the *Daily Mail*, the uneasy balance in TV between 'quality' programmes such as *Tinker Tailor Soldier Spy* or *Brideshead Revisited* and those that were prepared to plumb the depths of inanity, cruelty and cupidity in the bid to drive up ratings. Given that TV was by far the most important mass medium, and the one from which the vast majority of people gleaned their news and opinions, this was an important struggle. As one commentator put it: 'The contest between education and TV – between argument and conviction by spectacle – has been won by television, a medium now more debased than ever before.'[6] William Bennett, the right-winger appointed by Ronald Reagan to lead the fight against drugs in the USA, made a similar point at the World Economic Forum in Davos, Switzerland, in early 1996, stressing that it was not just industry but people who had been hollowed out by the free-market revolution of the 1980s. Bennett bemoaned the lack of religious faith and virtue in modern capitalist society, and drew attention to the American talk shows in which people are routinely humiliated – even to the point where some have committed suicide – simply to entertain prime-time audiences.

This, then, was the world as it confronted Labour and the Democrats in the early 1990s. To Clinton and Blair, the political paths followed by the two parties had been remarkably similar. Callaghan and Carter had been trapped between defence of the post-war system and the sense that cultural change was making their efforts useless. Foot and Walter Mondale, in 1983 and 1984 respectively, were representatives of the old guard, seemingly unaware that the right had peeled away layers of their supporters. Mondale's defeat at the hands of Reagan was as comprehensive as Foot's by Thatcher; he won only his home state of Minnesota and the District of Columbia. Kinnock in 1987 was an updated version of Foot, just as Dukakis was a mark-two Mondale. It was boom time in the Anglo-Saxon world, and Thatcher and Bush were unbeatable. Even so, the outlook for the left was not entirely bleak. The Democrats controlled both houses of Congress, while Labour maintained a strong base in local government, and in 1989 won its first national election in fifteen years when it triumphed in the poll for the European Parliament. The right, although successful in general elections, never secured more than 44 per cent of the popular vote in Britain; Reagan beat Mondale by 59–41 per cent but the turn-out was little more than 50 per cent. Winning the presidency was made more difficult for the Democrats by Republican encroachment into the south from 1968 onwards, as innate conservatism started to have more of a bearing on elections than historical southern antipathy towards the Republicans dating from the Civil War. This trend was interrupted but not halted by the choice of a southern Democrat, Jimmy Carter, as the presidential nominee in 1976. The calculation for the Democrats at the start of the 1990s was that they needed another southern candidate, but also had to win back the Reagan Democrats in the states of the north-east and the Middle West that contained a large number of electoral college votes. Labour made a similar assessment. It wanted to win back the aspirational working classes: the voters who had ensured that it held onto seats such as Harlow, Hemel Hempstead and Crawley in the 1970s, but who had defected to the Conservatives in 1979 and showed scant sign of coming back.

BACK WHERE THEY BELONG: TONY AND BILL TAKE OVER

Any criticism of what Blair and Clinton sacrificed to get into power has to be tempered by one fact: they won. Fourteen years after suffering its worst defeat since the 1930s – a defeat in which they were forced back into their strongholds in northern England, Scotland and Wales – Labour inflicted an even bigger humiliation on the Conservatives, who won just 165 seats. As one Labour minister put it three months after the general election: 'We have done as much for working people in 100 days in office as we did in eighteen years of opposition.' Blair wanted to be the first Labour prime minister to enjoy two full terms, and it was obvious from the moment his landslide was secured that he was already preparing for another campaign in 2001. After Clinton's re-election in 1996, the Democrats were hopeful that another southern candidate, Al Gore, would step up from vice-president in the election of 2000 and give the Democrats their longest period in the White House since the twenty years of the Roosevelt–Truman presidencies between 1932 and 1952. An assessment of the Blair–Clinton axis has to start from the judgement that they were right about some things. One was that the parties of the left could no longer appeal solely to the collectivist urge, but had to respond to the rise of individualism and construct – in the Gramscian sense – a hegemony of forces. Blair said at the Labour party conference in 1995:

Let me talk to you about my generation. We grew up after the Second World War. We read about fascism, we saw the Soviet Union and we learned to fear extremes of Left and Right. We were born into the Welfare State and the NHS, and into the market economy of bank accounts, supermarkets, jeans and cars. We had money in our pockets never dreamt of by our parents. We travel abroad. We have been through the sexual revolution of the 1960s. Half the workforce are now women, and the world of work has been revolutionized by science. We built a new popular culture, transformed by colour TV,

Coronation Street and the Beatles. We enjoy a thousand material advantages over any previous generation; and yet we suffer a depth of insecurity and spiritual doubt they never knew.

Here was the heart of Blairite thinking, which covered most of the political spectrum. It was conservative in its acceptance of individualism, centrist in its assertion that the Welfare State and the NHS were part of a political consensus, and leftist in its acknowledgement that people felt uneasy, uncomfortable and insecure. Labour's task was to reassure, while at the same time posing no threat to those who were enjoying the fruits of the consumer society. Blair summed up his philosophy thus: 'Socialism to me was never about nationalization or the power of the state; not just about economics or politics even. It is a moral purpose to life; a set of values; a belief in society, in co-operation, in achieving together what we are unable to achieve alone.'

This theme constantly recurred in the run-up to the general election. Even a speech to sportswriters to celebrate the eightieth birthday of Sir Stanley Matthews was used to bemoan the trend towards questioning decisions and berating the referee. There needed to be more emphasis on the team, less on the individual. And, in an address at Southwark Cathedral in January 1996, Blair said:

I see two futures open to this country. In one, Britain's communities follow the process that has occurred in some places in the US, where the affluent have retreated into fortresses with private security guards, leaving the rest to lie in ghettos of low opportunity, crime and insecurity. But the cycle of decay and economic underperformance continues. That is the *Blade Runner* scenario.

That is not the sort of Britain I want to live in in the twenty-first century. And that is not a future in tune with Britain's basic instincts. We are a country that supports the underdog. We are tolerant. We are great adventurers. We are patriotic, but we will always stand up against aggression against someone else.

Blair was certainly right about the trends in the United States, where eight million people already live in gated communities and fifty million – almost one in five of the population – form what are known as common-interest developments, protected by security guards. But the speech was also significant for its clear echoes of the main tenets of the post-war system – solidarity, full employment, responsibility, decency. In a way, it could be seen as a reiteration of the Bevanite home–adventure idea discussed in an earlier chapter.

However, there was a crucial difference. Blair and Clinton wanted to create the 'good society' but without the controls on capital which existed during the 1950s and 1960s and which even conservatives like Eisenhower and Macmillan saw as necessary. The problem for both Labour and the Democrats was, as one critic put it, that they were the parties of government at a time when government everywhere was in retreat. This was certainly true of the big issues of state – controlling the economy, ensuring full employment, taming capital, protecting workers. But it was expressly untrue when it came to social policy, where the big state was forced to concentrate its attention. Clinton and Blair were prepared to get tough with everybody – everybody, that is, except the financiers and big business. John Kennedy took action in his presidency to prevent US Steel from raising prices; there was never the slightest hope that Clinton or Blair would step in to prevent downsizing. Instead, they took the 1960s mixture of economic intervention and social liberalism and turned it on its head, pushing social authoritarianism into the vacuum left by the surrender of economic policy to the dictates of global capitalism. Neither man was prepared to offer what had been taken for granted in the 1960s – full employment, rising real wages, an expanded Welfare State – but Clinton was happy as Arkansas governor to withdraw driving licences from high-school dropouts, and Blair was keen on curbs on drinking, bans on cigarette advertising, a campaign for children to inform on shops that sold alcohol to under-age customers, and contracts in which parents would pledge to provide twenty minutes of reading practice with their children every night.

Instead of an independent economic policy, Clinton and Blair had what Edward Luttwak perceptively called 'central bankism', acceptable perhaps in times of high inflation but dangerous during periods such as the 1930s and the 1990s in which labour and resources were abundant. Luttwak wrote in the *London Review of Books*:

It must be fully recognised that the power of central bankers is so great because it is so broadly based. First, they are sustained by almost all responsible professional opinion, as they were in the 1930s. It is therefore foolish to criticise Greenspan or any of his foreign counterparts personally. They do not decide anything of their own volition. They merely exemplify, apply and enunciate a consensual doctrine as unchallengeable within its own premises as the Immaculate Conception. In the second place, central bankism attracts both right-wing and conventional left-wing support, not to speak of the centre, whose opinions coincide with the centre of gravity of respectable professional opinion.[7]

Luttwak's conclusion is that the economic philosophy of Democrats and Republicans, or of Labour and Conservative, is interchangeable; they are all central bankers. This is both true and dangerous: true because there is scant evidence that either Blair or Clinton will challenge the prevailing orthodoxy – low tax, low inflation, decision by technocrat, trickle-down; dangerous because democracy becomes sterile and ultimately meaningless if there is no clash of ideological belief. Britain once had a clear divide between the party that supported business and the party that supported employees. That did not mean that Labour in the past was anti-business, merely that it represented a particular interest. Among his first actions, Blair handed power over interest rates to an unelected central bank and invited the chairman of one of Britain's biggest multinational companies to become a minister.

As we shall see in a later chapter, taking the politics out of economics has deprived the left of anything significant to say about coping with insecurity. Central bankism, management consultancy, a messianic faith in education topped off with the language of concern, counselling and group therapy do not add up to a real alternative to the free-market right.

Of course, there was always the single European currency to differentiate Blair from Major and Thatcher. But here, too, he had a problem. Blair's overt Atlanticism increased his scepticism about monetary union, a project he saw not only as slightly archaic but also as containing enough potential instability to deprive him of the much sought-after second term. In this, he was as one with some of America's leading economists, who argued that joining the single currency in the first wave made no sense for Britain. Rudi Dornbusch described it as 'bad news – like finding out your mother in law has a twin sister'.[8] Paul Krugman's verdict on the Maastricht treaty was that 'a group of highly dignified, serious people, sitting at their baize-covered tables with their bottles of mineral water, created an agreement that sounded good on paper but on closer inspection was sheer nonsense'.[9]

What Britain needed in 1997 was a policy that put the needs of the domestic economy first. Indeed, that had been the whole point about leaving the ERM. But the Conservatives had been hidebound by their belief in flexibility and deregulation, by their failure to see that insecurity and inequality were debilitating. Labour's historic task was to concentrate on home – on job security, decent wages and alleviating poverty – before even giving a thought to embarking on the adventure of monetary union. But this was something

Blair was philosophically incapable of doing. Clinton, like any good global technocrat, was a strong backer of monetary union, and wanted Britain to join. Blair had turned Labour into the party of the City and the transnational corporation. Where once the City was seen as a problem, now it was lionized as a strength and a source of invaluable invisible earnings. Where once the focus of economic policy was on the national, now it was on the inter-national. As one observer put it: 'British politics has been stood on its head. The Conservative party, traditionally the party of financial and overseas interests, has been replaced by Labour. Instructed by its new friends in the City, Labour has become the party of financial – that is pre-Keynesian – orthodoxy.'[10] Or as Lester Thurow once pessimistically observed, elections in the West had effectively become popularity polls dominated by trivia and decided by who looked best on TV: 'Left wing parties may still get elected if Conservative parties mismanage the political process badly enough, but they have nothing positive to offer.'[11]

The main reason why neither Blair nor Clinton had anything 'positive to offer' was that neither was remotely left-wing.

CHAPTER FIVE

A LONGING LOOK ABROAD (2):
THE BRITISH LEFT AND
THE EUROPEAN UNION

It [the process of European integration] is a journey without end for the
journey is the end.
Norman Lamont, former Chancellor of the Exchequer

The EU is not about international co-operation; it is about over-riding its
constituent members and creating instead a single European state. It
seems that, with every passing day, the size of that single state grows, as
the eyes of capital and commissioners look east and to the south in search
of ever cheaper and less trade union organised labour.
Will Podmore and Phil Katz, *Sovereignty for What?*, Podmore, 1997

It is not worth risking the UK's future prosperity for an untried,
politically-inspired dream advanced by a Continental political
and economic elite.
Brian Burkitt, Mark Baimbridge, Philip Wyman,
A Price Not Worth Paying, Campaign for an Independent Britain, 1997

There was a threat to employment in Britain from the movement in the
Common Market towards an economic and monetary union. . . .
This threat has been removed.
Britain's New Deal in Europe, HM Government, 1975

Labour's Chancellor of the Exchequer – the first in eighteen years –
addressed the conference before lunch on day one of its deliberations. His
speech had been eagerly anticipated for at least twenty-four hours; the previous night, Birmingham's restaurants and hotel bars had buzzed with
discussion as to the likely content of Gordon Brown's speech. When it came,

it was warmly received. No one minded that his late arrival meant a late lunch. The Chancellor was the conference hero.

But which conference? Not the Labour conference, not even the Trades Union Congress, this was the Confederation of British Industry conference, annual gathering of the corporate clans. Once, a Labour Chancellor would have faced an Arctic reception on such an occasion; in the mid-1970s, the CBI was reported to be planning an 'investment strike' in protest at Labour policies. That, however, was water under the canal bridge at Birmingham on 10 November 1997, where the hot topic was Europe and its proposed single currency. The top men of multinational business and industry applauded as Mr Brown announced plans to prepare Britain for economic and monetary union. Even the regional morning paper, the *Birmingham Post*, joined in the spirit of things, printing a special CBI edition that declared: 'A city fit to lead Europe'.

There was one guest speaker who refused to be swept up by the Europhoria and who blurted out some uncomfortable truths about the likely impact of the euro: 'Before the CBI shakes hands with the TUC on a single currency, you should fix them in the eye and ask if they are prepared to tell their members that they might have to accept a pay cut.' The speaker was not himself from the trade-union movement. He was William Hague, leader of the Conservative Party. Next morning, the headline in the *Guardian* announced: 'Hague's Labour manifesto'.

Of course, labour manifestos used to be issued by Labour ministers, but not any more. In a mirror-image of the European Union's modus operandi, New Labour and its big-business supporters had concluded that Britain would join the single currency. Parliament would execute and the people would conform. This is the European way: the centre decides, the circumference follows. Regardless of the costs, regardless of the destructive impact on jobs and living standards, the drive for British Economic and Monetary Union membership had started.

THROUGH TRAIN COMING:
THE INESCAPABLE EURO-LOCO

The Treaty on European Union, signed at Maastricht in the Netherlands at the end of 1991, died on 2 June 1992 at the hands of forty-eight thousand

Danish voters who swung that country's referendum to a 'no' vote. Article R of the treaty was unambiguous: Maastricht had to be ratified by all parties, and the Rome treaty, to which Maastricht was an amendment, laid down that this ratification would proceed through each country's own constitutional arrangements. Two legal courses of action were available to the European Commission and the member-states after the Danish vote. The first was to draw up a new treaty; the second was to do nothing and simply bury Maastricht. Anyone who believed that the Community (as it then was) would meekly follow the legal route had clearly spent little time observing the behaviour of this extraordinary institution. Transforming a 100-yard reverse into a 200-yard advance had become something of a speciality in Brussels since at least the mid-1980s. Time and again, events that, according to foreign policy experts (especially British foreign policy experts), ought to have killed for good the idea of a 'united states of Europe' were skilfully pressed into service to drive the process forward. There was the accession of Spain and Portugal in 1985 ('loosening' the Brussels grip, apparently), the reunification of Germany in 1990 (detaching Europe's most important member from the whole project), the Gulf war in 1991 (reasserting Britain's role as the primary military ally of the United States), the war in Yugoslavia in 1991–92 (exposing the sham of a 'European' foreign policy). As for EMU, the central feature of the drive to European unity, this scheme defied death more often than the hero of the 1960s children's TV show, Captain Scarlet. Last rites were given at the start of the depression in 1990, and again after the lira and sterling were blasted out of the Exchange Rate Mechanism (ERM) in mid-1992. A year later, when the remainder of the system collapsed, undertakers stood ready to make the necessary arrangements. In 1996 and 1997, as German unemployment approached five million and government attempts to raid the country's gold reserves to ensure it met the conditions for EMU were fought off by central bankers, the air was thick with demands that EMU's guardians face facts and call the whole thing off. But, like an alien being in a cheap science-fiction film, EMU seemed to draw a hideous strength from the attacks and crises that beset it, and – at the time of writing – is planned to go ahead as per timetable. Devotees of the Soviet 'long-wave' economist Nicholai Kondratieff were delighted to note the crushing effect of the depressionary forces of the 1990s and their uncanny parallels with the 1930s. Then, as now, the biggest victim of the 'downwave' was a multinational empire (the British Empire then, the Soviet Union now). Then, as now, property prices entered free fall, trade unions retreated, monetary 'soundness' was enshrined as the over-riding economic priority and chronic unemployment was seen as regrettable but unavoidable. There was even the common factor of a crisis within the British Royal family (Mrs Simpson then, Princess Diana now).

In 1987, tipsters would probably have offered very poor odds on the likelihood of the European Community/European Union (the former is a subsidiary of the latter) surviving such a crushing downward swing. Based on three rickety legs of an inherently unstable 'milkmaid's stool' (Commission, Parliament, Inter-Governmental Council), the Union was almost tailor-made as victim of the slump. But anyone taking a bet on its imminent demise would have been well advised to check the features of those institutions that survive the 'downwave'; whether the British Royal family or the De Beers diamond cartel (both, at the time of writing, battling through for the second time this century), a common characteristic of the survivor is a certain ruthlessness.

So it was to prove with the Danish referendum. Having given the wrong answer when first asked, the Danes were to be offered a second chance to get it right. Nobody bothered to pretend the Danes would have been given the opportunity to reverse a 'yes' vote; the rerun of the referendum was presented as a triumph for European diplomacy. So-called 'opt-outs' of dubious legal validity were attached to the treaty, allowing Denmark some leeway on provisions covering the single currency, defence, common citizenship and judicial co-operation – and, in May 1993, the country duly held a second referendum and voted 'yes'.

The story does not end there. Denmark's Europhiliac establishment itched to ditch the opt-outs. On 15 November 1995, the *Daily Telegraph* reported thus:

The architect of the Edinburgh deal [the opt-outs were agreed in the Scottish capital], former foreign minister Uffe Ellemann-Jensen, remains unrepentantly pro-European to his toes – on a recent television appearance he revealed a pair of socks adorned with the EU circle of stars motif – and he will not take no for an answer. 'The opt-outs were created against my advice and for a psychological reason. Since then things have changed.'

For a 'psychological reason', read 'to fool the voters'.

Matters were arranged rather more smoothly in France, whose own referendum, held on 20 September 1992, delivered a marginal 51.05 per cent 'yes' vote, seemingly swung, mysteriously, by the ballot boxes flown in from France's West Indian possessions. It could be, of course, that French overseas voters had been swayed by an outburst by Commission President Jacques Delors on 28 August at Quimper in Brittany: 'There's no place in a democracy for people who call for a No.'

Much the same attitude conditioned the British government's handling of ratification. On 23 July 1993, the House of Commons voted by a majority of forty to clear the way for ratification. The air was thick with allegations suggesting MPs had been blackmailed and physically intimidated into voting with the government; the allegations were never denied.

In Germany, the Constitutional Court ruled on 12 October 1993 that the Maastricht treaty could be ratified by the Germans only with due recognition that it was subordinate to national law. Germany's political Establishment has responded to this ruling by ignoring it.

The simple fact was that Maastricht was not going to be allowed to fail. Members of the blood brotherhood of Europe's elite had sworn themselves to its preservation. No number of Commons defeats, referendum reverses or court rulings would be allowed to thwart the grand design. In the legal world, actions such as the repeat Danish referendum would be struck out as 'abuse of process'. But in high European politics, changing the jury, changing the question, shifting the courtroom and nobbling the witnesses – the dirtiest tricks of the rogue prosecutor – are routine practice, as is the offering of sweeteners to the jury. In the case of Maastricht, one of the biggest sweeteners was the concept of 'subsidiarity', the idea that every governmental decision ought always to be taken at the lowest possible level. Jacques Delors had been interested in the concept since 1975, but it was during the Maastricht negotiations that it began to sound like the idea of the moment. Written into the treaty, subsidiarity appeared, from the British perspective, to provide the mechanism whereby 'competences' were returned from Brussels to national capitals. Indeed, subsidiarity allowed Britain's Conservative government to claim that Maastricht had been a decentralizing treaty. On 7 October 1992, during the Tory Party conference, the president of the Board of Trade, Michael Heseltine, told activists: 'The whole history of the European Community has been to advance by centralization to Brussels.' A heckler called: 'It shouldn't', to which Mr Heseltine replied: 'Then what the heck are you complaining about when John Major has reversed the process?'

Quite how a treaty that took European competence into defence, foreign affairs, police and judicial matters and – critically – economic and monetary control had 'decentralized' Europe was a mystery. Charles Moore, editor of, first, the *Sunday Telegraph* and, later, the *Daily Telegraph*, commented on 3 April 1994 that, in claiming Maastricht to have been a decentralizing treaty, 'the Government is . . . living a lie'. On a separate occasion, he wrote of the Prime Minister and the Foreign Secretary Douglas Hurd that they spent sufficient time with other European leaders to know that their claim that Europe was moving Britain's way (i.e. towards subsidiarity) was simply not true.

Mr Moore's bafflement in the face of such deceit is understandable. Yet it discloses an incomprehension of the blood brotherhood in action. Given that Maastricht had to succeed, then the means by which it was sold to various European electorates were of at most secondary importance. In his book on the subversion of Italy, Philip Willan described how many of that country's secret service personnel regarded their first loyalty as being to the Atlantic Pact Security Office, NATO's security wing.[1] Secret protocols, attached to the NATO treaty and signed by Italy, required the Rome Establishment to guarantee its 'international alignment within the Western bloc by any means, even if the electorate were to show a different inclination'. Perhaps similar annexes are attached to the Rome and Maastricht treaties – or perhaps they need not be. Whatever the truth, the mentality is identical: European decisions have to be insulated as far as possible from democratic challenge.

Nor does one have to be a crazed conspiracy theorist to note that, as regards British politics, opposition to European integration tends to have an adverse effect upon a politician's career prospects. Mrs (now Lady) Thatcher's post-1988 disillusionment with the Community/Union led swiftly to the exit of a Prime Minister considered impregnable only a year before her resignation, someone whose stances on economic and diplomatic policy had been said to have been triumphantly vindicated by the events of 1989–90.

Murkier still were the rumours and lies that swirled around John Major's ill-fated Chancellor, Norman Lamont, in the wake of Britain's September 1992 exit from the European Exchange Rate Mechanism. Mr Lamont made it clear he had never approved of ERM membership and considered sterling's expulsion to be a liberation, allowing him to pursue a 'British policy'. Shortly afterwards, a number of rumours did the rounds, including an extraordinary story in the press, supposedly emanating from an off-licence in London's seedy Paddington area, alleging the Chancellor had made a late-night purchase of cheap champagne and king-size cigarettes, the clear implication being that he was illicitly entertaining a lady friend. Mr Lamont proved his innocence, but before further inquiries could be made, the Nigerian off-licence assistant who had supposedly supplied the story was dismissed by his employer and deported, robbing the media of the chance to inquire how an illegal immigrant had been able to concoct a story so plausibly close to the Chancellor's rather fey cheroot-smoking lifestyle as to fool political correspondents and parliamentarians.

The damage was done, and Mr Lamont was said to be a political liability. He was sacked, and replaced by Kenneth Clarke, who not only had been a fervent supporter of ERM membership but was keen for Britain to join the single currency. With Mr Lamont went his short-lived post-ERM 'British policy'. Mr Clarke declared his intention of meeting the Maastricht conditions for single currency membership and budgeted with that end in view. Downing Street presented Mr Lamont's dismissal as a regrettable necessity forced upon the Prime Minister by the Chancellor's lack of political 'feel'. But more recent evidence suggests the pro-European Mr Clarke was being lined up for the Treasury well before May 1993. Marking the fifth anniversary of devaluation, the BBC documentary *Black Wednesday* carried an interview with Mr Clarke in which he recounted the events of 16 September 1992. Three men, he said, had attended on the Prime Minister at his temporary HQ in Admiralty Arch (10 Downing Street was being repaired after an IRA mortar attack). Two of them – Trade President Michael Heseltine and the Foreign Secretary Douglas Hurd – had a clear interest in sterling's fate. The third, Mr Clarke himself, was Home Secretary, a post primarily concerned with police, prisons and the judiciary. His presence was not explained. The net result of Lamont's character assassination was that, within ten months of the total discrediting of Britain's involvement in European currency schemes, Britain had a Chancellor full-heartedly committed to the single currency.

Nor is there any sign that Norman Lamont will be the last front-rank politician to suffer the Euro-jinx. More recently, Labour's Foreign Secretary Robin Cook – one of the Cabinet's staunchest opponents of the single currency – was hit by disclosures of problems in his private life, albeit disclosures with rather more basis in fact than the Lamont off-licence story.

As for 'subsidiarity', the one and only piece of evidence supporting the Major government's contention that Maastricht was a decentralizing treaty, Charles Grant notes in *Delors: Inside the House that Jacques Built*, 'Delors never came up with a list of competences for the EC to hand back to member-states.'[2]

But by then, of course, the various juries had given the 'correct' answers.

WIDER STILL AND WIDER: DOES SIZE MATTER?

We open with the above brief tour of the Maastricht 'ratification' to give a flavour of how the European Union conducts itself in reality. On paper, the Union may be very many wonderful things; on the ground, it is a-legal, coercive, deceitful, it treats even its own rules as temporary expedients and lumbers forward, oblivious of opposition. These features are especially true of the Union's central cadres in Brussels, Strasbourg and elsewhere, but are displayed in almost equal measure by the its 'sub-officers', the diplomatic and Foreign Ministry personnel of the member-states and the elected politicians whom they supposedly serve.

Completing the 'triad' are the big-business interests of Europe, what has been called 'Europe Inc.'. Commenting on a report of that name from the Amsterdam-based Corporate Europe Observatory, Colin Hines, working with the International Forum on Globalization, wrote in *Tribune* on 25 July 1997:

[A] little-known organisation, the European Round Table of Industrialists [ERT] , is the driving force behind the idea of an internal market in Europe, the Maastricht Treaty and the deflationary, social-welfare-cutting convergence criteria of the proposed single currency. . . . Big business is flexing its huge, undemocratic muscles to shape Europe for its own ends . . . the centralisation of power in Brussels undermines national democracy and gives multi-nationals an enormous advantage over social movements.

Among the ERT members listed by Mr Hines were British Petroleum, Shell, Daimler Benz, Fiat and Siemens. In Britain, pro-Union groups such as the

Action Centre for Europe and the European Movement have been bankrolled by corporate interests including David Sainsbury, Robert Bosch and the financial group Robert Fleming.

There is plenty of human traffic among these three arms of the Union. Ex-BP chairman Lord Simon became a Labour trade minister in 1997; the previous year, with a typically Bruxellian contempt for any view the voter might take, he confided to a conference: 'Let me tell you a secret. Britain will join the European Monetary Union.' Moving the other way, Douglas Hurd, Foreign Secretary at the time of Maastricht, left politics to join NatWest Markets, the securities arm of NatWest Bank. On 20 November 1996, he used a platform offered by Telegraph newspapers to defend Britain's membership of the Union on what seemed to be the sole ground that business would benefit: 'the . . . [European] Commission is prising open closed markets, chipping away at state subsidies. . . . Telecommunications, aviation, energy . . . Britain . . . stands to benefit'. An old rule in the insurance business holds that one should never write one (dodgy) piece of business on the basis that it will lead to another (more profitable) piece of underwriting. Hurd's law dictates the opposite course: tangible national interests and sovereign rights ought to be cashed out in return for the hazy, sometime-never hope that some British company may someday be allowed to run an air service or a bank or own a telephone cable. National freedoms that can never be bought back are to be exchanged in one-time deals for transitory commercial gains.

Not only is Hurd's law dubious in principle, but it has never worked in practice. British membership of the Union has proved an economic disaster: a small trade surplus prior to joining has swung round into a colossal deficit, and the fishing industry, a mainstay of the British economy, has been pushed to the brink of extinction. This catastrophe is always explained away as 'proof' that Britain has been insufficiently 'positive' about membership. On the contrary: submersion into the single currency would leave unemployment as the sole adjustment mechanism for troubled national economies.

Unsurprisingly, Europe's redistribution machine is tilted against ordinary people and in favour of vested interests, principally finance (key beneficiary of the 'sound' money policies of Maastricht), industry (key beneficiary of the removal of capital controls) and agriculture (which takes directly from millions of poorer consumers in terms of inflated food bills and taxpayer-supplied subsidies). None of this, of course, would appear to be what one might call 'left-wing' and, indeed, for many years the British left was the advanced guard of opposition to British subsumption into the Union. By contrast, as Will Podmore and Phil Katz note in their study *Sovereignty for What?: Why Stopping European Monetary Union is Just the Start*,[3] the Conservatives were enthusiastic Europeans from 1961 through Mrs Thatcher's Bruges speech of 1988 and, in essence, afterwards, until the 1997 election. In 1983 Labour was committed to withdrawal, and withdrawal as a last resort as recently as 1987. Only after the election of that year did policy shift markedly towards Euro-enthusiasm, initially through policy review documents. In the 1997 election, Labour was decidedly the more pro-Bruxellian of the two major parties, although this stance was modified by assurances that the leader, Tony Blair, was actually a Eurosceptic (he penned an article for the *Sun* newspaper on St George's Day suggesting he would slay the dragon of Europe).

To an extent, Labour's Europeanism has been driven as much by social as by ideological factors. Since the 1950s, advocacy of European integration had been as much a touchstone of middle-class respectability as advocacy of unilateral disarmament had been a touchstone of middle-class dissent. The movement opened the 1980s by embracing the latter and ended it by embracing the former, this second action demonstrating to the electorate how far Labour had moved since the 1950s.

Nevertheless, on the surface, no relationship ought to look less likely than the flourishing affair between the British left and the European Union. Yet our opening, cataloguing the behaviour of the Brussels machine and its satellites, is not the whole story. States and quasi-states can behave badly without invalidating their structure or existence. Few would suggest dismantling the United States of America or the Republic of India in response to the malefactions of President Nixon or the state of emergency declared by Mrs Gandhi. While a sort of institutional version of 'by their fruits' is a useful tool in political analysis, it is not the only tool. Judged as an objective piece of machinery, it could be that the Union contains a potential perceived by the left for redirection towards social-democratic ends. Just because the EU currently operates as a combined clearing house and executive arm for capital and the continent's 'securiocracy' is perhaps no reason to assume it will always so operate. It may presently mandate slash-and-burn free-market policies, but perhaps a change of directorate will mean a change of direction.

In assessing this possibility, we need to break down the various aspects of the Union and judge them against traditional left-wing values and ideals. And the obvious starting point for such an exercise is size. The Union is not big simply because the preordained political zone adds up to a geographically large area (as may be said to be the case in China, Brazil and India); it is large by design. 'Widening' is an institutional imperative. First the Carolingian 'six' expanded to take in Britain, Ireland and Denmark, then Greece brought the Union its first non-Roman official alphabet. The Iberian countries followed, as did Finland, Sweden and Austria. Not only have the Carolingian bounds long been burst, but talks are currently under way to admit non-European countries such as Turkey.

Big may or may not be beautiful. But is there any relationship between the size of a political unit and its potential as a delivery mechanism for social-democratic aims? An off-the-cuff response – comparing, for example, Norway with the United States, or Denmark with Turkey – would be a resounding 'no'. But a pro-Union social democrat may well counter with Canada, or even Greenland. More seriously, many on the left embrace the Union as not so much a counterweight to the global market but a fencing-in of a large chunk of it. Effectively, they have bought the 'large area' (*Grossraum*) thinking of many continental economists, detailed extensively in John Laughland's book *The Tainted Source*,[4] and adapted it to the era of instant money transfers and 'globalization'. To this way of thinking, a big political unit, by enclosing within its frontiers a sizeable percentage of the total assets and activity of the global economy, will then be able to call the shots in a leftist sort of way in its dealings with multinational industry bosses and currency speculators. After all, the advantages of being 'multinational' diminish as the number of nations shrinks. Leverage over capital increases mathematically as the territorial jurisdiction expands.

Thus Ken Jackson, general secretary of the Amalgamated Engineering and Electrical Union, addressing the Trades Union Congress on 10 September 1997, was reported by the Press Association as follows:

[He] said a one-money Europe was a chance to end 'casino capitalism' in which workers' livelihoods were put at the mercy of currency traders. . . . 'If we had a single currency . . . [we would have] a unique chance to call in the chips on this "casino capitalism". My union has the courage to stick by its position on Europe. For unions to do otherwise is an unacceptable gamble with their members' future.'

Where national governments were pitifully outgunned by global capital, in other words, a 'big' multinational government would compete on at least equal terms. This was the thinking that had helped propel the British Labour movement into a pro-European stance at the end of the 1980s. On 17 November 1991, the *Sunday Times* detailed leader Neil Kinnock's conversion to the European ideal:

Berlin's declaration of the Confederation of EC Socialist Parties, taken at the rebuilt Reichstag building, set out the basic line: the left would fight to prevent the takeover of the European single market 'by purely economic forces'. What was needed was the urgent application of a range of interventionist policies to remove inequalities in living, push through social directives so far blocked by Britain, introduce the right to a minimum wage and strengthen trade union powers.

Both 'social dumping' and competitive tax cutting would also be ruled out in the unified Labour/Euro-socialist Europe: '"The introduction of binding minimum rates [of income tax] could be the most appropriate form of co-ordination," said the Kinnock-endorsed declaration.'

Most appealing of all, perhaps, was the prospect of 'Europe-wide reflation'; were the whole bloc simultaneously to boost demand as an unemployment-reducing measure, it would be big enough and ugly enough to resist both trade deficit problems and the unwelcome verdict of the speculators. That such Euro-Keynesianism would require the alignment of not only the economic cycles within the Union (a prospect that faded rather than improved as the 1990s ground on) but also the political cycles (given that all twelve, fifteen or sixteen member-states would need simultaneously to be governed by left-leaning governments) seemed not seriously to disturb the Labour leadership's new faith.

Simplified, the British left's enthusiasm for Europe can be summarized in the German trade-union slogan: 'The union makes us strong.' Forces in the world antipathetic to social justice are powerful because they are large and rich; forces working for social justice need to organize themselves into political units that are also large and rich. In the words of Transport and General Workers Union general secretary Ron Todd to the TUC on 8 September 1988: 'The only card game in town at the moment is in a town called Brussels.' Or, to quote Charles Grant again on Jacques Delors: 'He tends to see the economy as a self-contained system, rather than one influenced by a significant external sector. He once asked a colleague why the 1992 [single-market] programme had failed to protect Europe from the effects of America's recession.'[5]

Two issues need to be clarified. First, is this 'fencing in' of the essentially hostile global economy likely to work in theory? Second, is it working in practice? On the first point, it is far from clear that a large unit is automatically better placed to order economic and social priorities within its borders than a small one. The People's Republic of China and the USSR certainly managed for many decades to seal themselves off from the world economy, but so did Albania and North Korea. The opening of the former Soviet Union to international capital has caused great turbulence, to say the least. By 1997, China's 'open door' policy had created great wealth in some areas but thrown tens of millions out of work. Smaller nations moving from command to market economies suffered similar dislocation; the point is that the large states were no more successful in controlling this turbulence than were the smaller ones.

In the West, it is true that the size of the United States market allows its policy makers wide scope for imposing certain controls and priorities, for example in the field of car-exhaust emission standards. It is unlikely that the legislature of a smaller unit, especially one with a struggling domestic motor industry – France or the United Kingdom – would have taken such action unilaterally. Yet such reluctance on the part of the smaller nations is itself a free political choice. There is no mathematical link between the size of the United States and its ability to call the shots on car exhausts: tiny Sark in the Channel Islands (with an area of two square miles) has banned cars altogether. Neighbouring Guernsey operates a dual pricing system for residential property, with a lower price for local people and a higher price for 'immigrants'. This radical interference with the market mechanism requires no 'fencing-in' of as large a slice of the international market as possible. Quite the opposite, it is the compact nature of the political community that makes possible the execution of policies that would be considered extreme or irresponsible in a larger unit. Elsewhere in the north Atlantic, the extensive transfer-payment mechanisms within Irish society (which include free power and telephone units for some elderly people along with free public transport) can be operated not because the Republic of Ireland is a large political unit (it is not) but because a consensus has been built around such redistribution.

But even were we to grant the Euro-leftist the 'big is better' argument, there is little chance that the 'large area' would perform on the day. Without (too much) caricature, this vision of the future would pen global capitalism into a series of large areas: the EU, USA, and a Far Eastern grouping headed by Japan or China. Those outside this charmed circle would be prevented from 'social dumping' by the creative use by the Union and its partners of the World Trade Organization and other agencies and by the writing into free-trade treaties of 'social' clauses. Businesses that threaten to decamp to low-wage countries would face ostracism. The EU itself would form just one part of a 'very large area', within which social standards would be protected.

One obvious objection to this radiant future is the sad fact that neither of the two putative 'global partners' – the USA or the Far East – shows any interest in such an arrangement. President Clinton has urged US workers to 'compete, not retreat', and the US-led North American Free Trade Association (NAFTA) contains within its borders a large piece of the low-wage world: Mexico. At the opposite point of the compass, any Far Eastern bloc that excluded China would scarcely carry much clout, whereas one that included China would lasso one billion poorly paid workers into the social protection stockade.

A second objection is purely practical: would even the largest of large areas – perhaps even a single world government – ever prove an effective counterweight to international capitalism? Professor Ian Angell of the London School of Economics told a conference in Lisbon in June 1997 that technology was outstripping all attempts at taxation and other financial enforcement by national governments. Dematerialized electronic cash, he said, would be beamed off into computer repositories in the 'global commons' – the sea bed or outer space. 'Off-planet banking', he said, is on its way.

Faced with such developments, even the most enthusiastic Euro-social democrat ought to accept that the drive to build larger and larger political areas as an attempt to impose social accountability upon international capital is a fruitless, tail-chasing exercise. This is not to advocate surrender in the face of global capitalism: far from it. But it is to accept that the large-area response is sterile, because of its fallacious – and, we may add, rather quaint – assumption that, in dealing with the financial interest, geographical size is an asset. In fact, political geography and the free market have little connection with one another. Attempting to 'fence in' and then tame the capitalist market is likely to prove as useful as fencing in the wind.

This leads to our second question: how, in practice, has the large-area approach worked? As we saw above, Jacques Delors, for one, was not overly impressed by the results. The single market seemed more, not less, susceptible to the world economy than had been the old Common Market. But this was hardly surprising, given that one of the first post-Maastricht acts of the European Union was to sign the General Agreement on Tariffs and Trade, after some huffing and puffing from the French about the need for cultural quotas. Acquiescence in GATT was just one symptom of what is a central flaw of Europeanist social democracy: the increasing power of the large area makes more worthwhile the capture of its decision-making process by big-business interests. This capture is already evident in the trend of Brussels policy making since the mid-1980s, from the single market through the deflationary ERM and GATT to the proposed economic dictatorship of central bankers represented by the single currency. As Podmore and Katz put it: 'Despite the earnest piffle of the Social Chapter, the EU is guided by the "free market" economics and the "slash and burn" industrial policy used by Thatcher in Britain.'[6]

Insofar as big business seems divided on Europe, it is divided only between which interest ought to predominate in the single-currency era: the financial interest or the big corporate giants. The former seeks to give over-riding priority to price stability and free capital movements; the latter is traditionally more attuned to the view of the EU as a large multinational venture charged with representing European industry in international fora and ensuring access to markets abroad while providing financial and other support within the Union. It is the difference between Europe as seen by Daimler Benz or Airbus and Europe as seen by SBC Warburg or Deutsche Bank. The difference is real but ought not to be overstated. This is a family quarrel, nothing more. Indeed, at the time of writing in 1997, the dispute seemed to be fading as the drive to Economic and Monetary Union gathered speed.

What did not fade was the 'capture' of Europe by big finance and big business. As noted above, Europe's 'social dimension' – much touted in the late 1980s as evidence to the British left that the Euro-water was warm and that it was time to take the plunge – proved indeed to be little more than 'earnest piffle'. Worse, 'social Europe' seemed to be developing along the same lines as 'social Britain', with ever loosening controls on capital matched by ever tightening controls on the individual. As unemployment reached crisis levels in 1997, Europe's social affairs commissioner Padraig Flynn busied himself with new regulations on sex discrimination and smoking in the workplace. The nightmare prospect loomed of three (at least) tiers of legislative activity – regional, national and European – all acting as vast law factories, churning out thousands of new criminal offences, supported by 'Europol' and the pan-European criminal-records computer system. As Richard Hoggart and Douglas Johnson noted in their own tour of the European horizon: 'We pass laws against racist behaviour . . . laws to prevent birds' eggs being taken from the nest or badgers being baited, laws against sexism, laws about discrimination and many more in a long list. . . . These laws . . . do not simply protect the social fabric at the expense of limiting the freedom of the individual. They positively try (to use Jane Austen's phrase) to screw the citizens into virtue.'[7] Such a powerful, large-area political unit had obvious appeal to the British left's traditional opponents in the imperialist wing of the Tory Party. In a staunch defence of Superpower Europe, Tory Euro-MP John Stevens wrote:

We [pro-Union Tories] . . . stand for the two greatest objectives of conservatism: maximising Britain's power in the world and minimising government's power in the economy.

We consider ourselves to be the inheritors of the Conservative Party's old imperial tradition. We are not frightened of being part of some grand common enterprise, provided we have a dominant role in determining its shape and purpose.[8]

This is an honourable position, consistent with the 'Greater Britain' strand of thinking that stretches back through Churchill and Disraeli to the very dawn of the modern British state. But, as we argued in an earlier chapter ('Cash is Fact'), we do not believe 'punching above our weight' to be the appropriate foreign policy stance of the left.

In summary, 'Great Europe', the large-area aspect of the Union, has nothing to offer in terms of the fulfilment of leftist objectives. Its supposed major benefit – the fencing-in of the theatre of operations of international capitalism – is chimerical, and its size lends itself to a foreign policy stance incompatible with the British leftist tradition. Whatever the supposed advantages of European Union to the British left, its size is not one of them.

SEPARATE BUT EQUAL: DOES FEDERALISM SET YOU FREE?

But if the large area has nothing to offer the British left, perhaps its counter-concept, federalism, will prove more bountiful. Here, the Europeanists are surely on firmer ground; from the municipal socialism of the early twentieth century to the rate-capped 'people's republics' (the big Labour-controlled conurbations of the 1980s), British leftists had periodically found local politics provided a more productive area of operations than the national variety. A truly federal Europe would allow for such local or regional experimentation on a grand scale. Furthermore, was not the concept of federalism itself an ideal to which all socialists ought to aspire? More than simply a more efficient form of government, could it not prove the hinge upon which a future human commonwealth might one day be constructed? The word itself grew from the same root as 'fraternity', 'fraternal' and other expressions of brotherhood. How could one be a socialist and not a federalist?

The appeal of the federal ideal lay partly in its symmetry. In a unitary state, the lower units are subordinate to the higher. In a confederation (such as the 1931–47 'White Commonwealth' or today's Commonwealth of Independent States in the former Soviet Union), the higher unit is subordinate to the lower. But in a federation, neither unit is senior or subordinate; each is supreme in its own sphere – in the words of the old Irish toast: 'Neither above you nor beneath you, but beside you.' Rough and ready federal-type arrangements date back to antiquity: examples would include the Athenian League and the (historically rather shakier) argumentative Greek nation that laid siege to Troy. In the Dark Ages, British chieftains federated and defederated as the fortunes of their war with the Anglo-Saxons ebbed and flowed. But it was the foundation of the United States in 1776 that saw federalism emerge as a fully formed theory of government. At the heart of the American political settlement was the supposition that all powers not specifically arrogated to the central government remained the preserve of the states, the precise reverse of the British system, under which local authorities are permitted to perform only specific functions prescribed in law, while the central government is unfettered save by Parliament.

The 'internal sovereignty' of the American states is – on paper at least – the most powerful example of the federal principle in action. Not all federations operate with this level of autonomy at the lower level; Malaysia is an example of one that does not, although most of its states boast their own monarch. And although purists would declare the equilibrium principle ('neither above you nor beneath you') to lie at the heart of federalism, most observers would grant that institutions can lie somewhere on a sliding scale of 'federality'. In the academic world, for example, a large state school would display few federal features: the teachers are local authority employees, as is the headmaster, and budgets, even when devolved, are under the ultimate jurisdiction of the Department for Education and Employment. A public school would lie a little further up the scale, with individual house-masters/mistresses wielding considerable autonomy in terms of rule making, discipline, ethos, charges and budgets. But the key functions of admission, expulsion and curriculum would remain at headmaster or governor level. Higher still is the Oxford college, with its own staff, premises and funds, sometimes greater than those of the 'central' university.

Furthermore, life in any society other than an absolute monarchy or totalitarian dictatorship is inherently 'federal'. Were a British prime minister to stroll into an operating theatre and light a large cigar, he could not refuse to extinguish it on the ground that he headed the political executive that, in turn, ran the National Health Service and could therefore behave as he pleased in 'his' hospitals. Nor could he insist his local library stock all his favourite books, or demand state-owned London Underground build a Tube line to his house. Persons, individual and corporate, enjoy 'reserved powers' simply by dint of living under the rule of law.

Federalism, while not an absolute standard, is nevertheless something more than this. It is a philosophy whereby only those functions that cannot be performed at the lower level are moved to the central authority. The American model suggests that these functions have a core including defence, immigration, an external tariff, the fighting of large-scale crime and the protection of the environment. But there is nothing fixed about this list. Canada, for example, has permitted tariff barriers among the individual provinces and Quebec has been granted its own immigration controls; West Germany had practically no federal police force prior to the Red Army Faction terrorist campaign of the 1970s; Australia has reserved education to the federal government but not the sort of single-market powers enjoyed by Washington, DC. The Soviet Union allowed (in theory) constituent republics to sign foreign treaties, something prohibited in the American constitution. Despite these variations, a country's membership or not of the federal family is not difficult to establish. Britain, France, Japan and Ireland are not federations; Belgium, Switzerland and the United Arab Emirates are federations. Is the European Union either a federation or a federation in embryo?

The immediate answer to the first part of the question would have to be that it is not. However wide the definition is drawn, 'federalism' surely does not include a structure in which two of the member-states possess atomic weapons and sit in their own right on the United Nations Security Council. As to whether it is an embryonic federation, the answer here would again have to be 'no'. The European Union is not a federation in embryo, it is a unitary state in embryo. Federations, as we have seen, are built on the principle that only those functions that must of necessity be discharged centrally are passed up to the federal level. Whatever the precise details, these would tend always to be 'big' things: war and peace, currency issue, external relations. Everything else, including the vast bulk of judicial and police functions and general law making, would remain at the lower level.

The EU has developed in precisely the opposite way. First, relatively minor powers passed to Brussels under the Treaty of Rome (farm support, food hygiene, external tariffs and trade relations). More substantial powers were handed over under the 1985 Single Act, establishing the 'single market': working conditions, health and safety, industrial support, some social policy. Maastricht established the single currency project, common foreign policy, common citizenship and the 'Europol' police office. It is true that the president of France or British prime minister retains the power to unleash a nuclear holocaust. But this (rather useless) prerogative is practically the only piece of unfettered discretion remaining to them, and will doubtless be absorbed into the European 'defence pillar' at a future Maastricht-type conference.

Federations ought not to behave as the Union behaves, laying down the law on everything from the wearing of seat-belts to the cleanliness of public beaches. A federal Europe would concentrate on defence, high diplomacy and the refereeing of the single market at the 'big end', striking down large monopolistic takeovers and covert national trade barriers. Union Europe concentrates on everything. A federal Europe would have no directorates for transport or social affairs or 'the regions'. It would not sponsor the making of television dramas depicting the British as psychopathic xenophobes (see *The Writing on the Wall*, BBC TV thriller in summer 1996), it would have no need of the Brussels propaganda department DG X.

The Union today is in an unstable position, poised between its unitary destiny and the enfeebled but still extant inter-governmental dimension. Two over-riding legal principles still – just – maintain the Union's status as an association of sovereign states: the Luxembourg Compromise (permitting any member to use a national veto) and the doctrine that membership rests upon the continuing assent of national parliaments. Every development since the mid-1980s has whittled away the national aspect of the Union; future developments look certain to complete the process. The failure of each stage is used to build momentum for the next stage: thus the single market was working poorly, so the single currency was essential. When this in turn fails to live up to expectations, a single government will be demanded. Federations represent settlements, enduring political contracts. The EU operates on a momentum principle, the accretion of power. Should the British left be sincerely seeking federalism, it would not find it in Europe.

But should it be so seeking in the first place? It is hard to grasp the great leftist principle that beats at the heart of federalism, at least in terms of federalism as it has been practised. For every imaginative attempt to use local autonomy in the service of social justice there is a Governor George Wallace or an Ian Smith, prime minister of the internally sovereign British territory of Southern Rhodesia. When Britain's one experiment to date in United Kingdom federalism, the half-century-old government and parliament of Northern Ireland, was closed down in 1972, most leftists were mightily relieved. Nor is a federal structure particularly compatible with the strong governmental measures often found necessary by left-of-centre administrations. As Ian Williams warned in his 'Letter from America' in *Tribune* on 26 September 1997: 'Britain's political structure is indeed hopelessly centralized . . . so looking to the US's federal structure is superficially attractive. But America's sclerotic politics, explicitly designed to thwart all substantial reform, are hardly the solution. The US has 80,000 separate units of government, each with its own chartered powers and degree of autonomy.' Interestingly, he added: 'Despite all the layers of government, the federal government has delegated a stranglehold over the economy to Alan Greenspan, an Ayn Rand cultist believer in the gold standard, who raises interest rates whenever he thinks that American workers are breaking the two-decade-long pay freeze they have suffered.'

The underlying question is not whether the European Union is federalist but whether anywhere is federalist. This is not to deny that federations can be governed well and successfully, but simply to question whether they live up to their own federalist ideals.

Penguin's publication *A Dictionary of Politics* notes, under the entry for 'Federation': 'The essential difference between a federation and a confederation is that the organs of a federation have a direct power over the citizens of its component provinces or states.'[9] Here is the flaw in the federal idea. To adapt Keynes's comment about control of the currency, we would say that whoever controls the constitution controls the people's rights and thus controls the nation; in a federation that is the central authority. This control is strengthened by the modern habit of signing declarations on human rights; in a recent case, Australia's federal government threatened action against the state of Tasmania, whose laws on homosexuality were said to be incompatible with Australia's treaty obligations. Even without such external justifications, the federal authorities, in particular the federal judiciary, are in effective control of the political process by dint of the fact that the people are citizens of the federation, rather than – as in the confederal model – of its member-states.

This flaw is seen most clearly in the United States. All powers not specified as belonging to the centre belong to the states, and yet the centre has taken powers over almost every aspect of American life. One clear example is drug policy. As reported by Ambrose Evans-Pritchard in the *Sunday Telegraph* on 22 December 1996, Washington, DC, reacted with a mixture of 'outrage and disbelief' when Californian voters approved the legalization of cannabis for medical purposes (effectively any purpose deemed therapeutic by the user): 'The . . . 10th Amendment . . . stipulates that all powers are reserved to the states unless specifically allocated to Washington – (very few are, and drug policy is not one of them).' Despite this legal handicap, he reported, the federal government's war on drugs 'has escalated to the point where it has become the chief activity of the US criminal-justice machine – and the prison-industrial complex that accommodates it'. Nor is this an isolated example. In the early 1980s, President Reagan's government threatened withdrawal of federal highway funds for states that refused to raise the drinking age to twenty-one.

It is sometimes said that power in the United States seesaws between the states and Washington over fairly regular periods, with the former losing powers during emergencies such as wartime or depression only to regain them as a predictable disillusion sets in with the ways of the capital city. This is highly misleading. States have lost powers – both de jure and de facto – almost continuously for the last century and a half. It is true that this process moves more slowly or more quickly at different times, but the trend remains in the same direction. The greatest of all scandals to engulf the American capital, Watergate, triggered the return of no significant powers to the states. Until recently, the death penalty was the most visible symbol of the states' autonomy. It is less so now that the federal death penalty has returned to prominence, in use for offences such as the murder of a federal officer on duty (the charge upon which Oklahoma bomber Timothy McVeigh was convicted).

That America has strong civic institutions and independent, not to say bloody-minded, local and regional government is beyond doubt. But that does not vindicate the claim that the United States is a federation of sovereign states. Indeed, the American system owes as much to staunchly stand-alone municipalities, police forces and sheriffs' departments as it does to the states. Federalism is a mirage even when the federalists are genuinely federal. When they are not – as in Brussels – it is a death-trap.

TEACHING THE WORLD TO SING: INTERNATIONALISM, THE BROTHERHOOD OF MAN AND BRUSSELS

There are those on the left to whom the European Union, as an international organization, is intrinsically a good thing, as are the Commonwealth, the United Nations, the World Health Organization and a raft of other worthy – not to say wordy – bodies.

The Union is more than happy to go along with this image of itself as some sort of cross between the International Scout Movement and UNICEF. But this hardly squares with the Superpower Europe that is touted as the Union's 'federal destiny'. Neither the UN nor the Commonwealth has a 'defence pillar', a binding court of justice, a 'national' flag or anthem. If the Union really is merely another international forum, it cannot simultaneously demand all the powers of a sovereign state. Friendship organizations do not need common foreign policies or large civil services.

In a similar vein, membership of the Union is not comparable in any way with membership of NATO or the UN. No individual would allow himself to be persuaded to sink his savings, household and personal identity into a commune on the ground that membership of the commune is really little different from his long-standing membership of American Express. Nor would he be likely to fall for the bogus mutuality in which the Britain-into-Europe debate is often couched: that every other family in the street is submerging itself into the commune is no reason at all for our householder to do likewise. The question of what Britain will 'do' should it reject the Union betrays the fallacious idea of the nation as some sort of multinational enterprise that needs to seek 'strategic alliances' in order to prosper.

The Union is no more 'internationalist' than our notional commune is 'neighbourly'. On the contrary: true internationalism, as with true neighbourliness, is voluntary, not coercive. We can do no better than to conclude this section with a quote from a Mr John Parfitt, of Gloucestershire, who wrote to *The Times* in June 1995 to comment on the European debate: 'I am blessed with many friends and relations but my respect and affection do not extend to asking them to run my household nor to lay uninvited hands on my bank account.'

We have spent some time examining what the European Union is and is not: the embryonic atomic-armed superpower run from a central control point in the interests of large-scale banking and industry with its deflationary single currency and economic dictatorship of central bankers is not, and could never be, the progressive, internationalist organization many on the British left believe it to be. They imagine it to be merely an accident that the history of British membership is entirely a history of Conservative governments, from application (Macmillan), to accession (Heath), the Single European Act (Mrs Thatcher) and Maastricht (Major). It is no accident. The Community/Union was seen on the right as a legal and economic mechanism for ruling out for all time the possibility of domestic radicalism by a leftist British government. Indeed, only when the threat of such radicalism receded, with the restructuring of the Labour Party in the late

1980s, did some Conservatives feel safe in criticizing the 'federalist' antics of Brussels.

A European Democrat (then the label for British and Danish conservative Euro-MPs) briefing leaflet from the early 1980s entitled *Britain and the EEC — Why Labour is Wrong* declared: '[T]he Labour left wishes to change the nature of British society . . . the British Labour Party says its policies are incompatible with EEC membership. This fact alone underlines the extremist nature of these policies!'

In 1975, the official leaflet of the pro-European group during the referendum campaign *Why You Should Vote Yes* hammered home the message that Europe was a counterweight to left 'extremism': 'What are the alternatives? Those who want to come out are deeply divided . . . Some want a Communist Britain — part of the Soviet bloc.' No one was suggesting one had to be a Communist to want out of the Community. No, no. Merely that the electorate might have noticed that the sort of people who advocated withdrawal tended to be of a certain type (Communists). Another European Democratic Group publication of the early 1980s, *Tradition and Reality: Conservative Philosophy and European Integration* by Robert Jackson, then a Euro-MP, again drew attention to the link between Community membership and the fending-off of left-wing policies: 'Nor can there be any doubt of the radically disruptive character of the changes to British society now proposed by the Labour party . . . and intimately associated with the determination to withdraw Britain from Europe.'[10]

There are those such as Tory Euro-MP John Stevens, quoted above, who continue to tout the Union's efficacy as a barrier to traditional British Labour policies; in the same article he declared: 'The [Labour] party is suspicious of an independent [European] central bank and knows government spending limits would undermine its dream to create for Europe all the interventionism of regional aid and state subsidies that the Tories have dismantled in Britain.' Similarly, the clear and present danger of the Union's philosophy and modus operandi to the prospects of the British left have long been noted. Tony Benn in 1979 noted that as far back as 1963 he had listed among his principal objections to British membership the fact that 'the Treaty of Rome . . . entrenches laissez-faire as its philosophy and chooses bureaucracy as its administrative method'.[11]

Nine years later, former Labour minister Eric Deakins was blunt:

When the free internal market is achieved by 1992, it will mean the end of any prospect of a Labour government being able to carry out radical, let alone socialist, economic and financial policies.

Tories, Liberals and Social Democrats recognised long ago that EEC membership would emasculate any Labour government and effectively neuter the Labour Party.[12]

The huge shift in Labour's position has lowered the volume on both sides; rather less is heard now (either from an approving or disapproving perspective) about the incompatibility of British left goals and the nature of Bruxellian Europe. Indeed, the currents of conventional wisdom run strongly in the other direction: Europe, it is said, is inherently social democratic and structurally hostile to laissez-faire Conservatism. Only the old moderate Tories – Edward Heath, Michael Heseltine, Kenneth Clarke – continue to find European integration an enticing prospect. The British left, meanwhile, slaps its thighs and guffaws at the primitive attitude it once took to what is a mighty engine of progress and social justice.

It is quite true – with the honourable exceptions quoted above and some others – that the left's aversion to Europe had shallow roots. Outside leftists disliked it because it looked a bit like NATO without the North Americans; traditionalists disliked it because it was run by foreigners (one Labour MP referred to German Chancellor Helmut Schmidt as a 'Hun' when he urged the movement to support Community membership); the trade unions feared a loss of muscle – outside Iceland (not a Community member) no organized-labour bodies in Europe wielded the punch of Britain's unions; inside leftists such as Barbara Castle opposed it (in part) because they suspected (correctly, according to John Stevens) that it represented 'east of Suez' (a quasi-imperial role) by other means; some opposed it for no better reason than that it was a cause dear to the hearts of Labour's social-democratic wing (so dear, in fact, that the strongest-hitting social democrats felt obliged in 1981 to form their own party, in part to protect Britain's continuing membership). It is true also that Conservative doubts about further integration have grown considerably during the last decade, to the point where the party has at times seemed likely to split asunder. But before anyone swallows completely the idea that the two great parties of the state have, with the end of the Cold War, exchanged positions on Europe, here are some basic facts:

- Right-wing Euroscepticism, as a quasi-movement, did not exist prior to the British left's adoption of free-market policies in the period after the 1987 election. As long as genuinely radical, anti-capital, anti-big-business policies remained a real danger, the right gave its full support to major development in the Community. Margaret Thatcher spoke in front of a European flag at party conferences, free-marketeer Lord Cockfield was sent to Brussels where he set about smashing all national barriers to trade. Her appointee at the Department of Trade and Industry, Lord Young, was an enthusiastic propagandist for '1992', the single market. Only when the domestic left-wing 'threat' receded did the British mainstream centre-right experience any doubts about 'ever-closer union'. The sordid fact is that the minimal social package that had always been mandated by Brussels (social action plans and other 'earnest piffle' have a much longer history than the British right would have us believe) gradually came to seem not the liberation from tooth-and-claw socialism it had once appeared but as a price that no longer had to be paid now the prospect of a 'hard left' government had retreated.
- Not one front-rank Conservative 'Eurosceptic' advocates a radical revision of Britain's relationship with the Union. John Redwood, the 1995 leadership challenger to John Major, was swift to rule out such a move. Current leader William Hague is similarly Euro-complaisant. Michael Portillo (seeking a return to Parliament at the time of writing) supports British membership of the Union.
- Conservative policy towards the Union is conditioned by the belief that Union institutions remain mired in the sort of wet, 'consensus' policies that dominated the Tory Party prior to 1975. So-called Euroscepticism ebbs and flows with Britain's success or otherwise in 'dragging Brussels into the real world'.
- Genuine Eurosceptics have, from Enoch Powell to (the converted) Norman Lamont, suffered career ruin for their beliefs. The British right is an unfriendly home for those opposed to integration into the Union.

None of this is coincidence or historical accident, any more than the Union's role as the political wing of European capital is simply a ghastly mistake that can be cleared up with bags of goodwill and a positive attitude. Europe is modelled on and operates as the boardroom of a multinational corporate concern. Its appeal to the British right, from the 1950s onwards, lay in its ability to lift out of the domestic democratic arena key issues – freedom of capital, control of labour, laissez-faire competition – upon which the right feared it was likely to lose the domestic vote. The right's Europhilia has cooled as its domestic vote-winning record on these issues strengthened during the 1980s and 1990s.

Sad to say, its appeal to the British left has followed a similar trajectory, in that the appeal of realizing at least part of the left's social agenda in behind-closed-doors deals grew strongly as the likelihood of gaining a domestic mandate for that agenda waned.

But this symmetry is misleading. If the negative implications of Union integration for the left and right are weighed against each other, the scales fall heavily to the left-hand side. Freedom of capital movement, low inflation, strict controls on public spending and borrowing, tough competition rules – these are the foundation stones of the Union. 'Social Europe', on the other hand, is, if not expendable, then certainly negotiable (the process of negotiating away social protection may well have begun with the Commission's white paper on growth, competitiveness and employment of 1993). Not only are 'backroom deals' on leftist objectives likely to be struck at the lowest common denominator, they are likely to be the first to be negotiated away at the behest of 'Europe Inc.'. In contrast to the laborious process of building a democratic consensus behind economic and social progress within a politically homogenous democracy, the trouble with making deals, Europe-style, is that, as with a card game, you are only as good as your last deal.

INTO THE MADHOUSE: EMU AND AFTER

Explaining his objections to a single currency, the former UK Chancellor of the Exchequer, Nigel Lawson said: 'I don't want us to join because it's, at best, premature and, at worst, extremely damaging. It is likely to be damaging while the peoples of Europe are not in favour of submerging their autonomy, sovereignty and loyalty into a wider European loyalty. To do it prematurely would be to strain the political fabric and give full rein to xenophobes and demagogues in every country in Europe.'[13] Lawson's basic argument was that monetary union was bad politics because it was bad economics. As someone who had a starring role in the Conservative Party's Twilight of the Gods in the decade between 1987 and 1997 he was well placed to speak out. Lawson's futile attempts to shadow the German mark in 1987 and 1988 lay behind the unsustainable boom of 1988 and the deep recession that inevitably followed. Shadowing the mark was bad economics; it brought the eventual downfall of first Lawson and then his mistress. Joining the ERM was even worse economics; it opened the trapdoor beneath first Neil Kinnock and, eventually, John Major. EMU is the economics of the madhouse; its political victims have yet to be named. But assuredly there will be some.

As Lawson put it when giving evidence to the House of Commons Treasury Committee: 'The main disadvantage of a single monetary policy is that the larger, more varied and disparate the union, the less likely it is that the monetary policy will be appropriate for all parts of the union at all times.'[14] Such objections were being brushed aside in 1997 as Brussels geared up for the single currency on 1 January 1999. Significantly, however, supporters were far less apt to point out the economic benefits of signing up than to deliver Cassandra-like warnings about the fragmentation of Europe should monetary union not go ahead. There was good reason for this; the economic benefits were largely illusory and almost certain to be outweighed by the costs. In the 1960s, when the two Harolds were rebuffed by Charles de Gaulle in their attempts to join the Common Market, there was a sound economic case for joining. The six founder members – Germany, France, Italy, Belgium, the Netherlands and Luxembourg – enjoyed faster growth, lower unemployment, bigger productivity rises and more rapid increases in living standards. The British policy-making Establishment – shuffling from fad to fad – cast envious eyes across the Channel where the Common Market seemed to offer the answer to all the UK's problems.

In 1973, the year not only of Britain's eventual entry into the European Economic Community but, coincidentally, also the last year of the Golden Age, there were 3,712,000 people unemployed in the countries that now make up the European Union. By the end of 1996, that total was exceeded in just one country, Germany, where unemployment was at levels not seen since the years before Hitler came to power. Whereas Europe's jobless rate in 1973 was half that of the United States, as monetary union loomed the eighteen million people on the dole meant that it was now twice as high.

There were high hopes in Brussels that the single currency would provide the miracle cure for this endemic problem. But such hopes were groundless. The EMU stool had three legs: the 'big is beautiful' concept of the 1960s, the worship of Germany from the 1970s and the anti-inflation obsession of the 1980s. All three looked a bit wobbly by the late 1990s, as small countries showed that, in economics at least, size does not matter, as Germany started to export jobs abroad by the tens of thousands, and as the global economy was haunted by the spectre of 1930s-style deflation.

Big business, of course, saw it differently. From the boardrooms of the multinationals, the single currency looked like a good idea. The stated reason was that only monetary union could unlock the treasures of the Single Market, by reducing transaction costs and removing foreign currency exposure. The real, unstated reason, was that monetary union offered a way of offloading risk from the firm to the worker. In the Age of Insecurity, this seemed only right and proper, not just to industrialists but to politicians, who were only too happy to give up one of the main instruments of economic policy.

As Britain found in 1992, the exchange rate is a powerful weapon. If a country loses competitiveness, a lower exchange rate is one way of restoring balance to the economy. Take away the currency weapon, and the options narrow down to three. First, workers in one part of the economy where productivity and growth are low can move to areas where they are high. This happens in the United States, but it beggars belief that there will be mass migrations of workers across the European Union, where there are considerable cultural and linguistic barriers to mobility. In an increasingly service-sector-dominated economy, it is not feasible for a bank clerk in Manchester to move to Madrid, unless he or she is a fluent Spanish speaker. On the last count, not many were.

An alternative mechanism might be a system of fiscal transfers, which would move resources from one part of the union to another. Again, this happens in the USA, where taxes in booming areas are recycled as benefits in other states. But for Brussels to fulfil the same role it would have to increase its budget tenfold, and the rich countries would have to be willing to bale out the weaker and poorer nations. Given that the West Germans grew increasingly unhappy at the higher taxes levied to pay for the reconstruction of East Germany, this looks improbable. When it is clear that neither migration nor fiscal transfers are viable, business will call up the third option – increased labour market flexibility to take the place of exchange rate flexibility. In short, workers will have to take cuts in wages if they want to keep their jobs.

Supporters of monetary union have, predictably, been dismissive of the new Euro-zone being beset by these sorts of problems. They have argued that the convergence criteria laid down at Maastricht mean that a one-size-fits-all approach to setting interest rates will succeed in bringing the countries of Europe close together. Britain, of course, has already had plenty of experience of a one-size-fits-all policy; it was called the Exchange Rate Mechanism. The one good thing about the ERM was that at least there was an escape route. But EMU is a construction without fire exits, a strange anomaly for Brussels, which is normally so assiduous in ensuring health and safety regulations are met to the letter.

Yet memories, it seems, are short. The Blair government signalled its intention in October 1997 to join monetary union some time early in the next century, provided five economic tests had been met. Few had any doubts that, when it came to it, Labour would say that the five tests had been met (or were on the way to being met).

OPENING THE SCEAN GATE: THE LEFT EMBRACES THE ENEMY

Whenever the dinner-partying classes congregate, the time will come during the evening when someone, upon hearing some piece of political or diplomatic activity of which he disapproves, will shake his head and utter the all-purpose cliché: 'The march of folly.' Since 1984, when American historian Barbara Tuchman published her eponymous survey of policies pursued ('from Troy to Vietnam') contrary to the self-interest of the pursuers, her original finely drawn concept of 'folly' has been so corrupted and diluted as to be applied to any action in the public world – from the poll tax to Hitler's invasion of Russia – that failed to achieve the desired results.[15] In the process, the original insight is lost. Before it is too late, let's remind ourselves of

Barbara Tuchman's criteria for 'folly'. One: it must have been criticized as counterproductive at the time, not merely in hindsight. Two: rogue decisions by individual rulers do not qualify. Three: a worked-out alternative must have been available.

The British left's Euro-affaire qualifies on all three counts. Considerable numbers within the Labour Party continue to fight the Bruxellian drift (point 1), yet the ruling group presses ahead, oblivious (point 2). As for point (3), the viable alternative, we turn again to Podmore and Katz: 'We want genuine internationalism between sovereign nations, trading and treating with each other on the basis of mutual respect for each other's territorial and political integrity.'[16]

At the heart of the left's approach to Europe is an imagined (not to say hallucinated) bargain: all the traditional tools of economic and social progress — indeed, the chief instrument of that progress, the nation-state — are to be exchanged for a share in an enterprise that may (it is hoped) choose to pursue such progress on a continental scale. But at the heart of this bargain is a fundamental error, the error of believing that the Union has, to date, acted on behalf of the forces opposed to social progress simply because the wrong people have been in charge. The Union is not, as the Labour leadership seems to believe, experiencing some sort of malfunction: the eighteen million unemployed and wave of takeovers and mergers represent the way it is supposed to work, as do the surveillance computers, the identity card proposals and the plans for Europol.

The left's new 'positive' approach to Europe is reminiscent of nothing so much as the behaviour of the board of a small but efficient friendly society experiencing a chronic loss of nerve in the face of a barrage of propaganda about 'market share' and 'undercapitalization'. Their faith in their enterprise destroyed, they seek merger with a giant insurance company, allowing themselves to be reassured that, deep down, it shares their values and that the 'unique ethos' of the friendly society will survive the takeover. But it will not. Friendly societies — actual or metaphorical — need strong roots, a cohesive membership and a leadership motivated by ideals greater than the pursuit of money and power. Euro-unionism is not so much a blind alley for the British left as a roaring furnace masquerading as a cosy log fire. In its searing heat nothing can survive but the 24-carat gold of international capital.

CHAPTER SIX

NO HIGHWAY: THE LEFT'S MYSTERY TOUR DOWN TWO BLIND ALLEYS

The Andorra of this play has nothing to do with the real small state of
this name, nor does it stand for another real small state;
Andorra is a model.
Max Frisch, notes to *Andorra*, Eyre Methuen edition, 1964

I was beginning to feel perceptive and understanding.
That was the point at which I should have packed my bags and
gone home.
Eric Ambler, *Judgment on Deltchev*, Hodder & Stoughton, 1951

'Ask me a riddle and I reply:
'*Cottleston, Cottleston, Cottleston Pie*'
A. A. Milne, *The Songs of Winnie-the-Pooh*, Dutton edition, 1994

Two of the many items that greeted British newspaper readers on the morning of Tuesday, 2 December 1997 were of particular social significance. The
first announced the appointment of Lord Jenkins of Hillhead as chairman of
a commission set up to suggest systems of proportional voting to replace
Britain's one-person one-vote tradition. Prime Minister Tony Blair was
reported still be to unconvinced of the need to alter the country's voting
method, but by appointing Lord Jenkins – former deputy leader of the
Labour Party, former leader of the short-lived Social Democratic Party and
a long-standing enthusiast for electoral reform – he seemed to be suggesting
he was less unconvinced than had been thought.

The second concerned the expulsion from a state school in Derby of two pupils who had refused to wear safety helmets on the bicycle ride to and from school. The wearing of such helmets was not a legal requirement, but the headmistress was claiming a locus standi on the ground that the boys' bicycles were parked at the school. Non-helmet wearers able to park their bicycles with friendly residents nearby escaped the headmistress's strictures. These expulsions came at a time of mounting official concern at the increase in the numbers of pupils excluded from school.

What connects a political grandee like Lord Jenkins with a pupil–teacher spat at an up-country school few people had ever heard of? Simply this: each of the two items dealt with one of the two main areas of activity for the modern British left, constitutional reform and social authoritarianism. Each, we shall argue, is fraught with danger for the left and represents a displacement activity that will ultimately damage the left-wing cause. But first we need to see how the left became attracted to such activity in the first place.

WE CAN'T BE HEROES: THE FALL OF THE WALL AND THE LEFTIST PERSONALITY CRISIS

Conventional wisdom has it that the earthquake in the east that brought down the Communist bloc in 1989 delivered a massive aftershock to the social-democratic parties of the West and that the resultant crisis of confidence forced top-to-bottom rethinking of social-democratic priorities, rethinking that has begun to bear fruit with the left-wing victories in Italy and the United Kingdom and the 1992 and 1996 election triumphs of President Bill Clinton. To the fair-minded observer, such a crisis of confidence may seem a strange burden for the constitutional, Western left to have had to bear. Were not key social-democratic post-war figures at least as steadfast in their opposition to Soviet Communism as their conservative opponents? Obvious examples include John Kennedy, with his 'missile gap' (1960), the Bay of Pigs invasion (1961) and the nuclear showdown over Cuba (1962), Lyndon Johnson and his escalation of the war in south-east Asia (1964–68), Harold Wilson and the 'Chevaline' programme to modernize (at great expense) the Polaris rocket force (1974), Helmut Schmidt (cruise missiles,

1977–83), James Callaghan (cruise and the neutron bomb, 1976–79), François Mitterrand (who presided serenely over a huge nuclear-test programme in the Pacific and made a point of inspecting the 'Jupiter' control room from which the *force de frappe* would be launched).

Nevertheless, such a crisis was diagnosed in the aftermath of the disintegration of the Soviet empire, and the diagnosis was, to an extent, self-fulfilling. And there were some who felt the impact of Soviet collapse could have been greater still:

It is striking how little reaction there has been in social democratic circles and parties to the sudden and, as far as I know, barely predicted, collapse of European Communism and the Soviet Union. . . . Historically the split between revolutionaries and reformers represented the partition of a single stream. . . . More important . . . is to note the de facto degree of mutual dependence which existed between social democracy and Communism. On the one hand, social democracy could be perceived as reassuringly moderate – a sensible middle way. . . . On the other hand, Communism acted as a magnet, pulling the whole spectrum of politics to the Left.[1]

The post-Wall crisis deemed to be facing Western social democracy was said to spring from three basic root causes:

- Given the collapse of Communism was at least as much an economic as a military (in Cold War terms) defeat, it was seen as proof positive that – contrary to social-democratic thinking – there were no 'good bits' in the Marxist-Communist programme that could be combined with Western liberalism to deliver 'the best of both worlds'. It was not so much that the Communist bathwater was taking the social-democratic baby down the plughole with it, rather that the emptying tub disclosed the fact that (contrary to social-democratic assertions) there never had been a baby at all, simply more bathwater.
- Linked to this was the blocking-off of alternatives for the previously feared combination of have-nots and disaffected intellectuals in Western societies. With Communism, so mesmerically attractive to generations of shopfloor agitators and university professors, now not only out for the count but pronounced dead by the ringside doctor, these groups had nowhere else to go. Thus the policing function of social-democratic parties with regard to their traditional client base was redundant: who needed to tempt Communism-prone social

groups with a 'third way' when there was no longer any second way? As recently as 1980, Christopher Booker wrote: '[A] year or two ago, when I was watching a Robert Kee TV film about life in East Germany, showing a society with full employment, no inflation, no taxes and cheap subsidised housing for all, I could not help reflecting that the picture Kee presented would probably now strike most people in this country as rather enviable.'[2] Now if it did or not it no longer mattered: there was no GDR, hence no 'actually existing' socialist lifestyle. There was, quite literally, no alternative.

- Of more concern to continental than British social democrats was a third root cause for the crisis, linked to the first and second. This centred on foreign affairs and the belief that social-democratic parties, while doubtless staunch on defence issues, had a special calming touch in negotiating with the lumbering nuclear-armed beast to the East. Free of the dogmatic anti-Communism of conservative parties, it was thought, the constitutional left could approach defence, detente and arms control with a reassuringly dull technocratic air, epitomized by a booklet published by the former British Foreign Secretary and leading light in the Social Democratic Party, David Owen. Its title mimicked that of a disarmament publication *Protest and Survive*, itself mimicking the British government's civil defence leaflet *Protect and Survive*. In true social-democratic style, Dr (now Lord) Owen rejected both positions: *Negotiate and Survive*.[3] This asset shone (if dullness can be said to shine) all the more brightly during the second Cold War, when a generation of moderate non-ideological conservatives (Richard Nixon, Edward Heath, Valéry Giscard d'Estaing) was replaced by a generation of crusaders, principally Ronald Reagan and Margaret Thatcher. But the Cold War was resolved on terms other than the social democrats': 'If there was going to be a single German state . . . it certainly wasn't going to be the sort of greater Federal Republic that Adenauer . . . had demanded, but a joint enterprise in which West Germany became less capitalist and East Germany less communist . . . [but] a stopped clock is correct twice a day. History rolled round to vindicate both Adenauer and Kohl, while the tormented theories of Social Democracy now seem but the fossils of extinct ideas.'[4] It was not simply that the social-democratic analysis of the Cold War – centred on 'easing tensions' and 'removing misunderstandings' – had been proved wrong. Rather, the utility factor of having social democrats in the foreign affairs arena had simply ceased to operate.

These, then, were said to be the main elements of the crisis confronting the centre-left at the dawn of the 1990s: a lack of both ideals and, at home or abroad, usefulness. But, in the conventional version, the story has a happy ending. Soul-searching, thinking the unthinkable, modernization and generally eating humble pie have all added up (in best business practice) to a restructuring of the centre-left. Out of the turmoil of the late 1980s, it has (in line with modern counselling advice) reinvented itself. The rejected spouse, distraught after the disappearance of a life-long other half, has – after a spell of moroseness followed by an energetic bout of personal reorientation – settled down with a far more suitable, steady partner: the 'social market', effectively the free market ameliorated both by admonitory measures to reintegrate the underclass into the economic mainstream and by assorted constitutional and institutional reform.

The truth, we believe, is a little more prosaic. Far from 'reinventing itself' after years in deep therapy, the British left had moved on to its new agenda some time before the first hammer smashed into the concrete of the Berlin Wall. The supposedly distraught spouse was already shacked up with a new lover by the time the old one moved on. Or, to vary the metaphor, the left, demoralized by a string of failures with regard to the cliff face of poverty, unemployment and economic reform, took up the less demanding hobby of fell-walking, striding the undulating moorlands of constitution-mongering and politically correct exhortation. It was never going to be easy to tilt the economic mechanism back in favour of working people and the poor. How much easier to hallucinate a big non-problem into existence and then offer to solve it. By the late 1980s the 'problem' in question had a simple name: Britain. The central article of the left's new faith was that it was the country, not the free-market economy, that was the cause of our discontent. Specifically, the nature of the British social and political structure was at the root of all that was rotten in the state. By their fruits shall ye know them: as a thorn tree cannot bring forth good fruit, neither could the decayed British system bring forth sound economic performance and social stability. Finance and business were, in this analysis, innocent, in the true sense of the word. As neutral forces, they flowed in whichever direction was mandated by the social and political mechanism.

We ought to declare at once that this analysis, insofar as it enthrones cultural above economic forces, chimes with our own. Any viewpoint that implicitly rejects the concept of politics and culture as mere byproducts of the economic system cannot be entirely flawed. The issue is not whether the revisionists started in the right place, but whether they then proceeded in the right direction.

From this central concept of rottenness in the state, two distinct schools of thought emerged. Broadly speaking, the first held British institutions responsible for the national malaise, the second pinned the blame on British people. These schools of thought produced the two main strands of centre-left thinking in the 1990s: the first urges institutional reform, the second social authoritarianism. The first demands wholesale demolition of existing political and civil structures, including Parliament, the courts, local government and company law, and their replacement with 'modernized' versions that are simultaneously 'rational' and geared to the generation of outcomes favoured by the left. The second demands the elimination of many established behaviour patterns and 'attitudes', whether public drinking, drug taking, failing to wash hands before eating, failure to wear rear seat-belts, smoking on trains or aeroplanes or anything else deemed detrimental to social hygiene.

These are parallel strands of thought but they are in no way mutually exclusive. On the contrary, the re-engineering of the political structure and the re-education of the public can be mutually reinforcing. The restructured political system will be able to provide legislative support for the remoulding of social behaviour and a re-educated public will provide a favourable climate of opinion for institutional reform. We now examine both these strands in turn.

'OFF WITH HIS HEAD': CONSTITUTIONAL REFORM AND OTHER DISPLACEMENT ACTIVITIES

The year 1988 was rotten for the left in Britain, coming after a number of rotten years and seeming likely to precede at least an equal number stretching into the future. Convinced the economic miracle had finally arrived, Britons embarked on a giddy spree of getting and spending, helped along by hefty tax cuts in Chancellor Nigel Lawson's spring budget. House prices soared 40 per cent, unemployment tumbled and industry, facing the first labour shortage since the early 1970s, contemplated such radical moves as the presentation of a friendlier face to female and ethnic-minority workers.

The Labour Party, dragged along in the wake of this roaring boom, was reduced to intermittent suggestions that interest rates ought, at any one time, to be one point lower than they were. Meanwhile, the other left, the breakaway Social Democratic Party that had carried the hopes of an entire generation of 'centrist' Labourites, was passing into history. Its 1981 launch had proved the day that had dawned too brightly; reeling from two disappointing general election performances, it was, by 1988, passing under the maternal wing of its erstwhile junior electoral partner, the Liberal Party.

But something was stirring in the undergrowth. On 30 November 1988, the *Guardian* reported the launch the previous day of a new political movement: 'the Charter 88 constitutional reform campaign is only the latest episode in a contemporary reawakening of British interest in civil liberties and in new forms of government.' The name consciously echoed the Charter 77 movement, set up eleven years previously to fight for civil rights in Communist Czechoslovakia. Some may have thought it bad taste to compare any political grouping in Britain with the brave individuals who made up Charter 77 and who, in the early months of 1989, were to face show trials, police beatings and jail terms. But such samples did not trouble those connected with Charter 88 itself, whose entire raison d'être seemed to be the belief that Britain itself was some sort of police state. At its launch, the organization claimed: 'The intensification of authoritarian rule in the United Kingdom has only recently begun.' The visitor from outer space, supplied with Charter 88's version of events, would have had no idea that the country had held a hard-fought general election the previous year or that it was generally considered one of the least repressive political regimes anywhere in the world with a proud history of practical, evolutionary democratic government. The 'authoritarian' tag, of course, was extremely useful, allowing as it did Charter 88 to reject accusations that it was making any direct comparison between the United Kingdom and the totalitarian regimes still extant in eastern Europe or ranking its own personnel alongside the heroes and heroines of Charter 77. At the same time, it allowed Charter 88 to pose as more than a study group urging modest but important improvements to what was already a sturdy and much-admired democratic constitution. Put bluntly, this stance allowed Charter 88 to bask in the seedy glamour of other people's misery and to play the part of some kind of resistance movement while its members ran absolutely no personal risks whatsoever.

This pseudo-underground chic was a feature of other organizations launched at the same time, including the much ridiculed 'June 20 Group', not an armed guerrilla band but a discussion circle founded in 1988, meeting at the Kensington home of playwright Harold Pinter and including writers John Mortimer, Margaret Drabble and Ian McEwan. Again in 1988, a magazine appeared called *Samizdat*, aiming to 'demolish the myth of a pro-Tory consensus and draw together the threads of the consensus that actually exists'. The title reinforced the impression that left-inclined intellectuals had retreated into some sort of collective dream world in which they were daily at risk of arrest or torture at the hands of the hated Tory junta (had they been so, they would doubtless have been delighted to discover a range of controls on police interview techniques, including mandatory tape-recording and the explicit right to legal representation, all thanks to the same junta's Police and Criminal Evidence Act of four years earlier).

But if they had so retreated, they kept their fantasies to themselves. What was striking about this booming 'constitutional reform' industry was the care taken – as in the Charter 88 example above – never explicitly to question Britain's status as a founder member of the family of free nations, but rather to suggest that this priceless heritage was somehow endangered by years of 'one-party rule' (a reverse euphemism for the electorate's regrettable tendency during the previous decade to return Conservative governments). In this way, Charter 88 and friends were clearly marked out from Tony Benn (in Britain) and Gore Vidal (in America), two very different men who nonetheless believed their respective nations were not really democracies at all. Tony Benn had argued for some time that Britain was, in fact, a sort of delegated monarchy, in which the prime minister exercised Crown powers. Gore Vidal alleged his home country had long ceased to function as a federal democracy and had mutated into a Caesarian dictatorship, the 'United State'.

Such interesting (in both the correct and the pejorative senses) ideas had no place in the literature of the constitutional reform industry. Messrs Benn and Vidal stated bluntly that A was really B and, in doing so, exposed themselves to the fierce heat of criticism and debate. The reform industry preferred instead to play mood music (as in the Charter 88 title), hinting that, whereas there were no direct comparisons, when you thought about it, lots of things about A were beginning to look rather too much like B for comfort. This nudge-nudge intellectual dishonesty was and remains a deep flaw in the very foundations of the constitutional reform movement. A kind interpretation would suggest this goes a long way to explaining the marshmallow intellectual substructure holding up (or failing to do so) the case for a bonfire of the institutions. A less kind interpretation would suggest the reform industry was one part of a wider attempt to rewire the political process in such a way that the neanderthal electorate could be largely by-passed. Key to this project was the replacement of a disputatious, partisan Parliament with a sort of National Synod of the great and the good, composed in part of regional assembly members and 'senators' either elected by constituencies so vast as to be meaningless or drawn from party lists. This project had made great strides even by 1997, under the existing system; Parliament's role as the 'High Court' had been largely hived off to the Nolan Commission and its spin-offs while the Prime Minister halved the number of his weekly appearances before MPs. The election of that year was notable for the number of television and radio studio and 'phone-in' programmes advertising themselves as the public's chance 'to have your say', a puzzling concept to those electors who had imagined their chance to have their say would come on polling day. The drive to reshape British democracy into a managerial consensus was at times uncannily reminiscent of the 'guided democracies' that sprouted in the Third World in the 1960s and 1970s in nations whose ruling elites had decided the 'Westminster model' was 'inappropriate'.

Enthusiasm for constitutional reform gripped the left in inverse proportion to the waning enthusiasm for economic reform. The 1983 manifesto had committed the party to full employment; the 1987 manifesto pledged sufficient reductions in the dole queue as to amount to the same thing. By 1989–90, the pledge had disappeared, to be replaced by a watery substitute: 'training and investment'. By contrast, the 1983 manifesto had been largely silent on the subject of constitutional reform, beyond a commitment to abolition of the House of Lords, an atavistic move driven far more by class conflict than by any burning desire to rewrite the constitution. Ten years later, the party was committed to Welsh and Scottish home rule, regional governments in England (if desired), an elected mayor for London (the first such directly elected public official), a referendum on electoral reform and staged restructuring of the House of Lords.

On one level, constitutional reform had evolved into the left's 'big idea', the counterweight to the Conservatives' free-market system. This system had been largely accepted as a given on the official left by 1997, so political energies needed a new outlet. But beyond this, institutional restructuring had, by the mid-1990s, begun to assume the pretensions of a grand unifying theory. Its most influential proponent, Will Hutton, now editor of the *Observer* newspaper, was able to join the dots marking just about every crisis and difficulty facing Britain in the 1990s and paint a picture of advanced institutional decay. The City, the 'winner-takes-all' electoral system, the public schools, the antique constitution and the 'Anglo-Saxon' structure of company law, all combined to create an unstable socio-economic environment obsessed with short-term returns (whether company dividends or election wins) at the expense of both sound economic growth and an organically sound society.

Even Britain's high divorce rates, it seemed, reflected the 'spot-market' mentality engendered by the system.[5] The country's highest-profile divorce, that of the Prince and Princess of Wales, was cited as evidence of the disintegration of the political system ('his [the Prince of Wales's] own difficulties start to magnify those of the state', Mr Hutton wrote in the *Guardian*, on 22 November 1995). And the emergency in Northern Ireland illuminated what was merely a lurid example of the nation's general political malaise ('This is the land of direct rule by executive agency, unsanctioned by popular vote', *Guardian*, 27 July 1992).

Mr Hutton was not always hostile to 'direct rule by executive agency'; he demanded just that with regard to independence for the Bank of England. But the great tidal bore of his advocacy tended to blur the confusions in his case, and, by extension, those of the reform case in general. When he discussed 'gentleman capitalism' was he lamenting its absence in the barbaric Anglo-Saxon 'spot market' or condemning its presence? Was he really blaming the liquidity of City markets for high rates of return (all evidence suggests returns drop as liquidity rises)? And was Britain really a 'quasi-feudal' society in any sense in which the word 'feudal' retained any meaning other than the symbolic?[6]

If Will Hutton concentrated his fire on the centre of things, other reformers found their inspiration in the regions. Throughout the reform industry, a central belief was that local government – despite plentiful evidence of corruption, jobbery and incompetence – was a good thing in itself and that nothing so disgraced the years of Conservative rule as the clamps it had placed on this splendid institution. Anthony Howard said of Mrs Thatcher 'one of . . . [her] memorials is virtually to have destroyed the power of local government in this country'.[7]

First came rate capping, later the poll tax and, midway between, the abolition of the metropolitan counties and the Greater London Council. This last was seen as an outrage and a display of megalomania of scandalous proportions. The truth was a little more prosaic. The six metropolitan counties had, in fact, very little work to do and owed their creation in 1972 more to the tidy-mindedness of a (Conservative) government dedicated to a two-tier municipal system than to any pressing need. In contrast to the shire counties, where the split between county and district responsibilities was reasonably even and logical, the boroughs and cities in the 'metro' authorities performed most important jobs, leaving the county councils with largely empty 'strategic' roles. The 1974–79 Labour government had itself considered returning full county-borough status to certain cities, but decided against another upheaval. In any case, the Tory government did not 'abolish' the metropolitan counties (which remain to this day), it merely abolished their county councils.

The GLC was a slightly different case, having been created in the mid-1960s, but even here most of its powers carried qualifiers such as 'reserve' or 'strategic', and it was difficult to see how it managed to keep 22,000 staff usefully occupied. None of this cut much ice with the reformers. Both Andrew Marr[8] and Simon Jenkins[9] tore into the over-centralized, 'nationalized' (in Mr Jenkins's phrase) British state and called for the reassertion of popular sovereignty from the bottom up.

These distinguished writers and their imitators deserve a vote of thanks. Not only has the gusto with which they approached their task contributed greatly to the gaiety of the nation, but they have kindled an interest in political economy among millions of people who would otherwise have been inclined to give the subject a wide berth. In such circumstances, it seems ill-mannered to venture that their proposals, in common with the helpful suggestions of the entire constitutional reform industry, are of almost heroic irrelevance to Britain's real problems. But, as Clive James once wrote of one academic's convoluted work on literary criticism, 'He is a very patient guide, but in the long run it is usually not wise to thank someone for offering to clarify an obfuscation which he is in fact helping to create.'[10] Similarly, we ought not to be too effusive in our gratitude for the efforts of the constitutional reformers: the terrible disease for which they offer cures exists only in their own imagination.

Even were their central contention to be correct – that, post-1989, the United Kingdom was the one remaining 'pre-democratic' state in Europe – it would be extremely doubtful whether this had any meaningful impact upon the national economy's ability to function in such a way as to guarantee choice, opportunity and social tranquillity. One of the fastest-growing economies – if not the fastest-growing economy – of the 1990s was Malaysia, a nation ruled by a rotating monarchy of regional sultans and governed by a party with a robust, pre-democratic (non-democratic, actually) attitude to political opposition. In 1997, the growth spotlight shifted from Malaysia to Latin America, a region not renowned for its rational political culture.

But is this contention correct? In summary, the charge is that Britain is not a democracy but a 'semi-feudal state' (Hutton, the *Guardian* of 21 January 1995). This semi-feudalism (or outright feudalism; Mr Hutton drops the qualifier in some of his writings) expresses itself, politically, in the centralized nature of political authority, vested in ministers wielding Crown powers. The packaging around this central fact serves to underline it: the unelected upper house, the established Church, the bewigged judges and, of course, the monarchy. And from this central fact flow baleful consequences: the arrogant, error-prone executive, the miscarriages of justice, the company law that exalts ownership over partnership, the preservation into the age of biotechnology and computers of Britain's hateful, hidebound class system. Cause and effect: a decaying yet viciously defensive constitutional settlement equals an organically unsound, unstable socio-economic environment.

Happily, there is an alternative: the modernized, rational European state, with its written constitution, booming economy, irreverent, energetic young people, generous subsidies to the arts and culture, superb public transport system and heartfelt commitment to human rights. The exact location of this magic kingdom has shifted considerably since the late 1980s: Spain enjoyed its moment in the sun as the 'California of Europe', hosting the 1992 Barcelona Olympics and Expo 92 in Seville. But corruption scandals and financial problems shifted the halo elsewhere. Germany was a paragon for many years, with its super-productive workers beavering away in 'stake-holder' enterprises, but unemployment touching five million in 1997 tarnished the image even in the eyes of fervent admirers. Least probably of all, François Mitterrand's France, with its huge public-works projects and ultra-fast express trains, enjoyed a period of approbation nearly equal to that of Germany until a black wall of evidence mounted suggesting the 'Socialist' party had, in fact, presided over a state so centralized, corrupt and riddled with abuses of power as to make Britain under the Conservatives look like Sir Thomas More's Utopia. More recently, the Republic of Ireland has been the model held up for admiration, with its 'tiger' economy, pop musicians and film stars and compassionate woman presidents. We wish the Irish people joy of their new status and urge them to enjoy it while it lasts, because it never does.

In the end, it matters not which country embodies the reformers' alternative. As Brian Walden wrote in 1990, it is the idea itself that matters:

The lure of Europe is that it will confer on us greater material prosperity. The public has heard tales of extravagant social services, enormous pensions, long holidays, high wages plus vast subsidies given to every activity under the sun, and it wants to dip into this bran tub. . . . The word is getting around that the Europeans have stumbled upon a group of benevolent overlords, who treat their people like fighting cocks. In an atmosphere of indulgence and brotherly love the good life is given to everybody, regardless of merit. Not only are personal requirements abundantly met, but public services are indescribably superb. Europeans travel dirt cheap on fast trains, when they are not lolling on unpolluted beaches where they spend most of their time.[11]

More recent difficulties in continental Europe – recession, strikes, the deflationary effect of attempts to meet the Maastricht criteria for a single currency – have dented this cornucopian vision, but have done next to nothing to throw doubt on the original premise, that Europeans are happier, healthier and wiser than Britons because they enjoy enlightened, reformed political constitutions.

It is true that the British constitution is full of oddities and that, were we starting anew, much of it would never see the light of day. It would be a brave constitutional draftsman who would press the case for Black Rod or the Duchy of Lancaster, or who would inform colleagues of a splendid notion called 'the Queen's speech' that he had dreamed up in the bath. The point is not that these curlicues exist but whether, first, their effect is to exclude Britain from the Western democratic mainstream and, second, if it is, whether what the left considers social and economic malfunction can be traced to this fact.

How different is the British constitution from those of its neighbours? It is tempting simply to note that seven of the fifteen EU members are monarchies and leave it at that. But this is likely to leave the reformers unbowed. They are never happier than when contrasting our own supposedly fossilized, out-of-touch Royal family with the go-ahead, democratized crowned heads of Europe. So a deeper examination is needed.

Perhaps it ought to begin in France, home of the sort of 'rational' democratic government advocated by the constitutional reformers. The French constitution dates back only forty years, yet the fundamental charge against the British system – that no one today would invent it from scratch – can be levelled with equal force across the Channel. Heading the structure is an executive president who, in contrast to his circumscribed American equivalent, enjoys ill-defined but sweeping powers, in particular with regard to foreign policy, defence and European relations (the 'reserved domain'). Parliament, prime minister and cabinet are liable to dissolution and dismissal at presidential whim. The assumption behind the system seems to have been that the same party would control the presidency and the parliament; when this failed to happen in 1986, the doctrine of 'cohabitation' was effectively made up on the spot. To this extent, the French constitution is as 'unwritten' as the British. Not only is there little horizontal separation of powers, there is little vertical separation either. Mayors routinely serve concurrently as parliamentary deputies or even prime ministers; this co-mingling of municipal and national politics has proved fertile ground for corruption as planning permission and local contracts have been made conditional on 'parallel finance' contributions (effectively, bribes) to governing parties.

Nor, contrary to myth, is France a secular state, either de jure or de facto. The president of France is automatically an honorary canon of the church of

St John de Lateran in the Vatican, regardless of his personal beliefs. French mayors routinely supply rent-free property to the Catholic clergy and most French public holidays are Christian festivals. France grants knighthoods, as does Britain. French fondness for unelected 'quango'-type authorities at least equals Britain's. In fact, France and Britain share many of the same constitutional vices and virtues.

Will next-door Germany stand up better to criticism? Is this not an enlightened model of federalism and devolution, built on the ashes of a murderous dictatorship? Yes, and no. Germany's national government is in many ways a model of the parliamentary system, but the country's 'federal' nature can be over-emphasized. As John Laughland has noted, German federalism combines a large degree of administrative devolution – effectively large-scale local government – with legal uniformity.[12] No German state, he writes, has anything like the legal autonomy Scotland has enjoyed within the 'over-centralized' United Kingdom. Furthermore, Germany, in its way, is no more secular than Britain or France. The government docks 'Church tax', along with other taxes, from the salaries of registered Catholics and Protestants. This is more than merely a useful service allowing people to make voluntary religious donations. It is a powerful tool allowing churchmen to threaten excommunication on those who deregister.

As Bernard Connolly noted, European Commission president Jacques Delors seriously considered a proposal to dedicate the Community to the Virgin Mary.[13] This may have been a splendid idea, but that it was genuinely contemplated does little for claims of Europe's rationalism in contrast to the archaic United Kingdom.

Britain's House of Peers is, indeed, a relic of an earlier, undemocratic time. But the introduction of life peers (political nominees) and the almost certain removal or abdication of the voting rights of hereditary peers make it, in essence, far closer to some other European upper houses than is commonly supposed. The Irish Senate, for example, is composed of eleven prime ministerial nominees, six members elected by higher-education institutes and forty-three members elected by panels organized on a vocational basis. Italy has actually introduced 'life peers' since 1993 into what had been a wholly elected upper house; the eleven life senators are past presidents and prime ministers (an echo of the British practice). Belgium's upper house is a hotch-potch of co-opted, indirectly elected and directly elected members, the whole membership calibrated in a sort of benign version of apartheid to reflect the three main ethnic communities in the country.

But beyond this trading of anomaly for anomaly, oddity for oddity, is the fundamental fact that any political settlement is prone to anachronism. The more recent constitutions are at greater risk of this: nothing dates as quickly as last year's political fashions. Take the Italian constitution, written in 1947. Article 1: 'Italy is a democratic republic founded on labour.' Article 32: 'The Republic . . . grants medical assistance to the indigent free of charge.' Article 36: 'An employed person is entitled to wages . . . in any case sufficient to provide him and his family with a free and dignified existence.' Article 44: 'The law provides measures in favour of mountainous areas.' Article 48: 'To vote is a civic duty.' Most ominously, Article 139: 'The Republican structure is not subject to constitutional amendment.'

Whether one admires the post-war social-democratic ideals contained in some clauses or laughs at the idea of 'rights for mountains', it is hard to avoid the conclusion that this is a terrible muddle, judged by the 'rational' criteria of our own constitutional reformers. Seemingly random matters that ought at any time properly to be the subject of democratic law making are cast in stone, whereas many matters considered in our time essential human rights (the rights of sexual minorities, for example) are not mentioned at all. This does not mean that the Italian constitution merely needs a little updating. The point is that all constitutions bear the carbon-dating of the era in which they were written. Often, the phraseology is vague enough to mean little in changed circumstances: Italy's being 'founded on labour' probably falls into this category. But sometimes, as with the second amendment to the United States constitution ('A well-regulated militia, being necessary to the security of a free state, the right of the people to keep and bear arms, shall not be infringed'), the fashions of the day can have seriously deleterious results down the years. Lest anyone think the Italian constitution is an isolated example, let us take a brief look at the constitution of Spain. It dates from 1978 – and this shows. Article 129 (2) enshrines the encouragement of co-operatives; Article 130 (1) enshrines the modernization of the economy with special regard to 'agriculture, livestock raising, fishing and handicrafts, in order to bring the standard of living of all Spaniards up to the same level'. Article 131 (1) covers planning and economic harmonization.

Alongside assorted nostrums from the 1970s sit the articles covering the

Spanish monarchy: these are worthy of the constitutional reformers' darkest fantasies about 'feudal' Britain. The King is 'inviolable and shall not be held accountable'; the succession shall follow 'the regular order of primogeniture and representation'; the Crown Prince 'shall hold the title of Prince of Asturias'. Elsewhere Spaniards are guaranteed the 'right to honour', a phrase that would draw derision from reformers were it to appear anywhere in a British constitutional document but is apparently quite acceptable in 'modernized' Spain.

The Spanish example – with its devolved regional governments – was frequently cited as Britain braced itself for the first great constitutional reforms of the Blair government, Scottish Home Rule and Welsh devolution. An interesting aspect of the 'reform' debate was the highlighting of a difference of outlook between two strands of reformers: those who believed a reformed constitution would provide a means to centre-left ends, especially economic regeneration, and those who believed a reformed constitution was a centre-left end in itself. In the former camp was Robin Cook, later Labour's Foreign Secretary, who said at the party conference in Blackpool on 3 October 1994:

I strongly believe one of the reasons for the stunted, stagnant performance of the British economy is that Britain is the most centralized country in Europe. With the collapse of the command economies of Eastern Europe, we are the only country with a government that still believes all decisions are best taken in the capital city. But Labour believes local communities have a better idea than Whitehall about how to get their economies moving. Labour will put the tools of economic development in the hands of the local community, local business and the local workforce.

The idea that reform of the political constitution will trigger reformed relationships throughout society, with particular regard to economic relationships, can be extrapolated from this position. Again, Europe is the template: there, it is argued, consensual political structures based upon proportional representation and coalition governments have worked in parallel with consensual company law structures in which owners of equity are merely one group of 'stakeholders' among many. No wonder, say the reformers, that the British Conservatives fought to exclude the United Kingdom from Brussels initiatives such as works councils: true industrial democracy is as frightening to British traditionalists as true political democracy.

But does such neat symmetry really exist? The 'Rhineland' capitalist model may or may not be a a vast improvement on the 'Anglo-Saxon' system, but is its transplantation to Britain a legitimate goal for the left? In terms of job retention, the ability of European workers to fight redundancies – whether at Air France or in the German coal mines – would seem to rely far more heavily on 'adversarial' industrial relations of the British type than on 'co-partnership'. One of the biggest industrial closures of 1997, that of the Renault plant at Vilvoorde, was carried through with full regard to the 'co-decision' process; sacked car workers must have looked enviously at the 'Anglo-Saxon' antics of French public-sector workers, who were able, through strike campaigns, to force a series of climbdowns by the pre-1997 cost-cutting right-wing governments.

Beyond this is the fundamental question of whether employees are, in the normal order of things, 'partners' in the companies for which they work. This is not to resurrect far-left battle-cries against the co-option and corruption of the proletariat, but to ask a simple question about the nature of employment in a free society. In Britain as elsewhere, 'enlightened' bosses and unions have periodically sought to 'swap' pay rises for job guarantees, signing binding deals stretching into the future under which a wage ceiling is balanced by a commitment to retain employment levels. But such deals tend always to be undermined by the simple fact that, short of 'bonding' the workforce, there is nothing to stop individual workers from shifting to better-paid jobs outside the closed economy of the company, an action that inevitably exerts upward pressure on wage rates within the firm. At some point, the realization dawns that such well-meaning deals involve swapping the unswappable. And the reformers' case is based on a wholly false analogy: staff and management are not different political parties whose interests are served by working together in some sort of 'coalition'.

Furthermore, the evidence that such 'partnership' is a guarantor of long-term success is patchy. It is doubtless true that, were the world a fairer place, 'hire-and-fire' companies would eventually lose out to 'partnership' competitors. But there is no evidence that this is so: for every BMW there is a Ford, for every Braun an IBM. What is certain is that – on the Rhine, the Mersey or the Hudson – the best way to bring the bargaining power of employees and employers into some sort of balance is to run the economy at something approaching full tilt and allow collective and individual bargaining to operate freely.

Furthermore, the much-admired 'Rhenish' model displays a level of financial secrecy and lack of transparency that one may have thought would appal the reformers. Meaningful financial numbers are routinely hidden from view; secret cash reserves are used to smooth out profit patterns. The man in the boardroom knows best; shareholders and workers need not worry their heads over complex financial matters. In September 1993, the giant Daimler Benz group reported losses for the first half of the year of nearly one billion marks. More shocking than the deficit was the fact that it came to light only because Daimler was planning a Wall Street listing and thus had to expose its accounts to proper scrutiny: under Germany's 'Rhenish' rules, Daimler would have reported a profit of 168 million marks. No one would have been the wiser, certainly not the 'social partners', the trade unions.

Aside from all these objections, there is little hard evidence that 'co-partnership' and its financial equivalent – 'long-term' relationships between banks and companies – have any real connection with a nation's political constitution. Nowhere in the world have finance and industry worked together more closely than in Japan, which combines a first-past-the-post voting system with an imperial figurehead. By contrast, no voting system is more proportional than that of the Republic of Ireland, a nation with no tradition of industrial co-partnership or of bank–industry alliances. And, in reverse, there is no evidence that proportionally elected governments will, in the final analysis, stand by Rhineland capitalism. The 1994 General Agreement on Tariffs and Trade was quickly shown to be incompatible with the Rhenish model, an incompatibility that will probably lead to the victory of the former over the latter. France and Germany together could almost certainly have blocked Europe's collective signature of GATT, particularly if backed by other 'stakeholder' member-states, such as the Netherlands. In the event, Brussels signed GATT with only the minimum of fuss.

But not all supporters of constitutional reform look to a rejig of governmental institutions to presage a rejig of economic institutions. To some, the reform itself was a left-wing goal in need of no further justification beyond that it 'devolved power' and 'reversed the centralizing trend'. In the Scottish referendum campaign, Tony Blair identified himself with the second strand; home rule, he said in Glasgow on 8 September 1997, was about modernizing Britain's constitution and bringing power closer to the people. Earlier that year, his government had confirmed with equanimity that the Scottish

Parliament would be empowered, should it wish, to reinstate the death penalty, the clearest example of the view that decreed the act of bringing power closer to the people to be a desirable end in itself. And the shadow of the gallows brings us, rather neatly, to the second major strand of post-1989 left-wing thinking: social authoritarianism.

COMMAND AND CONTROL: NATIONALIZING THE BRITISH PUBLIC

An episode of the Granada TV series *Cracker* opens with the main character (Robbie Coltrane) sitting in the back of a black taxi. The interior of the passenger cabin is plastered with prohibitions: no smoking, please keep your feet off the seats, no food or drink to be consumed in this vehicle, no cheques or credit cards, do not distract the driver, and so forth. After an argument about Coltrane's smouldering cigarette, the driver sniffs the air and demands to know if Coltrane has broken wind. Why? demands Coltrane. Is that banned as well?

The scene will have struck a chord among people of all habits and persuasions. One had only to travel on London Transport in 1997 to verify the trend spotted by *Cracker's* scriptwriters. Admonitions, warnings and penalty announcements filled almost every available surface inside buses and Tube cars. Five years earlier, London Transport had actually produced a glossy brochure detailing all the activities banned on its property, vehicles and rolling stock, and distributed this must-read publication through ticket offices.

All this is of a piece with the development we examined earlier, that of the relaxation of state control over capital and the tightening of state control over individuals. In Britain, until 1997, this process had been associated almost exclusively with the Conservative government (we say 'almost', because Labour-controlled local authorities had made their own contribution to the control culture). Would the eviction of the Tories mark a reversal of this policy, or an intensification?

Once, the question would scarcely have needed asking. Past Labour administrations had presided over a marked withdrawal of the state from huge areas of private activity, a process that seemed almost to parallel the worldwide withdrawal of British forces from former colonies. Although it is a mistake to lump together all the changes of the 1960s as 'liberal reforms' (neither the abolition of capital punishment nor the legalization of abortion fits into this category: both represent, in their different ways, quantum changes in the conception of the 'good society'), it remains true that the state's flag was hauled down as fort after fort was abandoned: prior censorship of the theatre, homosexual activity between consenting adults, strict restraints in literature, the cinema and television. The age of majority was lowered to eighteen, simultaneously putting the Gretna Green marriage industry out of business and lifting the burden of *in loco parentis* from the shoulders of university staffs.

In the 1970s, James Callaghan and his deputy Michael Foot effectively shelved a plan to make the wearing of seat-belts compulsory, Callaghan on populist grounds, Foot on libertarian grounds. Nor did Labour ministers sanction such withdrawals only in cases concerning progressive middle-class desiderata. It is true that 'Ernie' and the legalization of off-course betting – two pieces of liberalization connected closely with working-class culture – were Conservative measures. But throughout Labour Cabinets of the time ran a strong streak of defence (not to say defensiveness) of the traditional pleasures of working people. In January 1971, the Fabian Society published a pamphlet *A Social-Democratic Britain* by that most middle-class of Labour bigwigs, Anthony Crosland:[14]

My working-class constituents have their own version of the environment, which is equally valid. . . . They want lower housing densities and better schools and hospitals; they want washing machines and refrigerators to relieve domestic drudgery; they want cars, and the freedom they give on weekends and holidays; and they want package-tour holidays to Majorca . . . eating fish and chips on previously-secluded beaches – why should they too not enjoy the sun? They want these things not . . . because their minds have been brain-washed and their tastes contrived by advertising, but because the things are desirable in themselves.

Twenty-odd years later, it seems unlikely that many of Labour's leading lights would regard these staples of working-class life as remotely 'desirable in themselves'. Those fish and chips, for example, would fail utterly to meet the latest 'healthy eating' guidelines, and all that sun could only increase the risk of skin cancer. Visiting Majorca may not necessarily be a bad thing, but only after visitors have read, marked, learned and inwardly digested assorted government leaflets on sensible drinking and the use of precautionary devices to prevent sexual infection, especially AIDS.

Two decades after Mr Crosland's untimely death in 1977, Labour was returned to power and the question posed above was rapidly answered: the victory of the left would mark an intensification, not a slackening, of the control culture. Within its first three weeks of office, Labour found time – amidst a heavy-duty diplomatic and political schedule that took in the EU summit in Amsterdam and the tortuous negotiations over the future of Northern Ireland – to propose a ban on tobacco advertising and sponsorship, launch a nationwide breast-feeding campaign, lecture the public on the need to fit 'hippo' devices to water tanks to cut consumption and announce it was considering making the fitting of bicycle bells compulsory to protect pedestrians. Shortly afterwards, the Minister of Public Health held a demonstration to show people the correct way to wash their hands before preparing food.

In part, the contrast between the new authoritarianism and the old live-and-let-live attitude marked simply a shift in Labour's electoral base. When Mr Crosland defended the sun, sea and sex crowd with their cheap holidays and fast food, he was defending his electoral base. Subsequent fragmentation of the social structure has shifted the movement's bedrock considerably; if the rather prim, politically correct new middle class of technologists, counsellors, 'health outreach' workers and consultants was insufficiently numerous to be described as Labour's new base, it could at least be described as its spinal cord. Once it would have been suicide for a Labour minister to lecture working-class constituents on their fondness for fizzy beer and Condor XX. Now it would be suicide not to.

This transformation has been reflected in the changing profile of the movement's leaders. Neil Kinnock, a man with genuine working-class roots, was the last to be at ease in the miners' benefit or working-man's club, with the blue jokes and smoky atmosphere. His own adoption of 'enlightened' social opinions, as with his unsuccessful attempt to give up smoking, were essentially private matters, part of the process by which a local boy made good. A companionable man who liked a drink, he confined his public lecturing to the subject of the alleged wickedness of the Tories.

The election of John Smith marked a change of emphasis. A Scottish lawyer, Mr Smith's great asset was said by newspaper commentators to be his 'bank manager' manner and air of general prudence. How well this would play with the English electorate (the key battleground in any election) was never to be tested. Nevertheless, during his short leadership, he developed what seemed to some observers an unfortunate habit of berating southern Britain for its alleged selfishness, not perhaps the most tactful piece of wooing when the south was mired in negative equity and the 'feel-bad factor'. A new message was playing, *sotto voce*: southern greed and selfishness had brought the country to its knees; the southern way, 'Thatcherism', had been given a chance and had produced an orgy of *enrichissez-vous* followed by the blinding hangover of recession; Scotland (deemed for some cultural or genetic reason to be 'more communitarian') would supply both the cure and the doctor to administer it: Mr Smith.

But it was not until Tony Blair succeeded Mr Smith in 1994 that Labour's social and political realignment reached what carpenters call 'dead plumb'. A barrister, married to another barrister, Tuscany-loving Mr Blair looked the sort of chap who would react with horror were Mr Crosland's package-tour hordes to threaten his holiday idyll. And his horror would not have been entirely motivated by concern for his own peace and quiet. It quickly became apparent that Labour's new leader was an unabashed social moralist determined to restructure British society along 'communitarian' lines. What this meant in practice, beyond a sort of compulsory togetherness presided over by social workers, was not easy to discern. Some derided him as 'preacher man', others accused him of sanctimony; these criticisms were like pellets from peashooters bouncing off the sides of the thundering Blair bandwagon.

Quasi-religious exhortation delivered in impeccably middle-class tones gave the new Labour leader the general demeanour of a house captain in a reputable Anglican boarding school, one whose study door was always open for boys with genuine problems but who gave short shrift to timewasters, those who smoked behind the bicycle sheds and those whose conduct generally could be described (in a favourite Blair epithet) as 'pathetic'. It was therefore unsurprising that, in January 1996, he chose Singapore (a large boarding school masquerading as a sovereign state) to deliver his speech lauding the 'stakeholder' society. Singapore's ferocious dedication to social hygiene has brought forth such innovations as the 'toilet police', a squad dedicated to arresting and fining those who fail to flush public lavatories (an alarm sounds to alert the squad). Other features of Singaporean life include state-sponsored match-making, a ban on chewing gum and widespread pro-hibitions of smoking.

In office, Mr Blair echoed another of Singapore's obsessions when his government advertised for a 'drugs czar' and announced that MI6, Britain's overseas intelligence service, would be assisting in the prosecution of the 'war on drugs'. Many a middle-class British executive had, in the past, admired Singapore's clean streets and low crime rate; now one of their number was in a position to try something similar at home. Like a business-man using fashionable 'benchmarking' techniques to measure his own company against the competition, Mr Blair seemed determined to transfer 'best practice', borrowed from nations like Singapore, to Britain.

Yet the authoritarian shift has deeper causes than Labour's new class iden-tification. Among them is the end of the affair between the British left and the urban working class. Stunned by the runaway success of Tory policies such as the 'sale of the century' of council houses, the party and the 'workers' began to drift apart. When, at the end of the decade, the intellectual backlash against the new working-class affluence began to gather force, Labour and its new core constituency in the social and corporate administrative classes was ready to respond. This backlash took a number of forms: 'green' con-sumerism, the concept of 'Essex Man' (an aggressive, amoral working-class individual made not-so-good), the (largely vain) efforts of some planning authorities to block new McDonald's outlets and to prohibit satellite TV dishes, the Home Office investigation into drunken disorder in white areas (delicately classified as outer-urban and rural), the moral panics over 'ram-raiding' and 'boy racers', the rushed legislation to ban the 'dangerous dogs' supposedly prized by the beer-bellied, know-nothing working-class male. In 1992, Tony Parsons tore into the new working class, with its tinned lager, computer games, football violence and bone-headed culture. 'Something has died in the working class, a sense of grace, feelings of community, their intelligence, decency and wit. The salt of the earth has become the scum of the earth.'[15] Theirs was the world captured unforgivingly by photographer Martin Parr in pictures such as *New Brighton* (1984) and *Videoshop* (1985): gung-ho consumerism set amidst overflowing litter bins and general squalor, the world of Martin Amis's super-slob darts player Keith Talent.[16] This back-lash swept up both the 'working' working class and the long-term unemployed or unemployable, the so-called 'underclass'. Indeed, the workers were depicted as underclass members with money – too much money for their own, or society's good. In work or not, they could only be called white trash.

Not only could Labour take great comfort from the new mood (the voters who had abandoned the party were never worth having in the first place), it could set itself the task of 'restructuring' this unhealthy, malfunctioning section of society without political risk. Indeed, by shading the re-engineering of the 'yob culture' into a generally tougher stance on crime, it could reap huge rewards. 'Tough on crime,' Tony Blair declared when shadow home secretary, 'tough on the causes of crime.' The 'tough on the causes' part was a blank cheque for a frontal assault on working-class attitudes and activity.

But it was not only to be the traditional proletariat that was to undergo 'attitude reassignment'. Britain generally, in the new thinking, was deemed a chronically traumatized and buttoned-up sort of place, one in need of a huge army of counsellors, anger-management experts and others. The nation, according to Susie Orbach, who shot to fame as the personal therapist of the Princess of Wales, lacked 'emotional literacy'. Just as, according to Tony Benn, the Conservative government's 1972 Industry Act had done the 'spadework for socialism', so the Tories' 1990 decision to allow GPs to recoup from local health authorities 70 per cent of the cost of hiring counsellors paved the way for the 'emotional control' culture of the late 1990s. The number of counsellors exploded – membership of the British Association for Counselling rose from 3,451 in 1987 to 10,700 by 1994 – and counselling 'experts' popped up in the unlikeliest places. Teenagers 'traumatized' by the dissolution of the pop group Take That in the early weeks of 1996 were offered telephone counselling, while BBC reporters covering the 1994 celebrations of the fiftieth anniversary of D-Day were offered help by their employer with any emotional stress they may have been suffering (some noted it was hard to understand how the event's original participants had managed to cope without the kindly ministrations of the counsellors).

Any doubts as to Labour's commitment to 'emotional literacy' were dispelled in the days and weeks following 31 August 1997, when the government effectively took charge of the national 'grieving process' following the death of Diana, Princess of Wales. Not only did this align the new government with 'emotional correctness', it highlighted a fundamental shift in the view of what was considered the central task of the state. It is quite true that the twenty years following the 1976 sterling crisis and accompanying austerity measures had been hard ones for the British people, enlivened only by an over-rich economic boom in the late 1980s. Once, a Labour government would have sought to bring this time of hardship to an end by promoting full employment and other measures to spread material prosperity and security. Now, it sought merely to spread a sort of vague spiritual uplift, assisted by sympathetic newspaper commentators who claimed that the mourning for the Princess marked a revolution in the national character. Some even suggested that, taken with the 1 May Labour election victory, the grieving for Diana represented some sort of slow-motion public uprising (continuing the insulting habit of comparing constitutional reformers to Czech dissidents, some commentary suggested the May election had been Britain's own 'velvet revolution').

Together, the tough stance on crime and the wholehearted promotion of 'emotional engineering' added up to an attempt to micro-manage the private lives of sixty million Britons, from hours spent on homework to diet, personal habits and public drunkenness. Seen through the eyes of the social authoritarian, British society is essentially a hierarchy of potential wrongdoing. To borrow the language of Orwell's Oceania, there are the 'proles', with their tobacco, cheap alcohol, propensity for violence and negative attitude to education and training, an 'outer party' permanently in danger of saying 'yes' to drugs and of failing properly to supervise their children's education, and an 'inner party' of high-achieving intellectuals who are prime targets for the temptations of money laundering, tax evasion and insider dealing.

Ironically, given that the tough-on-crime part of the equation drew the most criticism from inside the left, a strict stance on law and order would, on its own, have been largely unobjectionable. Labour is not and has never been a liberal party; the above-mentioned withdrawals from interference in private lives were practical, carefully calibrated moves taken in the light of public-interest considerations, rather than ideologically driven legislative priorities. In office, the party has taken a hard line on security issues, sending the SAS into Northern Ireland, passing the Prevention of Terrorism Act, standing firm on the 'Colonel B' affair and ABC secrets trial and raising police pay via the Edmund Davies review. Labour has always been well aware both that its traditional supporters take a generally illiberal view of law and order and that they are the principal victims of crime, a fact right-wing opponents will use ruthlessly (as Richard Nixon did to such devastating effect in the 1968 election) should there be any sign of excessive 'softness' towards criminals.

Firm application of the law without fear or favour has, on its own, no connection with the control culture. Indeed, it is the antithesis of it. But to combine stern policing of the public space with state-sponsored re-engineering of home and private life is to risk the transformation of a law-based society into what *Living Marxism* magazine has described (with some exaggeration) as an 'open prison'.

This danger is heightened by the apparent adoption by Labour of the 'balance-sheet' approach to civil liberties, the idea that each right carries attached an equal and opposite responsibility. On 13 June 1997, Tony Blair told an audience in Worcester: 'Rights and responsibilities go together.' But they do not. No responsibility attaches to any right other than a general responsibility to respect the same rights in relation to other people. Rights and responsibilities are different things; irresponsibility is no disqualification for the exercise of a right.

Linked to this false maxim is the suggestion that the acceptance of any palliative economic measures put forward by the state – job retraining, to take an obvious example – immediately entangles the recipient in a web of obligations to it. In its report of the Worcester meeting, the *Herald* stated: '[Mr Blair] stressed there would be stiff punishment for those who spurned improved opportunities and pursued a life of crime. He summed up the government's law and order philosophy by saying: "Don't be surprised if the penalties are tougher when you have been given the opportunities but you don't take them."' Hitherto, the chief justification for a court sentence had been that the offender deserved it. Now, it seemed, the very existence of state schemes for personal improvement would increase the severity of the offence. In a letter to the *Guardian* on 15 September 1997, Jonathan Calder wrote: 'Labour is effectively recasting unemployment as a form of individual delinquency.'

Just as firm application of the criminal law is antithetical to the control culture, so is the routine operation of the civil law, the law that regulates relationships among private individuals and companies. At the heart of the civil law is the notion of the first and second party (as in 'plaintiff' and 'defendant' or 'respondent'). Were a man to pester his secretary for sexual favours or were a cigar *aficionado* to burst into the living quarters of a fresh-air fiend and puff wildly, then a wrong would have been committed in both cases. The aspect of the control culture that goes by the title 'political correctness' is uninterested in first and second parties. Instead, it conjures into existence entirely hypothetical third parties, whose rights and interests require safe-guarding by the state machine and its social administrators and police. Given that these third parties do not exist, and cannot speak for themselves, no measures can, at the end of the day, be considered too severe for their protection.

Thus, in the United States, workplace romances (that is to say, entirely consensual relationships between colleagues) are discouraged (to say the least). The *Evening Standard* reported on 6 November 1997 that some City firms were beginning to follow the American lead. Thus large sections of hotels must be given over to no-smoking rooms, lest a notional future guest be offended by stale tobacco smoke. Drinking in public places must be pro-hibited by law, lest some of those drinking prove to be notional teenagers. Sweets must be removed from supermarket till areas lest a notional parent be notionally nagged by a notional child into buying confectionery that may adversely affect the child's health.

Not only are all these examples drawn from areas once regarded as the exclusive preserve of commonsensical relationships between first and second parties – whether the handling of office romances or the parent's response to the child's demands for sweets – or even the preserve of the thoughtful first party (the hotel manager insisting all rooms be properly aired and vacuumed between guests), they are symptomatic of the shifting into the private realm of the type of conflict properly belonging in the public realm. In other words, as we argue elsewhere, those in the public realm, having appropriated wrongly the rubbing-along, consensual manner of the workplace or family home, seek to uncover conflicts in the private realm that are either non-existent or amenable to endless compromise and informal agreement.

But then this is of a piece with social authoritarianism. The new 'com-manding height' of the economy is the British psyche: the underclass is to be made to buck its ideas up, while those in work are subjected to 'team-building' and 'attitude appraisal'. In other words, the state is seeking to remould what George Orwell's Winston Smith described as the few square centimetres inside the skull.

DEVOLUTION: THE TWAIN MEET

On 11 September 1997, the Scottish people voted in favour of a local parliament with limited taxation powers. The first of the great constitutional reforms promised by the new Labour government was now on the slipway. Papers enthused about the country's 'day of destiny', but the truth was a little more humdrum. Scotland's new internal government was to be given a rag-bag of functions and responsibilities, the selection of which was a poor advertisement for 'rational' constitutional reform (the parliament would, for example, have control over the death penalty but not over abortion, vehicle licensing or financial services). Nor was there anything especially rational about Labour's constitutional blueprint in general: different assemblies were planned for Scotland, Wales, Northern Ireland and Greater London, and the party's response to the 'West Lothian question' (why ought Scottish MPs to be allowed to vote on matters affecting England when those matters, in Scotland, would be decided by the Scottish parliament?) was to pretend it did not exist.

But if the Scottish authority and allied innovations were unlikely to prove set-piece defences for constitutional reform, there was little doubt that they would prove mighty engines of the control culture. Scotland's parliament, in particular, looked likely to turn out new criminal offences in Detroit-style volumes. A thousand new regulations, covering drinking in public, drug taking in private and smoking in telephone boxes, could be predicted with little chance of contradiction by events. Scotland, with its new legislative class itching to start work, marked a key point of fusion between constitutional reform and social control.

There is a case for wholesale constitutional reform, flawed though it is. There is a case also, equally flawed, for attempting to impose the culture of the social-administrator and management class on society as a whole. It could even be argued that, in certain times and places, such projects may legitimately be taken up by the left. But two danger flags should be noted. First, there is not and will never be anything specifically 'left-wing' about either project. Neither can ever be a central policy plank or a substitute for hard thinking or genuine ideology. Second, each of these projects is a terminus, not a corridor. We wrote earlier that constitutional reform was hugely irrelevant to Britain's real problems (we would say the same of social authoritarianism). They may be relevant, but only if the proponent believes the problem to be either the British constitution, full stop, or public lifestyles, full stop. Neither leads anywhere else. They are both blind alleys.

CHAPTER SEVEN

LET'S HEAR IT FOR KARL MARX: INEQUALITY AND INSTABILITY IN THE MARKET ORDER

Government, the economy, schools, everything in society is not for the
benefit of the privileged minorities. We can look after ourselves. It is for
the benefit of the ordinary run of people, who are not particularly clever
or interesting . . . not highly educated, not successful or destined for
success – in fact are nothing very special. . . . Any society worth living in
is one designed for them, not for the rich, the clever, the exceptional . . .
the world is not made for our personal benefit, nor are we in the world
for our personal benefit. A world that claims that this is its purpose is not
a good, and ought not to be a lasting, world.
Eric Hobsbawm, *On History*, Weidenfeld & Nicolson, 1997, p. 9

On a global scale, the combination of poverty, population growth and
environmental degradation increasingly threatens the security of nations.
from *Politics of the Real World*, Earthscan, 1996

. . . the capitalists . . . can then pretend to be the 'wealth creators', the
people who 'provide work' for others. In fact what they have done is
steal the product of the labour of others – and then forbid it to be used
for further production unless they are allowed to steal again.
Chris Harman, *Economics of the Madhouse*, Bookmarks, 1995

It started as a trickle and turned into a flood. As if to prove the old cliché that
despotic regimes are at their most vulnerable once they take the first stum-
bling steps towards liberalization, the policies of openness and restructuring

introduced by Mikhail Gorbachev sealed the fate of Communism in the Soviet Union and Eastern Europe. At first, it was just one or two brave East German and Hungarian families piling into their ancient Trabants for the flight to the West; within weeks the aerial shots of the central European plain looked like the Second World War newsreel footage of refugees fleeing from the Blitzkrieg. Shortly after that the arc lights picked out the young Germans taking sledgehammers to the Berlin Wall.

Ever since that chilly autumn night in 1989, the name of Karl Marx has been forever tarnished. One by one the bastions of Marxism – the hardline dictatorships in Africa, the peasant regimes of south-east Asia, the client states in Eastern Europe – have succumbed to free-market capitalism. Political elites in countries like India, that used to have a foot in both camps, have now embraced laissez-faire solutions to their problems with full-blooded enthusiasm. Outside Cuba and North Korea, it would be hard to find anybody to say a good word about the founder of Communism. Marx was wrong, and that is the end of the story.

But of course it is not. Marx was wrong about a lot of important things and many of his fundamental errors were obvious years before the end of the Cold War. Karl Popper was clinical in his demolition of Marxism's claims to be scientific, pointing out in *The Open Society and Its Enemies* that the only countries to embrace Marx's doctrines were peasant economies unable to claw their way out of feudalism. The developed industrial states that were supposed to be ripe for revolution proved remarkably immune to the certainties found in the pages of *Das Kapital*, and became more so as the oppressed proletariat – far from signing up for the class war in response to ever greater immiseration – became richer and more contented.

Marx's work – which he liked to compare with the discoveries of Newton and Darwin – was in reality one part history, one part economic analysis, one part naive futurology. He failed to predict just how pliable capitalism would prove to be; far from passively waiting for the masses to turn the streets of Manchester, Berlin or New York into rivers of blood, the capitalist class made concessions, big concessions. The franchise was enlarged, welfare states were created and then extended, trade-union activities tolerated. For the most part, these reforms were pushed through by conservatives, not radicals. It was Bismarck who introduced the first state pension scheme; Churchill who as a Liberal in Asquith's government pushed for social reform in Edwardian Britain; Franklin Roosevelt who established a welfare safety net in the United States in the 1930s. America's example is illustrative. If ever there was a nation that had the ingredients for revolution it was America in the late nineteenth century, with its robber barons and hordes of impoverished immigrants. But the Homestead Acts were passed to give settlers in the virgin territories of the West free land, and severe anti-trust legislation was passed to curb monopoly power. The tradition continued after the Second World War with the GI Bill, designed to provide veterans with the chance of a decent education so that they could enjoy their share of post-war prosperity. The Civil Rights legislation and Lyndon Johnson's Great Society programme in the 1960s were based on the same philosophy. In Johnson's native Texas it would have been called putting a chicken in every pot; today it would be dubbed inclusiveness. The doctrine of ensuring that everybody had a stake in the system applied both externally and internally, reaching its zenith with the twin-forked Marshall Plan and Welfare State programmes after the Second World War.

Capitalism's deft footwork meant that Marxism remained a fringe sect in the West. Only in those European countries where democracy was tainted by defeat in war – Germany after the First World War, France and Italy after the Second – was there any real risk of a Communist takeover. Even then, the revolutionary mood quickly dissipated.

Yet the determined way in which the West fortified itself actually reinforced one of Marx's main arguments, namely that capitalism is inherently unstable if left to its own devices. That was certainly true of the period in which Marx was writing, when the wild gyrations of the business cycle meant booms and busts arrived with alarming regularity. The fact that in the ninety years between Marx's death in 1883 and the end of the post-war Golden Age in 1973 capitalism became more humane strengthens one of Marx's other key points: that societies are shaped by struggle.

We shall argue in the rest of this chapter that the collapse of Communism at the end of the 1980s was hastened by the adoption in the West – particularly the United States and Britain – of a more aggressive form of capitalism. America's massive military build-up in the 1980s and the willingness of Margaret Thatcher and Helmut Kohl to deploy American cruise missiles at British and German bases exposed the bankruptcy – both economic and political – of the Soviet Union. But once the external threat was removed, once there was only one model of global development on offer, capitalism quickly forgot the accumulated history of a hundred years. No longer were welfare states seen as bulwarks against Communism, a worthwhile price for keeping the workers content and peaceful. All of a sudden – and despite the fact that the West was richer than ever before – welfare states became an intolerable burden on capitalism, siphoning off investment and energy with their insatiable demands for benefit payments. By the mid-1990s, it had become one of the axioms of Western thought that Germany was being eaten away from the inside by the high non-wage costs – fringe benefits, sickness pay, unemployment insurance – doled out to its pampered workforce. Whereas in the 1970s, the seven- and eight-week holidays enjoyed by the Volkswagen workers at Wolfsburg were seen as proof positive of the German productivity miracle, by the late 1990s they were decried as the outward manifestations of Germany's Euro-sclerosis. John Sweeney, the head of the American trade union movement, put the move to a harsher form of capitalism well when addressing capitalism's annual talking shop – the World Economic Forum in Davos, Switzerland – in early 1997. In the 1950s and 1960s, Mr Sweeney said, some of the nastiness of capitalism was tempered. There was a fair share of the spoils for everyone. Now there was a lack of concern in boardrooms about the impact on workers of downsizing and falling real wages. 'Once we grew together; now we are growing apart', he said.

THE RADIANT FUTURE: CAPITALISM'S NOMENKLATURA CLEANS UP

In a strange way, having finally emerged victorious in the Cold War, capitalism started to ape some of Communism's more egregious characteristics. The right's band of tame academics – as inured from the effects of the Age of Insecurity as any party apparatchik under Brezhnev – could be relied upon to claim that free-market economics were not only desirable but inevitable. The destabilization of companies, communities, even whole countries, such as Mexico in 1995 and Thailand in 1997, did not shake the faith in the scientific rationale behind the free movement of globalized capital, any more than the millions starving to death in the famines of the 1930s made Stalin question mass collectivization. Having started as a pragmatic set of beliefs that could be changed as circumstances dictated, capitalism hardened into a dogmatic and monolithic creed that brooked no opposition. Just as the Soviet model would bring the joys of the workers' state to South Yemen and Mozambique, so free-market capitalism would bring peace and prosperity to all corners of the globe.

Thus far, actual performance has not lived up to the propaganda. The United Nations Human Development Report has shown that there are actually more people living in absolute poverty than there were in the early 1970s. Two communiqués were released by the Group of Eight summit in Denver in 1997: an economic declaration that talked in glowing terms of the strength of the global economy and a political statement which ran to nineteen pages and ninety-one paragraphs. The political statement outlined the problems facing the new world order – ageing populations, the despoiling of the environment, the spread of infectious diseases, unsafe nuclear installations, transnational organized crime, illicit drugs, terrorism, human cloning, reform of the UN, threats to democracy and human rights, nuclear proliferation and conflicts in Africa, Hong Kong, the Congo, Haiti, the Middle East, Cyprus, Albania, Afghanistan, Korea and Burma. In the circumstances, it was just as well that the G8 was so optimistic about the global economy; otherwise the list of problems might have been longer than the *Encyclopaedia Britannica*.

A rather more accurate assessment of the true state of the world came in David Korten's book, *When Corporations Rule the World*:[1]

- in 1992 the top 1,000 chief executive officers in the USA received on average 157 times as much salary as the average worker, compared to forty times as much in 1960. Between them, they received $3.8 billion, up by 42 per cent from the 1991 figure;
- the top 1 per cent of American earners receive more income than the bottom 40 per cent combined;
- the top 400 richest people listed in *Forbes* magazine had a net worth in 1993 of $328 billion: put into context that was equal to the combined GDP of India, Bangladesh, Nepal and Sri Lanka, four countries with a combined population of one billion;
- 70 per cent of world trade is managed by 500 corporations, and 1 per cent of multinationals own half the stock of foreign direct investment.

The global elite – the people who make the decisions, fly first class, stay in five-star luxury hotels, attend Davos each year – have certainly thrived. To the extent that the G8 is an extension of this global elite, its prognostications are accurate. But to the vast majority of people – the 36 per cent of British white-collar staff who voluntarily work more than forty-eight hours a week because they are frightened of being the first to leave the office, the parents in America who on average spend 40 per cent less time with their children than they did thirty years ago – the world has become a rougher, tougher place. Moreover, the claims by the G8 (or the WTO, the World Bank, the IMF, the majority of chief executives and the entirety of the political class in the West) are false. The claim to have found the miracle cure for all economic ills is belied by the record dole queues lengthening across Europe, the recrudescence of the soup-kitchen culture in America, the banana producers of the Caribbean bankrupted by the WTO's insistence that the former colonial powers, Britain and France, should not be allowed to give trade preferences to poor, one-commodity economies, the destabilization of economies in Latin America and south-east Asia made possible by the elimination of controls on capital.

Little wonder then that the belief in progress is now confined to a small segment of the population. The American economist Robert Frank has coined the phrase 'Winner Take It All' markets, in which the fruits of growth become concentrated in an ever smaller number of hands. It would be more accurate to call them 'Winner Take It All, All The Time' markets, because the global elite never loses. What happened to Goldman Sachs and the other blue-chip Wall Street houses when their investments in Mexico looked like turning sour in early 1995? Would they lose the billions in 'hot money' they had recklessly lent to the Salinas government to finance Mexico's current account deficit? Of course not. Within days a US-broked $50 billion IMF package was conjured up to ensure that there was no systemic threat to the West's banking system (shorthand for Wall Street losing its shirt). The Mexican people, naturally, did not have it quite so easy. They had to learn the errors of their ways via an IMF austerity package that led to an 8 per cent contraction in the economy, an increase in unemployment of one million and a 40 per cent fall in investment. The country's debt to the IMF and the USA has been repaid, but wages are not expected to return to their pre-collapse level until 2000 and unemployment affects a quarter of the workforce. To the global community, Mexico is a success story. And so it is, just as a gambler would consider a casino a success if he doubled his money every time the roulette wheel landed on red and if he got his stake back when it landed on black. For some, the risk has been taken out of the risk business. But not everybody has been so fortunate. Elsewhere, among those with no chance of ever enjoying a golden handshake or parachute, there has been a loss of belief in progress. A MORI poll in 1995 asked respondents whether they expected their children to enjoy a better life than they had. For most of the post-war period, children have confidently expected to be better off than their parents, and they have been right to hold that view. But there is no longer such optimism about the future. By a majority of five to one (60 per cent to 12 per cent) the MORI survey found that people expected life to be worse for their offspring.

Such a response was hardly surprising. For twenty years, first blue-collar and then white-collar workers were told that inequality was not only inevitable but desirable. Living standards could rise for all only if the already rich were provided with the right incentives to invest and innovate. Trickle-down theory became the orthodoxy and provided a rationale for the biggest increase in inequality for more than a century. Those who complained that the sleek denizens of the boardroom were seeing their share-option packages soar in value because they were axing rather than creating jobs were said to be guilty of the politics of envy. But it was not just inequality that led to a far more pessimistic mood than in earlier decades. There was also the sense that the dice had been loaded in favour of the boss. All restrictions on the free movement of capital were swept away, trade unions were tamed with a mixture of legislation and unemployment, and the provision of a social wage through the Welfare State came under both financial and ideological attack. Put simply, if workers were unemployed, it was their fault. If they were not too slothful or too stupid to get a job, then they were too unproductive or had priced themselves out of work. Companies had to compete in the real world and there was no room for sentiment, or for unions that might fight for higher wages and oppose the smooth workings of the flexible labour market. Flexibility, in this context, meant one thing and one thing only: 'You're sacked.' The new approach, sanctified by the phrase 'management's right to manage', applied across the board, even to organizations such as the NHS where it was not apparent where the cut-throat competition was coming from. In fact, most of the claims about the West being swamped by low-price imports from the 'tiger economies' of south-east Asia were spurious, as Adair Turner, director-general of the CBI, had the grace to admit. Mr Turner said that the main reason for downsizing was that technology was making it possible for firms to computerize large parts of their operations, thereby increasing profitability and returns to shareholders. His views are borne out by the available evidence. Less than 5 per cent of the West's trade comes from outside the twenty-nine-nation Organization for Economic Cooperation and Development. More than 80 per cent is accounted for by the European Union, North America and Japan. However, these were seen as trifling, nit-picking objections. For cheerleaders of the new order, the decisive agreement was that – *pace* Marx – the globalization of capital was scientific and immutable. It is with this claim that we will begin our analysis.

DAY OF THE VOODOO MAN: MARKET GURUS AND PHONEY SCIENCE

Economics is not a science. Many economists – particularly those who believe that decisions on whether to get married can be reduced to an equation – see the world as a complex organism that can be understood using the right differential calculus. Yet everything we know about economics suggests that it is a branch, and not a particularly advanced one, of witchcraft. Analysts on Wall Street and in the City are accorded the exalted status of sages, yet all too often resemble the quack doctors rumbling through the Wild West with their medicine shows. The virulence of recessions and booms are nearly always underestimated and even short-term forecasts are often woefully inaccurate. One highly paid economist with a US-owned firm in the City once admitted that the forecast he sent out to clients for the UK trade figures was calculated by adding up the deficit for the previous three months and dividing by three. 'Since I've started doing that my record has improved', he acknowledged cheerfully.

Even if it were a science, modern economics is fundamentally different from other disciplines. It is axiomatic that the global economy is shaped by certain rules: that low inflation leads to stronger growth, that there is a level of unemployment below which inflation will start to take off, that low taxes stimulate investment and growth, that making rich people poorer is not the way to make poor people richer. These assertions – for they are just assertions – will be examined more closely below. But what can be said from the outset is that in all other branches of science, the creative process is influenced by struggle and conflict. Progress is made by testing ideas continually, not by constant reiteration. In psychoanalysis this notion was encapsulated in Jung's theory of the libido, where the psyche is dynamic and in constant movement. The libido flows between two poles, and the greater the tension between the two poles the greater the energy. Jung argued that without tension there was no energy, and that healthy individuals were characterized by the libido flowing between thinking and feeling, extroversion and introversion, progression and regression. Once one extreme is reached, the libido passes over into the opposite. In Jungian terms, the world could be divided between the extrovert West with its aggressive materialism and the more introverted and contemplative East. However, the self-regulatory function of the Jungian libido is not applicable to globalization; there is no contrast of opposites in a world where the cultural hegemony of Walt Disney, Rupert Murdoch and Coca Cola is only matched by its vapidity. Yet an outlet has had to be found somewhere. So whereas the dominant economic model is becoming more extrovert, so the people who live and work in it are becoming more introvert, retreating into the self in an attempt to find the elusive secret of personal happiness.

If the new order has a few problems with Jung, one might consider that it would be on safer ground with Darwin. After all, Darwin's theory of evolution is seen as support for the survival of the fittest, and helps to explain why it has been inevitable that Western capitalism should first emerge victorious over Communism and then spread to every corner of the globe. In truth, this is a very one-sided interpretation of Darwin's work. His famous study of the Galapagos Islands is really about adaptability and biodiversity. As one recent book highlighted, there were no woodpeckers on the islands, but other birds gradually developed some of the characteristics of woodpeckers to find food. Under the triumphalist global model, the Galapagos pseudo-woodpeckers would be seen as hopelessly outdated and inefficient. The solution would be the building of a land bridge to the nearest mainland – Ecuador – allowing South American woodpeckers to be imported. The process would be policed and monitored by the WTO to ensure that there were no unfair restrictions on the export of Ecuadorean Picidae, until the last indigenous birds were killed off.

But in many ways, the greatest opponent of the supremacist global model would be Marx's old adversary, Popper, whose core belief was that only through criticism could knowledge advance. It could be positively harmful, Popper stressed in *The Open Society and Its Enemies*,[2] for people blindly to accept the status quo; rather, a policy was merely a hypothesis that had to be tested and, if necessary, modified or corrected. Popper had the totalitarian regimes of Nazi Germany and Stalinist Russia in mind when he extolled the virtues of democracy, which he saw as the transmission mechanism for the rectification of mistakes. In open societies, there would be pressure for reform when the cost of bad policies proved to be too high, whereas the absence of democracy in closed societies condemned their rulers to making even bigger mistakes in the future.

One study of Popper argues that the Austrian-born philosopher was a classic social democrat. There is something in this assessment. Popper's vision was of political pluralism, a system of checks and balances in which it was seen as right and natural that different views and conflicting aims should be accommodated. He was also stimulated by the paradox of freedom, in which absolute freedom gave the strong the right and the ability to dominate or enslave the poor.

We must construct social institutions, enforced by the power of the state, for the protection of the economically weak by the economically strong . . . this, of course, means that the principle of non-intervention, of an unrestrained economic system, has to be given up; if we wish freedom to be safeguarded, then we must demand that the policy of unlimited economic freedom be replaced by the planned economic intervention of the state. We must demand that unrestrained capitalism give way to an economic interventionism.[3]

Popper, seen in this light, is part of a liberal tradition that stretches back a century and a half. Thinkers like John Stuart Mill were believers in capitalism and repudiated Marx's prescriptions, yet could see that mid-Victorian industrial society was in need of reform. Dickens is normally taken as the great chronicler of the injustices of the period, although one of the vignettes from Marx's old collaborator, Engels, is just as telling, and somewhat less long-winded. Engels discloses how he strikes up a conversation with a solidly bourgeois Mancunian about the terrible slums in the city. The middle-class gentleman listens politely and, at the end of the exposition, raises his hat and says: 'And yet there is a great deal of money here. Good morning, sir.'[4] Mill laid the philosophical foundations for the move to a more interventionist economic policy to promote the general welfare of the nation. 'I know not why it should be a matter of congratulation that persons who are already richer than anyone needs to be, should have doubled their means of consuming things which give little or no pleasure except as representatives of wealth.'[5] Mill believed in the state as an active force, an instrument of civilization that could help smooth out the economic cycle. In this he was adumbrating not just an alternative vision to Marx's class war but a harbinger of the ideas propounded by Keynes and Beveridge a century later.

I confess that I am not charmed with the ideal of life held out by those who think that the normal state of human beings is that of struggling to get on; the trampling, crushing, elbowing and treading on each other's heads, which form the existing type of social life, are the most desirable lot of human kind, or anything but the most disagreeable symptoms of one of the phases of industrial progress.[6]

In his way, Mill shared Marx's perfectly correct view that industrial capitalism contained an in-built bias towards instability. Where they differed is that Marx saw revolution as inevitable while Mill saw reform as possible. Mill was proved right. There was no inevitability about capitalism's collapse. Even Eastern bloc economists shared this view. The Hungarian economist, Eugene Varga, was stripped of his academic rank by Stalin after asserting that capitalism had been given a new lease of life by the Second World War.[7] The move to a more activist state meant that there would be no return to the anarchy of unbridled capitalism, and that meant that capitalism would be more stable. Not much is heard these days of Eugene Varga, since his view that capitalism works better when it is acting as a bulwark against revolution and discontent is as deeply unfashionable now as it was in the years when the Iron Curtain came down across central Europe.

However, plenty is heard of another Hungarian, George Soros, who, after reportedly making a billion pounds from the frenzied speculation that led to sterling's enforced departure from the ERM, came up with a classic Popperesque critique of modern capitalism. In an article for *Atlantic Monthly* he warned that open societies required the clash of ideas.[8] By contrast, the fact that laissez-faire was becoming ubiquitous was leading the West down the path to closed, intolerant societies in which only material success matters.

Soros had been right about sterling and the ERM, and he was right again about the weaknesses of modern capital. Indeed, to the extent that he was both a speculator and a man dedicated to saving capitalism from itself, he was the Lord Keynes of our times. But the crucial difference was that politicians and other economists were forced to listen to Keynes by the length and depth of the Great Depression, even if they were not willing disciples. In 1930, as the West started to count the cost of the stock market bubble that had burst in 1929 Keynes had looked forward to a day when 'The love of money as a possession – as distinguished from the love of money as a means to the enjoyments and realities of life – will be recognised for what it is, a somewhat disgusting morbidity, one of those semi-criminal, semi-pathological propensities which one hands over with a shudder to the specialists in mental disease.'[9]

This – Freudian psychoanalytical jargon notwithstanding – was strong stuff, but three years and 25 per cent unemployment later, it was matched in Franklin Roosevelt's inaugural address in March 1933. 'The money changers have fled from their high seats in the temple of our civilization. We may now restore that temple to the ancient truths. The measure of the restoration lies in the extent to which we apply social values more noble than mere monetary profit.'

Roosevelt made his address less than six weeks after Hitler came to power in Germany and as the Soviet Union embarked on its second five-year plan. For those who believe in the theory of long Kondratieff waves in the world economy lasting fifty or more years, this marked the low point in a twenty-year downswing for capitalism, the crisis that marked the shift from deflation to reflation and the birth of a new technological paradigm based on cars, air travel and consumer durables. Similarly, the mid-1990s could be seen as the end of a prolonged downward lurch that began with the oil crisis in 1973 and will only be remedied once the new technology – this time based on computers – is harnessed to more congenial economic policies. This, sad to say, still looks some way off. Communism was one of the victims of the downswing of the 1970s and 1980s, so there is no longer any concern that a Soviet-style command economy offers growth without unemployment. Soros was given the traditional welcome for a prophet: he was ignored.

The counter-argument was based on Francis Fukuyama's book *The End of History*, in which he claimed that liberal capitalism and liberal democracy had, like Gary Kasparov, cleared the chess board of all the opposing pieces. It was checkmate, not just in the here and now, in the 1990s, but for ever. Those who said that there were places where the free-market and the money-making ethos could not and should not go were dismissed as Utopian dreamers out of touch with the 'real world'. Those who said that a system built on enriching the many at the expense of the few was flawed were told that a system of incentives for the talented was already starting to bear fruit and would bring even greater prosperity in the future, provided there was no return to the 'politics of envy'. To those who said that the present-day global economy did not compare very favourably with the post-war Golden Age, the riposte was that the real Golden Age for capitalism was not 1945–73 but 1870–1914, an earlier era of globalization that would have led to rapid growth had it not been truncated by war, protectionism and dirigiste policies pursued by nation-states in the first half of the twentieth century.

We explore the causes and effects of the hollowing out of Western culture and society by unrestrained modern capitalism in other chapters. Here we will confine ourselves to judging the record of the laissez-faire revolution in terms of inequality, poverty, growth and investment. In 1923, Keynes said that the capitalism he wished to protect and nurture was proving only 'moderately successful'. It is unlikely that he would be as generous today.

Indeed, Keynes would be alarmed that in the West unemployment was back to levels last seen in the 1930s, and that the gap between rich and poor was wider than it had been a hundred years earlier. But the main architect of the post-war economic settlement would have been horrified that rising inequality and longer dole queues had been short-term policy goals of the new right, 'the price worth paying' in Norman Lamont's memorable phrase for a reinvention of classical, pre-Welfare State capitalism. In a particularly candid interview for a television documentary, *Pandora's Box*, on the British economy granted before he became chief economic adviser at the Treasury, Sir Alan Budd said that the Marxist interpretation of the mass joblessness in the early 1980s was that policy makers had actively sought to create a reserve army of the unemployed in order to quash organized labour. The jury may still be out on whether the loss of jobs during the early Thatcherite period was class war or crass stupidity, but no such doubts apply on the laissez-faire approach to inequality. This was intentional, both in Britain, where income inequality increased more than in any country other than New Zealand (a country which became the test-bed for right-wing ideas that even Mrs Thatcher would not try) and Ronald Reagan's America. On the right, anti-egalitarianism was seen as a long overdue corrective to the levelling down of the 1970s. High achievers, it was said, were being stifled by redistributive tax systems that took money from the rich and either handed it directly to the poor or used it to keep wastrels in subsidized state-funded jobs. An alterna-tive strategy was proposed – which became known as 'trickle-down' – in which lower levels of income tax and state spending would unleash the creative impulses of risk takers. Given the right incentives, entrepreneurs would set up businesses, invest more, employ people in 'real jobs' and raise growth levels. In the immortal words of *Private Eye*, it would be 'trebles all round', because by enriching themselves, the wealth creators would enrich everybody. Wealth would trickle, perhaps even cascade, down the income scale. As with every other policy in the 1980s and 1990s this had its own soundbite: 'You don't make the poor richer by making the rich poorer.'

One did not need to be Karl Popper to see that this was a hypothesis and not a scientific fact. However, years of repetition – particularly in the news-papers owned by some of the main beneficiaries of trickle-down – hardened it into an iron law. The belief that high taxation damages incentives for 'risk takers' has become part of the language of politics, even though in Britain those on the right look back to the first two terms of Thatcherism – before income tax for the rich was cut from 60 per cent to 40 per cent – as the Golden Age of post-war Conservative rule. Labour has been critical of trickle-down economics and one of its priorities on coming to office in 1997 was to tackle the problem of the underclass, the 20 per cent of households lacking one earner, by narrowing the gap between rich and poor. However, Labour was reluctant to go down the redistribution route, eschewing even a higher marginal rate of tax on those earning more than £100,000 a year. Redistribution had been the theme of Tony Crosland's book *The Future of Socialism* in 1956, which marked Labour's transition from a party of nation-alization to a party in which the spoils of an economy enlarged by Keynesianism would be divided more equally. But to the Blair modernizers, redistribution sent out the wrong messages to voters because it signalled that the party wanted to cap achievement and enterprise. It was quintessentially

Old Labour, and was expunged from Labour's vocabulary by Blair and Brown, who argued that in the modern world equality of opportunity rather than equality of outcome was what really counted. Labour had its own sound-bite – a hand-up not a hand-out – and argued that the only way to help the members of the underclass was to bring them back into the labour market via a Welfare to Work programme offering subsidized jobs, education, voluntary work or a place on an environmental task force.

What is interesting about both these policies – trickle-down and opportunity trickle-down – is that they both chime neatly with the prevailing economic orthodoxy, which assumes that if there are problems they must be on the supply side of the economy. As such, if there is unemployment it is not because there is a shortage of demand caused either deliberately or inadvertently by the government, but because the workers are paid too much, are lazy or feckless, or lack the skills to compete in the global economy. The alternative interpretation is that the causes of economic malfunction lie almost predominantly on the demand side. People are no lazier or more stupid than they were in the 1950s and 1960s, but they are less protected by unions and the law has been changed to give the employer the whip hand over the employee. On the other hand, the economy has been run with an in-built deflationary bias for twenty years while at the same time skewing the rewards of slower growth towards the better-off. Seen in this light much of the economic rationale for the post-Keynesian era can be exposed for what it is – mythology dressed up as truth.

MORE MYTH THAN HITS: THE RECORD, LIVE AND UNCUT

Let us begin with the myths of trickle-down. Myth one is that Anglo-Saxon economies have been transformed for the better by the policies followed since the mid-1970s. The American and British economies have, according to this theory, rediscovered their vim and vigour as a result of the combination of the reduction in inflation, tax cuts, and reforms of labour markets.

Here are the facts. That there has been a sharp increase in inequality is not in doubt. According to a recent book written by three economists from the Institute for Fiscal Studies: 'From 1977 there has been a continuous rise in inequality. . . . By comparison with the preceding 20 years or so, this level of change and continuous increase was unprecedented. Indeed, such a change appears to be historically unusual when judged against a longer period'.[10]

The Dutch economist Jan Pen pioneered a graphic way to depict inequality by a 'parade of giants'. This shows how income distribution would look if every individual had to pass a particular point in one hour, with each given a height according to his or her income. The latest IFS calculations for the UK make the average income proportionate to the average height of 5 feet 9 inches. As the parade begins, the first few people passing by would be upside down. They would be self-employed people with negative income and no state benefits. After that the dwarfs would start. For the first twelve minutes the people coming into view would be less than 2 feet 10 inches in height. That is, one-fifth of the population would be on less than half average income. At the half-hour point the height would have increased to 4 feet 9 inches, still denoting incomes of well under the mean. At thirty-six minutes the 5 feet 9 inches mark would be reached. After that heights would start to rise quite rapidly. At forty-eight minutes the people passing in the parade would resemble the tallest basketball players at 7 feet 8 inches, by fifty-four minutes they would be almost 10 feet and by the last minute giants of 15 feet 6 inches would stride by. In the last few seconds the merchant bankers and the chief executive officers would come into view, but you would have to crane your neck to see them. They would be as high as Nelson's column.

It is not just that there is inequality in modern Britain: the giants in Pen's parade are becoming taller and the dwarfs more numerous. The narrowing of the income gap in Britain after the Second World War is illustrated by the decline of the domestic servant, which became unaffordable for the upper middle classes in an era of high marginal tax rates. The popularity of the TV programme *Upstairs Downstairs* in the early 1970s was explained, in part, because it seemed such an Edwardian period piece, with its small army of parlour-maids, butlers and cooks. Income shares remained remarkably stable in the 1960s and 1970s, with a slight narrowing in the 1970s as a result of redistribution and incomes policies. But after 1979 there was an extremely sharp divergence. The bottom decile of earners took a 4.4 per cent share of income in 1976–78, the last three years of incomes policies. By 1991–93 this had dropped to 2.9 per cent. Despite all the complaints about the lack of incentive for high achievers to work, the top 10 per cent still took 21.3 per cent of income in 1976–78. By 1991–93 they were taking more than 26 per cent of the cake.

The centre of gravity of the population has also shifted. Back in the early 1960s, the heaviest concentration of incomes fell at 80–90 per cent of the mean. In other words, Britain's income distribution was comparable to that in most of Europe today, with millions of people clustered around the middle of the range. But by the early 1990s there had been a dramatic change, with the peak of the distribution falling at just 40–50 per cent of the mean. One-quarter of the population had incomes below half the average by the early 1990s as against 7 per cent in 1977 and 11 per cent in 1961. At the other end of the scale the number of people on three times the mean income had almost doubled – from 600,000 to one million between the early 1960s and the early 1990s. Where then is the evidence that trickle-down has enriched Britain from top to bottom, from rich to poor? There is none. Wealth has trickled down, but only from the super-rich to the rich. Elsewhere, low pay and poverty have burgeoned.

Trickle-down was justified by the notion – to quote President Kennedy – that a rising tide lifts all boats. This has simply not happened. To continue the metaphor, one end of the boat has been raised high out of the sea while the other has been plunged under the waves, making the boat seem increasingly precarious. Depending on the measure used, up to 14.1 million people live on 50 per cent or less of average income, an increase from 7 per cent to 25 per cent of the population since 1977.

Part of the bill for poverty has been picked up by the state, which provides 80 per cent of the incomes of the poorest decile and a quarter of the income for those in the fifth decile, people in the middle of the income distribution. There is some irony in the arguments made in the late 1970s that state spending was crowding out more productive investment, given the exponential rise in social security bills since that time.

The social security system is blatantly redistributive. As the IFS notes, of all the components of household income only social security has an equalizing effect. This is a point Labour ministers might like to take on board the next time they are intoning the new soundbite, that there is no long-term gain from taxing the rich simply to increase benefits for the poor. The logic of this is that it might be better for the poor if benefits were reduced, but that would simply have the effect of making the income distribution even more unequal than it already is.

But, to repeat an argument much used in recent years, it may be that the economy as a whole has benefited from inequality even if not everybody has yet begun to share in the new era of prosperity. Again this is hard to substantiate. Growth rates, investment rates and productivity rates are all lower now than they were in the Golden Age, and there is evidence that the trend rate of growth – the underlying growth rate – has also decreased. Britain's growth rate in the 1970s – the 'bad old days' – was 2.4 per cent. In the 1980s, it fell to 2 per cent: hardly an impressive performance, though the argument was that the shake-out in the early 1980s was necessary to clear away all the dead wood. But, it was argued, Rome was not built in a day, and it would take time for trickle-down to have an impact. However, the force of this argument is somewhat lessened by Britain's growth record in the 1990s, which at 1.2 per cent per year on average has been lower than in any period since the war. Rome may not have been built in a day but it did not remain a handful of hovels on the banks of the Tiber for the first five hundred years after Romulus and Remus.

Perhaps there are particularly British characteristics at work here. Maybe other countries have fared better with trickle-down. In the United States, for example, the top-bracket income tax rate averaged almost 90 per cent in the 1950s, then fell decade by decade to 80 per cent in the 1960s, 70 per cent in the 1970s, 39 per cent in the 1980s and 35 per cent in the 1990s. And have the forces of growth been unleashed by a new wave of entrepreneurship? It would not appear so. Growth averaged 4 per cent in the bountiful Eisenhower decade, accelerated slightly to 4.4 per cent in the 1960s, fell back to 3.2 per cent in the crisis-ridden 1970s, dropped to 2.8 per cent in the first ten years of trickle-down under Ronald Reagan and George Bush, and has continued to drop to 1.9 per cent in the first half of the 1990s. There has been a relationship between the marginal rate of tax and growth, but the correlation has been negative. Cutting the top rate of tax for the rich and widening the gap between rich and poor has led to a slowdown in growth.

A similar relationship can be found outside the developed West. A thirteen-nation study found that the poorest 10 per cent of the population in Indonesia commanded almost 4 per cent of national income, whereas in Brazil the poorest 10 per cent enjoyed less than 1 per cent.[11] Yet in the period between 1980 and 1993, Indonesia grew by 5 per cent a year, while Brazil had negative growth. Countries with anti-poverty strategies – mainly those in south-east and east Asia – grew much faster than countries – mainly in Latin America – where the levels of inequality were high.

There have been signs recently that some of the high priests of the laissez-faire creed are starting to have second thoughts about inequality as they sift through the economic statistics. In the summer of 1997, the free-market-supporting OECD stated heretically in its annual *Employment Outlook*: 'Countries with more deregulated labour and product markets do not appear to have higher relative mobility, nor do low-paid workers in these economies experience more upward mobility. Equity concerns about increased earnings inequality cannot be dismissed simply with an appeal to increased labour mobility.' Stripped of jargon, this means: 'We got it wrong.'

The OECD went on to admit that for many workers low pay is a chronic condition, and that this is especially true of the Anglo-Saxon economies where the gap between high and low earners has widened appreciably. The UK and USA have more persistent low-pay spells, but appear to reap little or no benefit from this trend. When low pay is defined as less than two-thirds of median earnings, low-paid workers in 1986 had averaged just under two years of low-paid employment in Denmark by 1991, but just over four years in the USA and the UK. There was a carousel effect, but not the one that the trickle-down supporters had envisaged. Instead of going from low pay to high pay, workers tended to go from low pay to no pay. As the OECD blithely admitted, this had potentially negative consequences for poverty and their productive capacity, as well as that of the economy as a whole.

Nor is this the end of the OECD's Pauline conversion. Not only had labour markets become more unequal but: 'A widespread and, in some countries, very sharp increase in the number of individuals perceiving employment insecurity took place between the 1980s and 1990s.' The OECD cannot understand this. It thinks there is a paradox because jobs are as stable in the 1990s as they were in the 1980s, and can only speculate that the explanation lies in the risk of separation from a job and the subsequent financial consequences. In other words, it's not just the threat of losing your job but the fact that the new one you get may be at much lower pay. 'Considering the characteristics of the new job, evidence from North America points to substantially lower earnings in the new positions, and, in general, it now seems more difficult to find a satisfactory new match.' This finding appeared to startle the OECD, perhaps because its economists can always be certain of moving on to a lucrative job at one of the proliferating number of multi-lateral organizations or at a finance house willing to pay through the nose for somebody with some inside information. But for many people, the financial penalties associated with losing a job were all too real.

One study of downsizing in the USA found that 12 per cent of those made redundant left the workforce altogether and a further 17 per cent were unemployed for two or more years.[12] Of the remaining 71 per cent, 31 per cent took a wage cut of 25 per cent or more, 32 per cent a cut of between 1 and 25 per cent, and 37 per cent found re-employment at no loss in wages. The outcome was much worse if the employee had climbed the corporate ladder and had fifteen or more years of seniority, lived in a low-growth area and was forced to switch industries. In those cases, the individual typically lost more than 50 per cent of the previous wage. This may help to explain why those with the highest level of education were found to be the most insecure. They had the most to lose. Significantly, job insecurity and inequality were lower in those countries with strong trade unions, centralized pay bargaining and generous levels of state benefits for the unemployed.

So if inequality has risen and its economic — let alone its social — consequences are not good, the question has to be: what should be done about it? The consensus view, shared by Christian Democrats and Social Democrats, Clintonites and Blairites, is that governments should aim for macro-economic stability, because that leads to low inflation. Low inflation is the prerequisite for higher growth. At the same time, administrations should embrace the new technology, raising educational standards so that the low-skilled workers displaced by the competition from developing countries can find better and higher-paid jobs in the so-called sunrise industries.

THE STABILITY MYTH

There is little evidence to show that low inflation leads to higher levels of growth. Nor is there evidence to show that inflation at levels of anything up to around 15 per cent leads to lower growth rates. The Bank of England once commissioned a study from an American economist, Robert Barro, to show that this was the case, but bend the available data any way he could, he could not come up with the desired result. Indeed, the experience of France under the so-called *franc fort* policy since 1983 shows that almost fifteen years of stability and low inflation have led to much lower growth rates and much higher levels of unemployment than in the days of expansion and devaluation.

In the mid-1980s, the trend rate of growth for the rich Western countries that make up the OECD was some 3 per cent. Now economists put it at 2.5 per cent. The actual growth rate during the 1990s has been well under 2 per cent, compared to 4 per cent in the 1950s and 1960s and 3 per cent in the 1970s. As one commentator put it:

In the last seven years, OECD growth has only matched trend or potential for a very short period. With this sort of growth record it is not surprising that companies have been delayering staff – have been downsizing. The trouble is that this sort of action feeds on itself and is very difficult to stop.

This quote comes not from a wild revolutionary, but from Richard Freeman, chief economist with ICI. He goes on:

It seems that the present policy focus on economic stability has deflected attention from growth and employment. I think it is not going too far to suggest that both governments and academia find growth too difficult whereas stability is not. But the empirical evidence – as far as I am aware – of the link between stability and growth is not strong. Governments and central bankers seem to have a touching faith that stability will bring its own cure.

Maybe policymakers have been misled by businessmen.

If there is one thing businessmen agree on it is that the greater certainty which stability brings will increase investment. Well, there has been reasonable stability in much of the OECD for a relatively long time but the record on productive investment has been dismal. I believe that slow growth is the key factor keeping corporate OECD risk averse.[13]

THE TECHNOLOGY MYTH

America's Silicon Valley has boomed over the past decade. The companies known as the New Titans have expanded and companies such as Microsoft and Intel are seen as the successors to the old giants such as Kodak and Ford. But this growth has to be put into perspective. Microsoft and Intel between them employ fewer than 50,000 workers, and all the New Titans together have a payroll of 128,000, one-third fewer than Ford in the USA alone.

The New Titans are put forward as evidence that downsizing does not matter. It simply means that some Americans are being forced to move to better jobs – General Motors may fire you but Microsoft will hire you, and Microsoft jobs are better. But, as the American writer Edward Luttwak wrote, it is not true that if GM fires you, Microsoft will hire you.[14] In 1995, the total number employed in computer and data-processing services – which includes everything from writing software to repairing PCs – stood at just over one million out of 114 million employed Americans. The number of Americans employed in the production of electronic and other electrical equipment actually fell slightly during the 1990s, from 1.7 million to 1.6 million.

There has been some evidence recently that skill shortages in high-tech industries – both in the USA and the UK – may be pushing up wages in those sectors. But the evidence over a longer period for the wages of engineers – who as problem solvers are supposed to be in demand from the new industries – is far less conclusive. The median salary of engineers, including fringe benefits, fell by 13 per cent in real terms between 1968 and 1995. The real increase in jobs in both the USA and the UK in recent years has been in poorly paid service jobs – personal services, security, retailing, health care, the self-employment in which someone who has been downsized starts up as a window cleaner or labourer. This, in itself, is a function of rising inequality, since the rapid increases in incomes for the rich have allowed them to employ a new servant class to clean their homes, protect their property, look after their children and wait on them in the grand hotels which have become the equivalent of the country homes of past centuries. In America, where 77.5 million of 114 million employed workers are non-supervisory (workers with no management function) employees, average hourly earnings stood at $8.40 in 1978. By 1994 they were down to $7.41.

THE EDUCATION MYTH

Against this backround of low growth and widening income disparities, it is not easy to see what the policy of 'education, education and education' is actually going to achieve. It may be that education is desirable in its own right – indeed it almost certainly is, provided that what is delivered is education rather than merely a training checklist demanded by business. It may be that education and training have a part to play within a package designed to improve economic performance. But on its own, raising educational standards will not be the magic ingredient that will ensure higher levels of growth.

Why should that be? First, supply does not necessarily bring forth its own demand. If it did, the establishment of a training school designed to churn out astronauts and rocket scientists would ensure that Britain had its own space programme. What actually happens, in a period of low growth, is that there are not enough good jobs for those with qualifications, and they start to take the jobs for which they are over-qualified, thereby displacing people further down the ladder. There is evidence that those at the bottom of the ladder are disadvantaged because of poor levels of attainment in literacy and numeracy. However, the government's education is not aimed at them specifically, but is rather concentrated on raising the average performance.

Second, as with stability and low inflation, it is hard to find proof which links educational attainment with growth levels. A recent study by Peter Robinson, of the LSE's Centre for Economic Performance, says that once the vast majority of the adult population is functionally literate – the case in most developed countries for many years – any link between the attainment of literacy and numeracy and economic performance is very hard to demonstrate.[15] He says that much has been made of a recent cross-country comparison showing that British fourteen-year-olds lagged well behind pupils from Singapore, Hong Kong, South Korea and Japan in a recent mathematics study. But what does this actually prove? America, which has the highest GDP per capita in the world, came out of the study as badly as Britain, and what possible influence could the performance of students at least two years away from leaving school have on economic performance? A more meaningful study carried out in 1982–83 showed that children in Hong Kong and Singapore did not have significantly higher scores in maths than those in England. 'Any notion that the impressive economic growth of these countries in the last decade or so is a product of past superior attainment in mathematics is not borne out by the evidence. Indeed, the relative improvement in the mathematics attainment of Hong Kong students has followed economic growth and not precipitated it.'

An even earlier maths study, carried out in 1964, shows that Britain was around average of the twelve countries that took part, making it hard to single out a lack of mathematical skills as the reason for an under-performing economy over the subsequent three decades. Finally, Britain's poor relative performance in the maths study was not mirrored in a similar science study, where UK students did well. Sad to say, there is no correlation between performance in science and growth either.

AND FINALLY . . .

History is littered with civilizations that have been brought down by extremes of inequality. In Ancient Egypt, Mesopotamia, Rome, India, China, Europe and Japan, gross disparities of income and wealth demolished what were once rich and cultured societies. At best, enormous inequality spawns peaceful changes; at worst, bloodshed and violence. Into these categories fall Czarist Russia, the Soviet Union, China, the Ancien Régime in France, the whole system of medieval feudalism.

In the modern world, there is an added complication. The examples mentioned above come from a pre-democratic time. And democracy has complicated matters. As Lester Thurow put it, because market economies have not produced enough economic equality to be compatible with democracy, all democracies have found it necessary to 'interfere' in the market with a wide variety of programmes that are designed to promote equality and stop inequality from rising. These have included GI bills, anti-trust laws, progressive income tax, unemployment insurance, welfare states, full employment.

Historically, democratic governments, not the market, built the middle class. . . . No matter how badly capitalism is treating you, these programs said, democracy is on your side. Democracy cares about capitalistic economic inequality and is working to reduce it. The combination worked. The potential conflict between capitalistic power and democratic power did not explode. . . . History also teaches us that the survival-of-the-fittest versions of capitalism do not work. The free-market economies that existed in the 1920s imploded during the Great Depression and had to be reconstructed by government. Maybe survival-of-the-fittest capitalism can be made to work, but no one has yet done so.[16]

Later Mr Thurow concludes of Clinton's economic policies:

Skill training for the non-college-bound is part of the answer, but it would have to be put together with growth policies that created the jobs and tight labour markets where real wages would once again start rising. Not knowing how to put such policies together and perhaps being unwilling to do so even if they did know, the political Left has nothing left to sell.

Once the honeymoon is over for Labour in Britain, it may become clear that Thurow is as right about Blair as he is about Clinton. This is an era in which a much more elitist form of progressive politics holds sway. This not only fails to address crucial questions of power and control, but does nothing to attack insecurity directly. Instead there is a vision of an opportunity society. Opportunity, not wealth, will trickle down, because as one student of the Labour Party argues: 'for the modernisers, however, equality is an out-dated concept with [it is alleged] its connotations of levelling down and dull uniformity. . . . It [Labour] must unequivocally affirm that its real objective is enhancing individual freedom by extending opportunities. Yet freedom, as a contemporary social democrat (Roy Hattersley) has argued, is only effec-tive to the extent that people have the resources to make real choices and this requires a substantial degree of redistribution. Or, as a socialist of more tra-ditional stripe (Tawney) observed, the existence of opportunities to rise depends "not only upon an open road, but upon an equal start".'[17]

In America, there are growing calls for a change of direction. One econ-omist described the state of affairs as a 'silent depression',[18] and this is borne out by the figures. US GDP growth in the 1990s has been the most sluggish since the 1930s. Real family incomes declined by 6 per cent between 1989 and 1995, only increasing in one year. In the 1930s real wages in the USA rose by 17 per cent, and were back to their 1929 level by 1935. The agony in the 1930s was felt by the unemployed millions, but they were still only a fraction of the population; the silent depression of the 1990s in the USA has affected 80 per cent of employed workers and at least 50 per cent of families. It has not been an unemployment depression but an income depression. Half the families in the USA have seen their incomes decline in the 1990s.

There is a real threat of populism unless solutions can be found to this problem. The discontents who flocked to Ross Perot and Pat Buchanan are testimony to that. What is needed, according to Luttwak, is 'a new political economy' that can 'promise more personal economic security to the broad masses of office workers, shopkeepers, industrial workers and government employees now threatened by efficiency and unemployment'.[19] This new political economy requires a repudiation of much that has happened since the mid-1990s. It means an understanding that inequality is a drag on economic performance and has to be tackled both through an expansionary macro-economic policy to create jobs and through a more progressive tax system. The era of great inflation is a thing of the past; each subsequent peak since that in 1973–74 has been lower than the last. There is a chance that technological advances could be the focus of a new era of prosperity, just as the car and the jet engine were at the heart of the post-war boom. But this will not happen by chance. It was not by luck that growth, incomes, investment and productivity soared in the three decades after the end of the Second World War. There was a catch-up process in which Europe and Japan closed the huge productivity gap with the USA during a period of reconstruction, but as Ajit Singh argues, this does not explain why there was no catch-up after the First World War when the productivity gap was just as large.[20] The explanation is that after the Second World War there was a political commitment to full employment buttressed by a social compact in which employers agreed that the fruits of growth should be shared with the workers and that business should shoulder its share of funding the Welfare State.

It might be argued that because both American and UK GDP per capita are the highest on record there is no cause for concern. But it is not just the level of national wealth but its distribution that matters. There have been four real depressions in the USA – in the 1780s, the 1840s, the 1870s and the 1930s. The top 1 per cent owned 27 per cent of wealth in 1870, 36.3 per cent in 1929, falling to 30.6 per cent in 1939 and 20.8 per cent in 1949. This share rose slightly to 24.9 per cent in 1969, and was back to its 1929 level by 1987. It now stands at 40 per cent plus.

Depressions can be seen as what happens when inequality gets out of hand in a market system. At one end of the scale there is a growth in poverty, which in turn leads to high debt as people struggle to maintain their living standards. They either borrow or consume less. At the other end inequality encourages bouts of wild speculation as the rich find themselves with piles of spare cash. Speculation leads to bubbles, and bubbles lead to crashes, as the inhabitants of Mexico and Thailand could no doubt testify. In the end inequality is bad for everybody, even the rich.

CHAPTER EIGHT

THE BIG ALTERNATIVE

Money obviously does matter, but – except to a minority, and to those
who haven't got any – it doesn't matter most.

Charles Handy

A backward
And dilapidated province, connected
To the big busy world by a tunnel, with a certain
Seedy appeal, is that all it is now?

W. H. Auden, *In Praise of Limestone*, May 1948

If human vices such as greed and envy are systematically cultivated, the
inevitable result is nothing less than a collapse of intelligence. A man
driven by greed or envy loses the power of seeing things as they really
are, of seeing things in their roundness and wholeness, and his very
successes become failures.

E. F. Schumacher, *Small is Beautiful*, Blond & Briggs, 1973

'Tell me', said Birkin. 'What do you live for?' Gerald's face went baffled. 'What do I live for?' he repeated. 'I suppose I live to work, to produce something, in so far as I am a purposive being. Apart from that, I live because I am living.'

'And what's your work? Getting so many more thousands of tons of coal out of the earth every day. And when we've got all the coal we want, and all the plush furniture, and pianofortes, and the rabbits are all stewed and eaten, and we're all warm and our bellies are filled and we're listening to the young lady performing on the pianoforte – what then?'

D. H. Lawrence posed this question in *Women in Love* more than eighty years ago. It is still awaiting an answer as the twentieth century draws to a close. Capitalism and democracy have emerged triumphant from the struggle against Communism and totalitarianism, largely because they have proved better at delivering 'the goods' than any rival system. But Lawrence's 'what then?' is as relevant now as it was when he was working on *Women in Love*, a time when the Edwardian era was dissolving into the horrors of the First World War and one phase of industrialization built on coal was giving way to another centred on mass production.

In a sense, Eric Hobsbawm was right in the sub-heading of his book *The Age of Extremes* to call this the short century, lasting but seventy-five years from the assassination at Sarajevo to the arrival in Eastern Europe of fast cars, fast women and fast money. Globalization is not a new phenomenon, for the period from 1870 to 1914 was as much a period of free movement of capital and rapid technological change as our own. For the pound sterling and the City of London in the last years of the nineteenth century, read the dollar and Wall Street; for the motor car and the telephone read the long-haul jet and the worldwide web. And just as the profound political and economic changes of the pre-1914 age challenged all the certainties of the mid-Victorian world, leading to revolutions in art, design, music and literature, so the twentieth century is ending with a search to find out where the modern phase of globalization is supposed to be leading us all: a world in which the question of production is solved once and for all, and all nations share in universal peace and prosperity? Or a soulless, standardized materialism in which the greed of the favoured few and a system skewed in favour of the rich and powerful drive the planet to the brink of extinction?

There is little doubt how Lawrence would have responded. Gerald is portrayed as the archetype of a man dominated by mechanistic urges; he is seen forcing his mare to wait terrified while a clanking goods train passes a level crossing; he wants to squeeze every last bit of production out of his mines; he wants to dominate. In the end he loses control of his life and dies alone, freezing to death in the high Alps.

That was then. Today, fires can destroy the rainforest of Borneo as if the island had been turned into Dante's Inferno, young men in the dealing rooms of financial institutions make millions from shifting money round the world in an ever more fruitless paper chase, eighteen million people are without work in Europe and more than a billion people are without the basic necessities of life – food, clean water and shelter. Lawrence would have seen this as a horrific example of dehumanization, of the triumph of the machine. And he would have been right. For years now, Lawrence has been deeply untrendy, far too hectoring and, to be honest, a little bit proletarian for these sophisticated times. But in many ways he was the prototype green, and he has found an echo in many a modern writer trying to make sense of it all. Take Charles Handy, for example, who says in his latest book: 'If we trusted ourselves, and our hearts, a little more and the dogmas of the disciplines rather less, we could regain control over the things which really matter'.[1]

The 'things which really matter' have not changed that much over the years. People still want a steady job, decent pay, a healthy environment, personal freedom and somebody to rely on if the going gets a bit tough. In short, they want security. But security is the one thing the modern system cannot deliver. Indeed, it seems almost proud of the fact that it cannot offer security. Security is bad. It stands in the way of the great god of international competitiveness, the economic imperative that dominates the West's business culture and justifies everything from the downsizing of bank clerks to the chopping down of rainforests. This is fine for those who can compete; for the big powerful nations, the corporations that dwarf many a small nation-state, the trouble-shooters, the analysts, the design gurus and the other fortunate few who make up the global elite. In an age where money and the pursuit of money have been turned into the sole reason for living, they will always do well. But for almost everybody else – the people and the nations who cannot compete in this cut-throat game – it is a frightening proposition.

Handy quotes some alarming statistics, as disturbing in their way as the destruction each year of 4 per cent of the Amazon rainforest or the widening gap between the world's rich and poor. America is the world's richest nation and its only remaining superpower. When the Berlin Wall came down it was to New York and Los Angeles that the citizens of those drab towns in Eastern Europe turned for their model of the good life. Yet, in the USA, 42 per cent of workers say they feel used up by the end of the day, and 69 per cent would like to lead a more relaxed life. Little wonder then that America is the therapy capital of the universe and that analysts are making a fortune out of unhappiness. One study by MIT, cited by Handy, found that depression at work was costing $47 billion a year, the same as treating heart disease. Another, by the US Institute of Management, came up with the findings that 77 per cent of managers reported their hours to be stressful,

77 per cent were worried about the effect of their work on their family, and 74 per cent about their relationship with their partner.

None of this is ever captured by the standard measures of economic achievement. Measured in the traditional way – by growth in per capita GDP – we have never been richer. Starting in the immediate aftermath of the Second World War, the line on the graph moves steadily onwards and upwards. By any of the accepted yardsticks we are better off than we were at the start of the 1950s, when most of the rationing necessitated by war had been scrapped. We live longer, we consume more calories, we all have TVs, most of us have videos, washing machines and telephones; car ownership has increased sharply, families that would once have taken holidays in Blackpool, Margate and Scarborough now head for Benidorm, Marbella and Sorrento.

But GDP per head is a crude means of assessing a society's well-being, missing out on all the texture that differentiates quality of life from standard of living. There is a reason why per capita GDP has attained such importance; it is easy to measure output, spending in the shops and the incomes of those in work, but very hard to put figures on concepts such as rising crime, social breakdown, pollution, spending on self-improvement and so on. And economists love to deal in hard facts and figures. They find nebulous concepts difficult, even though for many people it is hard to square the insecure and anxious lives they lead with the notion that they are much richer than they were ten or twenty years ago. In recent years, some radical economists have tried to incorporate some of these 'nebulous concepts' into an all-embracing measure of well-being called the Index of Sustainable Economic Welfare. For all its obvious flaws as seen from the standpoint of a statistician – how to put a cost on habitat loss or rising inequality, for example – the ISEW provides a better picture of what has happened to the West in the fifty years since the war. In the 1950s and 1960s the ISEW rose in tandem with per capita GDP. It was a time not just of rising incomes, but of greater social equity, low crime, full employment and expanding welfare states. But from the mid-1970s onwards the two measures started to move apart. GDP per head continued its inexorable rise, but the ISEW started to decline as a result of lengthening dole queues, social exclusion, the explosion in crime, habitat loss, environmental degradation and the growth of environment- and stress-related illnesses. By the start of the 1990s, the ISEW was almost back to the levels at which it had started in the early 1950s. There is no doubt in our minds that the ISEW provides a better guide to what has been happening in the global economy, with its movement since the early 1970s first helping to explain the rise of the right under Thatcher and Reagan and the later swing back to the left culminating in the victories for Clinton, Blair and Jospin in a seven-month period between November 1996 and June 1997. There was no guarantee that this shift would be permanent: electorates everywhere were fearful and migratory, prepared to punish parties that failed to answer a deep-seated need for a safe anchorage in the storm-tossed 1990s. For, as almost every commentator agreed, this was a turbulent, disjointed decade. We may be richer; but are we happier?

Lawrence, Schumacher, Gandhi and Handy would all say no. Some of the things that would sway them are hard to quantify: the one in seven children in the UK whose asthma is believed to be aggravated by pollution, the exact number of people who are homeless, the doubling of crime since the end of the 1970s. Although by no means a Marxist, Lawrence was convinced that the machine age would be destroyed by its own internal contradictions and that the world would then be recolonized by an elite (Lawrence, his disciples and some suitably noble savages) who had proved themselves worthy of redemption. Gandhi shared Lawrence's fear of man's subservience to the machine, once saying:

I want the dumb millions of our land to be healthy and happy, and I want them to grow spiritually. . . . If we feel the need of machines, we will certainly have them. Every machine that helps every individual has a place, but there should be no place for machines that concentrate power in a few hands and turn the masses into mere machine minders, if indeed they do not make them unemployed.[2]

Fritz Schumacher was convinced that the world – or, at least, the rich part of it – was living beyond its means, and urged an end to the hedonistic gobbling up of non-renewable resources. In *Small is Beautiful*, written in the early 1970s, he made some dire forecasts, most of which, sadly, have proved to be underestimates. Like Lawrence, he would be shocked to see how his warnings have gone unheeded.

Handy, while sharing Churchill's opinion that democratic capitalism is probably the least bad system available, has serious doubts about where it is heading. He, too, sees a spiritual hollowing out, in which Man has become a prisoner of the 'money myth' and he argues that the limits to growth are not so much environmental and economic as psychological and philosophical. We disagree with Handy. All four of the factors he mentions are proving or will prove to be limitations on growth. But where we do concur is that it is the money machine that lies at the root of the Age of Insecurity, and that only by restoring money to its rightful subordinate position will the deep-seated problems of unemployment, poverty, exclusion and environmental degradation be tackled.

JOURNEY TO THE END OF THE NIGHT: THE 1990s AND BEYOND

The twentieth century began with a decade that, in retrospect, seems utterly at odds with the barbed wire and the machine guns of the Somme, the searchlights over Nuremberg and the purges of Stalin's Russia. Similarly, it has closed with a decade that jars with the recent past. The 1980s were, even at the time, self-consciously a reaction to the thirty years of Keynesian plenty that had gone before; the 1990s have often seemed to be a 'virtual' decade, in which history has been abolished, tradition counts for nothing and everything is in a state of flux.

For our fortunate elite – the well-heeled, the able, the peripatetic intelligentsia with their Rhodes scholarships and their PhDs from Harvard and Stanford – it has all been hugely exciting. They have travelled the world (club class, at the very least) like latter-day Richard the Lionhearts, suffused with a crusading spirit. In place of a lance they have had a laptop, instead of a shield they have grasped a mobile phone and a flipchart containing one word: change. Rarely a day goes by without the public being told that they have to change – change the way they work, change the way they cast their vote, change the way they communicate, change the way they show their emotions, change the way they look after their bodies, change the way they think about welfare. Everything, in short, can and should be changed about the way we live our lives, apart, that is, from the economic system.

Free trade, free movement of capital, privatization, low taxes, flexible labour markets: these cannot be questioned. They are, quite simply, above argument. The current orthodoxy does not quite suggest that late twentieth-century free-market capitalism has attained a state of perfection. That would indeed be foolish, for it would suggest that there is no real role for the small army of skilled technicians who keep the machine running at full throttle. Instead, there is always a case for some tinkering with the mechanism – a bit more competition here, a touch of education and training there, a rethink of the benefit system thrown in for good measure – and this is what is on offer in the racks of books on management theory that line today's bookshops.

But since the current model of development is believed to be omnipotent and omnipresent, there is little or no analysis of what the machine is for or what would happen if it broke down. In our view, this is a serious mistake, and could perhaps turn out to be a fatal one, unless swift action is taken. The slow growth, the high unemployment, the crippling debt burden for the developing world, the loss of habitat, the rise in crime, the bouts of severe foreign exchange turbulence do not suggest to us that this is a machine where judicious use of the oil can or – to use the modern metaphor – some repro-gramming will suffice. This machine is more like the nuclear power station in *The China Syndrome*: a good idea in principle, yet bedevilled by the most serious of design flaws and teetering on the brink of a geological fault. As we have detailed earlier in this book, some of the Panglossian claims for global capitalism have been undermined by the chronic unemployment in Europe, the social breakdown in America and, in particular, the foreign exchange crisis and pollution cloud that engulfed south-east Asia in the late summer and autumn of 1997. The humbling of the tiger economies of Thailand, Malaysia, Indonesia and South Korea by currency speculators and the smog that descended over Jakarta, Singapore and Kuala Lumpur as a result of forest fires burning out of control served notice that the downside of globalization was the financial instability caused by trillions of dollars sloshing around unchecked in financial markets and a cavalier attitude towards a fragile ecosystem.

The losers, as always, were the ordinary people of the region, those choking in the fumes or faced with years of economic austerity imposed by the International Monetary Fund. In Britain, the 1990s was the decade in which the demolition gangs of the free market finally smashed up the post-war 'home'. Between 1990 and the end of 1996, one million people lost their homes through mortgage company repossession as 390,000 proper-ties were seized. A further one million-odd properties were estimated in 1996 to be stuck in 'negative equity', according to securities group UBS.

Personal bankruptcies in England and Wales hit a peak of 36,794 in 1992 and by 1997 seemed to have 'stabilized' at 22,000 a year, three times the 'crisis' level reached during the first post-war recession, that of the mid-1970s. Business insolvencies, measured as the number of receivership and administration orders, totalled 23,439 for the years 1990 to the end of 1996, and even this huge figure – compiled by accountants Deloitte & Touche – is an underestimate as the data include Scottish business failures only from 1991. And unemployment became a mainstream social experience: by the latter part of 1997, it was calculated that one in five men and one in eight women had suffered at least one spell of joblessness during their working lives.

Little wonder that some people were asking whether there was not a saner way of ordering the world's affairs. We believe that there is, and the rest of this chapter will be spent looking at what could and should be done.

Lawrence provided the answer to his own question in his poem 'The Triumph of the Machine', written near the end of his life, in which he looked forward with relish to the day when 'the last factory hooter sends up the last wild cry of despair as the machine breaks down'. Then, Lawrence said, the world would be unshackled from industrialism. As a poem, it is great stuff; as a political prescription it leaves a lot to be desired, not least in that attempts to return to a preindustrial state – Pol Pot's Cambodia springs to mind – have not been especially encouraging. From the vantage point of 1997, it looks unlikely that Western capitalism will collapse, but if it did it would take most of us with it. What, then, is to be done?

OPTION ONE: LIE BACK AND THINK OF GATT-LAND

An answer of sorts is to leave everything to market forces. Free-marketeers have long argued that capitalism is a self-regulating organism which, left to its own devices and unhindered by meddling politicians, would achieve a benign equilibrium. There is something to be said for this argument, even though most of the recent evidence has suggested that imperfections in the market mechanism have resulted in equilibria that deliver unacceptably high levels of unemployment, waste, poverty and damage to both the social and ecological realms. For those on the left, it is not easy to see why there should be a progressive case for market forces. But consider what happens in the world of nature, where an increase in the population of lions means that the antelope herds dwindle. But the lions can only flourish if there are enough antelope to prey upon, so gradually the lion population starts to fall and the antelope population starts to rise. Now think of the lions as capital and the antelope as labour. Capital has had the upper hand over labour since the mid-1970s. Trade unions have been hunted down like antelope by the Masai, unemployment has risen, insecurity has risen. But, there comes a point when deflation becomes a hindrance for capitalism, because the system depends for its survival on satisfying consumer wants on an ever increasing scale. Multinational corporations need customers with money in their pockets, and gradually the pendulum swings back towards fuller employment and stronger unions capable of recolonizing some of their old grazing grounds.

One attraction of this thesis is that it is dynamic. It recognizes that there are conflicting forces that are in a state of constant struggle with each other, as opposed to the notion that there is now one supremacist model of development in which everybody is on the same side. Another is that the championing of consumer power in the laissez-faire revolution of the late 1970s and early 1980s has led to a situation in which the emancipated consumers can extract concessions from their liberators. Financial deregulation, for example, allowed more people to own their own homes, take out personal pensions, start up savings schemes. Many of these people were naive and gullible, and many of them were ripped off. But such was the public outrage against some of the more egregious examples of wrongdoing in the financial sector – Barlow Clowes, Robert Maxwell, and the almost systematic way in which personal pensions were sold to individuals in good occupational schemes – that by the end of the 1980s a reaction had set in. The financial sector knew that those companies that did not clean up their act would see their customers drift away to those that did. Market forces would out in the end. Similarly, Shell was forced, by a consumer boycott in Germany, to back down over the plan to dump the Brent Spar oil rig in the North Atlantic. The growth, particularly among young people, of an interest in how products are made and the working conditions of those who make them means that many corporations fear more than anything else the loss of their 'right-on' image. The Nike shoe company, for example, wants to maximize its profits and charges premium prices for its running shoes and trainers. But it is acutely sensitive to accusations that its pursuit of the 'bottom line' is at the expense of workers in Indonesia paid only a dollar a day in plants where unions are banned by law.

One economist has argued that consumer power means that it is possible to construct a demand curve for labour standards. Consumers in the West are not indifferent to the way in which goods are made and would pay more for products that have been made by a workforce treated properly. Take two identical T-shirts, one produced in an ethnically cleansed village, the other under normal conditions where the workers are free to join a union and have the right to strike. 'At the same price most consumers would choose the shirt made under better working conditions. Most would pay a modest premium for that shirt. But as the premium rises, the number willing to do so will fall. This gives us the demand curve for labour standards.'[3]

Mr Freeman's argument is that governments should consider legislating for labels on goods explaining how they have been made. This would not offend those for whom the free market is sacred, since perfect information for consumers is seen as vital if the market is to work properly. We could eventually see consumers as the agents of what the Austrian economist Joseph Schumpeter called 'gales of creative destruction', in which the power of unfettered business will be challenged and eventually toppled by the consumer power unleashed by laissez-faire policies in the late 1970s and 1980s. Some signs of this were already apparent by the end of the 1990s. Food production and animal hygiene were being cleaned up as a result of the outbreak of BSE among British cattle herds, a disease that would never have developed had regulations in abattoirs and for the manufacturers of animal feedstuff not been relaxed in the 1980s. The new Labour government also took a Freemanesque line on pension mis-selling, publishing tables of those companies failing to move quickly enough to compensate clients who suffered financial losses as a result of being advised to move into personal pension plans. To complete the picture of an age willing to admit that it had got things seriously wrong in the 1980s, the Treasury minister put in charge of the clean-up campaign was one Helen Liddell, a former executive for Robert Maxwell, the biggest pension cheat of the lot.

A THIRD WAY: THE SEARCH GOES ON

The textbook theory behind the free market approach may be impeccable, but in practice the world simply does not work like that. Consumers do not have perfect information and the notion of perfect competition requires a large number of small firms none of which is able to dominate the market. Are Microsoft and Intel minnows in the big pool of computer technology? Are Toyota, BMW and General Motors really so tiny and inconsequential that they cannot carve up markets between them? Is it really true that Goldman Sachs and J. P. Morgan are but innocent bit players in the world of global finance?

The reality is that the ideology of laissez-faire is so hedged around with absurd assumptions as to make it nonsensical. Massachusetts Institute of Technology Professor Paul Samuelson, for example, once wrote an elegant defence of free trade, so elegant that he won the Nobel Prize for Economics for it in 1970. Other economists purred their approval of Professor Samuelson's superb argument, while ignoring assumptions that the man in the street might consider relevant to the case. For Professor Samuelson's thesis to hold good, it has to be accepted that there is no government, gainers compensate the losers from trade, capital and industry stay at home and do not set off round the world in a desperate search for the lowest wages, wages in the domestic economy are the same in every industry, and the country does not have a trade deficit. In the circumstances, Samuelson might as well have added a sixth assumption, that the moon is made of green cheese.

It does not matter whether free market theory is breached once or one hundred times, nor is it material whether the hole in the argument is big or small. Once the principle is sullied, there can be no optimal outcome, no perfect equilibrium. The existence of a state with a role that extends beyond establishing property rights and the rule of law would, in itself, be enough to make the whole free market argument tendentious. But modern capitalism is also marked by the existence of oligopolistic firms, which, far from responding to price signals from consumers, actually create their own demand through advertising and a range of marketing techniques. The abiding belief of free market theorists is that business provides what consumers want it to provide; the reality is that consumers buy what business wants them to buy. The global trading system is driven not by the guiding light of David Ricardo and the theory of comparative advantage but by the bludgeoning power of the three big players – the United States, Europe and Japan. This is not free trade; it is old-style mercantilism in a different guise.

The knowledge that nothing approaching a perfect system exists – or is ever likely to – has restored some self-confidence to progressives. They no longer believe that the state can or should try to run the economy, and accept many of the changes – privatization, tighter curbs on the activities of unions, the move towards lower marginal rates of income tax – that have taken place since the mid-1970s. In particular, they never seek to challenge the culture of big business. The movers and shakers of the corporate world are not just tolerated by the new parties of the left but welcomed with open arms into top slots in government. Clinton and Blair have offered business most of what it wants – NAFTA, GATT, WTO, a single currency, flexibility, deals on investment – while business has to concede not even the smallest of the demands made by labour for more secure terms and conditions, union rights and higher pay.

While never challenging the right of business to press ahead with its strategic agenda for greater liberalization, the new left is prepared to argue that the imperfections in the laissez-faire model have given rise to market failures that ought to be tackled by governments. Given that even the right believes there is a role for the state, the real question then becomes the sort of role it should be. Progressives have to admit that there is something wrong with the system. Otherwise they would not be able to call themselves progressives. But their analysis is woolly and unsound. Advocates of the third way believe that modern capitalism is doubly flawed; high levels of long-term unemployment and social exclusion show that it cannot deliver optimal outcomes, while at the same time its creed of individualism and disdain for the public realm has hollowed out Western society and caused a moral crisis. As one writer put it:

We have a universal market, but it does not carry with it the civilizing effects that were so confidently expected by Hume and Voltaire. Instead of generating a new appreciation of common interests and inclinations – of the essential sameness of human beings everywhere – the global market seems to intensify the awareness of ethnic and national differences. The unification of the market goes hand in hand with the fragmentation of culture.[4]

But, having reached this point, the case against global capitalism reaches an abrupt halt. There is no hint that the left should be trying to roll back the power of business and completely change the nature of the system. On the contrary, all that has happened is that Mrs Thatcher's most baleful legacy to the West – the phrase 'there is no alternative' – has been accepted as one of life's certainties. To be sure, those progressives in Britain and America who are in power feel a sense of malaise. But their response has been rather like that of Gladstone who, with his forays to rescue the fallen ladies of the night in Victorian London's demi-monde, sought to save capitalism from itself.

Both Bill Clinton and Tony Blair are, of course, avid believers in the third way. While accepting that the power of government to act has been seriously circumscribed by the power of financial markets and the footloose nature of capital, the Democrats in the USA and the Labour Party in Britain have sought to build a new consensus around the idea of a limited interventionism underpinned by the philosophy of communitarianism, a term coined by the American writer Amitai Etzioni. It is not hard to see why Mr Etzioni has become fashionable among the third-wayers since his entire philosophy has been based on building a bridge between the demands of the individual and the needs of society.

In the contemporary West, there is an urgent need to rebuild a sense of personal and social responsibility, a sense that we are not only entitled but must also serve, that the individual good is deeply intertwined with the needs of the common good. . . . The West is in the cold season of excessive individualism and yearns for the warmth of community to allow human relations to blossom.[5]

Mr Etzioni has become to Blair and Clinton what Hayek was to Mrs Thatcher. Blair's speeches are replete with the need to balance 'rights and responsibilities', and the way in which individuals can draw strength from a set of collectively shared assumptions, traditions and family values. To symbolize his commitment to family values, one of Blair's first decisions on winning the 1997 election was that his family move into Downing Street with him (the bigger flat above Number 11 rather than the cramped accommodation above Number 10) – the first time children's voices had been heard in the corridors of power for fifty years.

To some, there was rather too much of the old-fashioned evangelizing preacher about Blair. His first party conference speech as prime minister talked in quasi-religious terms of 'beacons of hope', rather as John Wesley might have thundered two centuries earlier about the need for his flock to renounce sin and prepare itself for Judgement Day. Labour's new creed was certainly based on concepts that Wesley would have understood – self-discipline, caring for others and hard work. Of the three, work was the most central. By the time Blair came to power, unemployment in Britain was falling, although it still remained higher than it had been when the Callaghan government left office in May 1979. However, joblessness was heavily concentrated in certain geographical areas and among certain groups of people, particularly ethnic minorities and the young. One in five households of working age had nobody in work. Moreover, the higher incidence of divorce and the increase in the number of single-parent families meant that there were one million lone parents bringing up two million children on state benefits, at a cost to the taxpayer of £10 billion a year. Labour's argument was simple. High structural unemployment and a lack of employment opportunities for single parents were linked to sink estates, crime, a tendency for men to abrogate their responsibilities and deep, entrenched poverty. Putting people back to work – or giving women the chance to work – would, by contrast, lead to higher living standards, a greater sense of personal dignity and responsibility, and help to restore communities.

The government's five-point programme for achieving this goal was laid out in full in October 1997.[6] Step one was to promote higher levels of growth and economic stability. Step two was to invest more in human capital, namely education and training. Step three was to help people off welfare and into work. Step four was to improve the workings of the market via a robustly Thatcherite prescription of tougher competition policy, regulatory reform and the outlawing of state subsidies to ailing industries. Step five was to create a fairer and more inclusive society by, among other things, introducing a minimum wage, modestly reforming labour law to give unions the right to be recognized where 50 per cent of the workforce wanted one and signing up to the European Social Chapter.

The Treasury's *Action Plan for Jobs* encapsulated the idea of the third way, incorporating something from the right (liberalization of markets) with something from the left (supply-side measures to combat inequality and unemployment directly) and something that both left and right could agree on: the link between economic stability and growth.

There is much in this new left programme that we can agree with; some of it, indeed, we applaud. The argument that the real enemy of the family has been the social breakdown associated with the failures of free-market economics rather than comprehensive schooling and permissive attitudes to sex seems to us to be closer to the truth. Western societies in the 1950s and 1960s were stable precisely because jobs were plentiful and pay was good. Workers were happy to see the taxes taken from rising real incomes pooled and recycled into the social wage – education, health, pensions and a safety net for the weak and infirm. The notion that the era of full employment spawned a dependency culture is simply not true. Working people were, often for the first time in their lives, able to fend for themselves and were proud of their independence. Communitarians say that their heartfelt desire is to return to this state of grace, but their ideas and actions tend to suggest otherwise. The sort of sturdy, self-reliant communities that Mr Etzioni and his followers yearn for will not come about unless there is real economic change. But fundamental economic change – of the kind forced on the West by the Great Depression and the Second World War – is the one thing the communitarians cannot offer. Instead, they propose to tackle the problem from the other end, meddling only peripherally in the activities of capitalism but forever seeking new ways to bully people into leading better lives. The charge levied against communitarianism – that it is a doctrine suffused with social authoritarianism – is well made. In the 1960s the state believed that its role should end when workers arrived home with their pay packets.

Communitarianism, by contrast, is not content that people should be left alone once they have entered the garden gate; it wants to know how they are cleaning their teeth and washing their hands, how many minutes their children are spending on their homework, how much fatty food they are eating, how many units of alcohol they are imbibing, whether they are having safe sex and whether, having had the safe sex, they are guilty of the even worse sin of enjoying a post-coital cigarette.

The package calls to mind the late Rabbi Hugo Grynn's dictum regarding the distinction between a genuine holy man and a cult leader; as the latter grows older, he said, he becomes progressively more interested in the contents of other men's souls and in the contents of his own stomach, whereas the former becomes increasingly interested in the contents of his own soul and of other men's stomachs. The Rabbi's words cannot help but come to mind as one reads of yet another trendy, expensive restaurant made famous by Labour's stage army of rich lawyers and business tycoons, all oozing sanctimony and tut-tutting over the lifestyles and 'attitudes' of the poor.

It seems obvious to us that – even allowing for its illiberality – this is a less successful recipe for the sort of society the communitarians claim to want than the mixture of economic dirigisme and social tolerance that gradually came into being during the first three decades after the war. We do not think such a recasting of policy is impossible, but it would require a fundamental shift in attitudes. Few of the people at the top in Clinton's Democrat Party or in self-styled New Labour have any first-hand experience of the politics of exclusion. They are strangers to unemployment and low pay, and are rather better acquainted with the *Michelin Guide* than *The Communist Manifesto*. That, of course, does not debar them from seeking a communitarian solution, either from a sense of social justice or because they personally stand to gain from an environment where falling crime rates bring down insurance policies, and savings from the cost of welfare can boost spending on state schools and the NHS.

They can see – as even Milton Friedman does – that a liberal society requires a 'minimum degree of literacy and knowledge', along with a 'widespread acceptance of some common set of values'.[7] But after that, as J. K. Galbraith pointed out in *The Culture of Contentment*, their commitment to social inclusion and the family is tempered by the knowledge that they personally are doing rather well out of the process of globalization.[8] Put another way, the case for higher marginal rates of income tax gets weaker and weaker the more money you earn.

Unfortunately, without a greater degree of scepticism about the wisdom of unfettered capitalism, the hopes of a thorough-going reconstruction of society along communitarian lines are unlikely to be met. This is because globalization is inimical to family values. The family is based around the intimate, the local, shared and traditional values. The global market-place is concerned with none of these things. It can see a point in family values and tradition but only so long as they do not stand in the way of the iron logic of the global market-place – the relentless search for the highest possible rate of return on capital. As one writer put it: 'The more closely capitalism came to be identified with immediate gratification and planned obsolescence, the more relentlessly it wore away the moral foundation of family life.'[9]

But during the 1980s and 1990s, globalization has attained an aura of invulnerability. Multinational companies are now widely perceived to be more powerful than governments, the state is seen as withering away and Bill Clinton found in 1992 that even being the head of state in the world's sole remaining superpower did not give him the clout to face down the bond market, which, as one of his closest advisers admitted with a mixture of awe and disgust, was more powerful than the Pope or the president. If all this is true, then we should be grateful for small mercies and accept that the incremental changes offered by the left's cautious, supply-side interventionism are the best that can be offered. We believe that more far-reaching solutions are not only necessary, but possible.

IT'S THAT MAN AGAIN: THE CASE FOR JOHN MAYNARD KEYNES

The very mention of Keynes is sufficient to send shivers down the spine of the global Establishment, so it is as well to state from the outset what we are talking about here – or, more to the point, what we are not talking about. Keynes has to be differentiated from Keynesianism, particularly the latter stages of Keynesianism when it was possible for Richard Nixon to excuse his loss of control over the American economy in 1971 with the comment: 'We are all Keynesians now'. With friends like Nixon, Keynes did not really need enemies. By the time of the stagflation that followed the Yom Kippur war of 1973, Keynes had become associated on the right with all the excesses of big government and stood accused of taking a cavalier approach to budget deficits, inflation and the tendency of state spending to crowd out private-sector investment. While this is not meant to be a history of the post-war West, it should perhaps be pointed out that Keynesian demand management achieved rather higher levels of growth and employment than the monetarist rigour that supplanted it. But that is not our point. Our real concern here is to show that the central thrust of Keynes's work was that capitalism was not a self-correcting system; rather, when left to its own devices it could lead to prolonged periods when output was low and unemployment low. Keynes's view, which we share, was simple: capitalism should not be left to its own devices.

In some respects, Keynes had it easy. His *General Theory of Employment,*

Interest and Money was published in 1936, just as the West was starting to emerge slowly from the slump and embark on the long slide into war. These two events – first the Depression, then the war – legitimized Keynes's approach. Left to its own devices, capitalism could lead to untold misery and waste; in wartime the state relegated the mill-owners, the coal magnates and the railway barons to secondary roles as it mobilized every possible resource for national survival. As a result, when the war ended it was unthinkable that the pre-Depression status quo should be restored. Keynes believed in capitalism; indeed, he was a famous speculator himself. But he did not believe that capitalism would thrive unless it was tamed and managed. This applied in both the domestic and the international spheres, with the state not only stepping in to boost investment in times of weak demand but also putting severe restrictions on the mobility of capital through exchange controls and the Bretton Woods currency system.

The right would argue that what happened over the next thirty years – comfortably the most successful period the world economy has ever enjoyed – was the result of post-war reconstruction, the opening up of world markets through successive GATT rounds, the pent-up consumer spending stifled by twenty years of Depression and war. In fact, the state of the economy is attributed to anything other than the blindingly obvious: that the West did well because Keynes was right and capitalism did have to be carefully managed. It could, indeed, be argued that had the disciples of Keynes followed their master's blueprint more scrupulously and only used deficit spending in economic downswings, then the upswing in the 1950s and 1960s would have been even more pronounced. Faced with the fact that its antidote to Keynesianism proved to be a quack doctor's remedy, the right has opened up a fresh line of argument. Even if Keynes had a point in 1936, the world has changed. The globalization genie is well and truly out of the bottle. Again, this is a highly questionable interpretation of events.

Let's start with Britain and ask ourselves what the Major government did on the evening of 16 September 1992. Black Wednesday was not just the day that the pound was ejected from the Exchange Rate Mechanism; it was also the moment when Keynesian economics was reborn in the UK. Major and his Chancellor did exactly what Keynes, had he been closeted with them in Admiralty House while Downing Street was refurbished after an IRA mortar attack, would have told them to do. First, they set about easing monetary policy, allowing the pound to fall by 15 per cent and cutting base rates from 10 per cent to 6 per cent over the next five months. Second, the annual Autumn Statement in November 1992 provided £750 million for housing associations to buy 20,000 empty houses, provided export cover to exporters to help them re-establish themselves in markets lost during the pound's over-valuation in the ERM, abolished the levy on the purchase of new cars to stimulate consumer spending, and boosted public spending by £1.5 billion. The Prime Minister summed up the new policy as a growth strategy. It was a Keynesian growth strategy and it worked like a dream.

Britain's rediscovery of Keynes was opportune, if long overdue, proving as it did what could be achieved if the right sort of macro-economic poli-cies were applied. But the UK was not the only country in which policy makers were starting to wonder whether monetarism was quite the cure-all that it had once seemed to be. America's recovery from the Gulf war reces-sion had been relatively rapid because the Federal Reserve deliberately kept real interest rates at zero for two years, ensuring that liquidity was injected into a banking system put in jeopardy by the lending spree of the late 1980s. That the Fed should have tried a classic Keynesian remedy should cause little surprise, since America was only ever an occasional dabbler with the drug of monetarism and even under Ronald Reagan followed an economic strategy that could best be described as military Keynesianism, in which increased defence spending had the dual impact of prosecuting the Cold War and reflating the economy.

More remarkable, perhaps, was the way in which Helmut Kohl set about fusing the two halves of Germany following reunification in 1990. Despite the fact that Germany had been one of the few countries that had not tried a Keynesian solution in the aftermath of the mid-1970s oil shock, Bonn came up with a classic piece of tax and spend: tax the rich people of West Germany and spend it on a reconstruction programme in the East. During the 1997 general election campaign, Blair repeatedly stressed that Keynesian tax-and-spend policies were finished. Presumably nobody informed Herr Kohl of that fact.

The final example of Keynes's relevance in this supposedly Keynes-free age comes from Asia. There have been three phases to the Asian miracle: the first saw the rise of Japan, the second the coming of age of the tiger economies of Taiwan, South Korea, Hong Kong, Singapore and China, the third the remarkable expansion in Indonesia, Thailand and Malaysia. Yet, when the region was beset by currency turbulence in the summer of 1997, it was the newly industrializing nations of south-east Asia that were first affected; the crisis began where there was most evidence of what Keynes called the casino economy. When the contagion did spread it was not because there had been too much Keynesian regulation of credit and capital flows but too little. The success of governments in Taiwan, Japan and South Korea in securing rapid growth was the result of a determined effort to build up export industries, both by keeping the exchange rate low and by active industrial policies designed to concentrate resources among a handful of favoured companies. Regardless of the credo of GATT, imports were curtailed so that domestic industries could be given time to flourish without facing the full blast of competition from overseas. Protectionism extended to service sectors that were heavily over-manned by Western standards, but which soaked up surplus labour in order that employment levels could be kept high. When things started to go wrong in the Asian economies in 1997, the IMF and the OECD were taken by surprise. Both had held the Asian 'tigers' up as models for developing countries.

Linda Weiss argues that the alleged impotence of the nation-state has been wildly exaggerated.[10] In part, this has been fostered by nation-states themselves, which have tried to justify unpopular policies by telling electorates that the dictates of the global market have left them with no choice but to bend to the prevailing mood. In part, it has been stimulated by the multinational corporations, which find that even shows of illusory power can help them to extract useful concessions from governments. She adds, rightly, that an additional problem is that many nation-states have made life even more difficult for themselves by following economic policies that have ensured year after year of slow growth and high unemployment. The potential for active fiscal policies has diminished as the state's resources have been concentrated on the long-term unemployed and the increasing number of families living below the breadline. Even here, the state has had to be careful not to overdo the largess. History suggests that the reluctance to pay taxes goes back a long way: witness the Boston Tea Party, the Peasants' Revolt and the wicked old Sheriff of Nottingham. But taxes are particularly unpopular when times are tough for those paying them, as they were in the past in times of famine and have been in the modern era when real incomes are rising modestly (as in Britain) or not at all (as in the United States). At a time when its resources are stretched and higher taxes are singularly unpopular with an enfranchised population, it is little wonder that governments would like to pretend that their power is being leeched away by the nasty corporations.

Again, we ask: *cui bono?* Who gains from the nation-state's crisis of confidence? High on the list of beneficiaries have to be international finance and multinational business. The more timid the nation-states become in their dealings with capital, the greater the manoeuvring room for capital. Some idea of big business's agenda for the nation-state can be gauged from an article in its house magazine, *The Economist*, on 29 June 1991. Ostensibly about Canada, the piece was titled 'The Post-modern Nation-state?', and conjured up this vision of that country's future: 'Perhaps the most important responsibilities in tomorrow's Canada will be municipal ones. . . . For those who like winter sports, Canada will always (unless global warming intervenes) be an attractive country. It will lead the way on issues like smoking in public. . . . It will provide jobs for constitutional experts. . . . It will also continue to have a truculent French-speaking minority.'

To be fair, the (anonymous) author did not advocate such a future for Canada, but merely extrapolated from current trends, and seems accurately to have identified the direction in which Canada – and other states, including our own – are being pushed, towards a future of glorified municipal activity (tourism promotion, bossy public-health rules) and endless bickering between ethnic groups. From the perspective of the boardroom, a mouth-watering vista opens up of a world polity atomized into thousands of city councils, all fighting like dogs for 'inward investment' under the watchful eye of the World Trade Organization, the international enforcement arm of big business.

Of course, this is just half the story. Like the cocksure teenager insisting on his indifference to the girl next door, big business lets it be known it can take or leave nation-states provided they stay out of the way of 'enterprise' and 'competitiveness'. But this is far from the whole truth. In extreme cases, wealthy multinationals can effectively dispense with any state whatever and operate in conditions of near-anarchy: the mining giant Lonrho employed 1,400 men-at-arms to defend its interests in Mozambique in the early 1990s, and in West Africa mercenary units have 'established stability' in diamond-mining areas, sometimes – it has to be said – to the relief of the local population. But these are exceptions – exceptions made possible by the steady profits earned by the companies concerned in peaceful parts of the world in which property rights are secured under the rule of law. Generally speaking, international capital needs the state as badly as ever: to enforce its contracts, to protect its property, to supply police, troops, customs officers, judges and the whole apparatus of civilization, as well as to provide docile, ready-trained workers with the 'right attitude'.

The reliance of multinational business upon the supposedly despised state was vividly illustrated when, in July 1997, the *Guardian* reported that a fraud case involving Denmark's Jyske Bank versus Scandinavian defendants and relating to property in Spain and Gibraltar was being heard in the High Court. No Britons were involved and the case was of no relevance to the United Kingdom, but Jyske decided to go to law in London and the defendants then became the responsibility of the British taxpayer; as much as £10 million was paid in legal aid.

Alan Grant, writing in the same newspaper in June 1996, turned the spotlight on that supposed bastion of tigerish free enterprise, the British airline industry:

Although airlines compete with each other on a superficial level, in reality all of them are dependent on massive, often disguised, public subsidies.

Airlines, unlike motorists, do not pay £2 a gallon in fuel tax. While earthbound traders pay tax and VAT on tobacco, perfume and alcohol, airlines trade 'duty free'.

Aircraft are designed so that all pollution is directed out into the environment and thus on to non-aircraft users. They monopolise land – such as Heathrow – appropriated from the country and gifted to a private company, BAA. Unlike people on the ground, they are not subject to any noise laws. And the customs and police officials necessary for the airlines' smooth operation are paid out of public funds.

Thus big business needs the state, in particular its judicial and security functions, and it needs also the valuable tax exemptions and subsidies that only the state can provide. Were states really to wither away, international capital would need to reorganize itself into a series of armed camps; multinational business would cease to exist in its current form and become something else.

But the states upon which capital depends need not be nation-states. Indeed, business would prefer it if they were not. Only the nation-state – by legal virtue of its sovereignty and the practical virtue of its social and political solidarity – can mount an effective challenge to international capital, which would find it far more convenient if authority were divided between neutered city-states and a handful of regional and global bodies such as the European Union or World Trade Organization. What better way to further this process than to declare that the 'old-fashioned' nation-state is impotent? The idea of the impotent state has been well documented, not least by William Greider in his book, *One World Ready or Not*. In almost 500 pages of relentless reportage, Mr Greider leaves the impression that modern capitalism is like a machine with no one at the wheel that is 'sustained by its own forward motion, guided mainly by its own appetites'.[11]

Mr Greider's book is a vivid expression of the Age of Insecurity. It conveys the sense that something is going terribly wrong with the world but nothing can really be done to stop it short of a cataclysm that changes attitudes and throws up an original thinker, as the 1930s threw up Keynes. We do not share this view. We do not believe that there is nothing that can be done, largely because we still believe in the nation-state. We start from the following premise.

I sympathise, therefore, with those who would minimise rather than with those who would maximise economic entanglement between nations. Ideas, knowledge, art, hospitality, travel – these are the things which should of their nature be international. But let goods be home-spun whenever it is reasonably and conveniently possible, and above all, let finance be primarily national.

There are no prizes for guessing which eminent economist was responsible for those words. But Keynes has never seemed more pertinent.[12] The nation-state is not the shrivelled-up old has-been that the denizens of the modern capitalist order would have us believe. It is perfectly possible, as one group of left-leaning economists argued, to run a big-government policy; the problem is not the absolute level of tax and spending but the gap between them.[13] As a more optimistic American than Mr Greider put it: 'It is within our means . . . to reclaim the power that we have yielded to the institutions of money and re-create societies that nurture cultural and biological diversity – thus opening vast new opportunities for social, intellectual, and spiritual advancement beyond our present imagination.'[14]

The key is certainly to reclaim power ceded to the 'institutions of money'. Indeed, later in this chapter, we will go further and suggest ways of downgrading the importance of money altogether. But the prime task is, as Churchill once said, to make finance less proud. Putting the handcuffs back on capital will assist in curbing the activities of the multinational corporations, which are growing in importance but are far from the untameable monsters of current folklore. Linda Weiss, for example, has extracted some interesting data on multinationals and their foreign direct investment (FDI) flows into other countries.[15] One myth is that multinationals are concentrating on building up manufacturing capacity in low-cost countries. This is wrong. Most FDI is in non-manufacturing – hotels, golf courses, department stores, banks, office blocks. Japan is easily the biggest source of FDI in southeast Asia and two-thirds of it goes into non-manufacturing. Moreover, a considerable proportion of the FDI that is in manufacturing goes on merger and acquisition activity. Overall, FDI is completely dwarfed by portfolio flows of the sort that brought Mexico to the edge of the financial abyss in 1995 and did the same to Thailand, Malaysia and Indonesia in 1997.

The other intriguing question Linda Weiss raises is whether transnational companies are as obsessed with cost as we imagine. If that were the case, she argues, why is not more FDI in developing countries? In 1991, 81 per cent of it was going to high-cost nations, up from 69 per cent in 1967. It could be that the size of the pot has grown so rapidly over the past quarter of a century that there is more than enough to go round, but Ms Weiss argues differently. She says that multinationals place a higher premium on fixed cost (machines) than on variable cost (labour), that new production methods yoke together suppliers and producers, leading to regionalism rather than globalism. Finally, there is an 'advantage firms derive from domestic linkages: national institutional frameworks which enmesh businesses in support relationships with trade associations, training and financial institutions, and national and local governments'.

What does this mean for the West? It means, quite simply, that big business is much more vulnerable than it would care to think. Most of its operations take place in the West, nearly all its consumers are in the West, and it relies heavily on the governments of the West to create the right conditions for the corporate interest to flourish. Domestically, this requires governments to keep unions on a tight rein, reorientate the education and training system so that it suits business, provide inducements for relocation in run-down areas and make only token protests when large companies gobble up their rivals in an attempt to dominate a particular market. Internationally, governments are there to cut deals for multinationals. This may mean negotiating trade liberalization deals; no one who was present as the Uruguay Round of GATT talks came to an end in Geneva in December 1993 could forget how the negotiators were being lobbied day and night by executives from Los Angeles, Lyon and Düsseldorf. Or it may mean acting as an attorney, as the United States did when it took up the case of the American company Chiquita at the World Trade Organization.

THE BIG ALTERNATIVE – GREEN KEYNESIANISM

Instead of looking at the world through the one-way mirror of big business, we should look at the sort of world we would like to see. We are not asking for much. We would like full employment, we would like a high-wage rather than a low-wage economy, we would like job security, we would like a fairer distribution of income both between and within countries, we would like to have some certainty that the planet will outlast us. Now ask whether the culture of big business helps in that process? Have free movement of capital, monetarism, free trade, the drive for a single currency, the World Trade Organization taken us any closer to our objectives or have they taken us further away? Unless you have started this book at the end and are working your way forward, the answer should be obvious.

Governments of both stamps in Britain and America sonorously insist that a low-wage economy is not the way forward for the West, yet by conniving in the great drive for international competition they ensure that this will precisely be the result. Governments everywhere shake their heads and whine piteously about habitat loss and global warming, then cede sovereign powers to multilateral bodies that will only hasten the process.

Multilateral organizations are certainly needed, but they should be multilateral organizations that are part of the solution rather than part of the problem. A good start would be to follow the suggestion of abolishing the WTO and setting up a General Agreement for Sustainable Trade policed by a Sustainable and Equitable World Trade Organization.[16] Fair trade should replace free trade as the prime objective. As for the Bretton Woods institutions, the World Bank, with its dismal history of building dams that no one wants and burdening the developing world with debts, should be closed. If there was ever a fat, overpaid, self-satisfied, complacent bureaucracy it is the World Bank. The International Monetary Fund could stay, but only if it were reformed to become the policing body for global capital, ensuring that it abided by the rules set by nation-states. Multilateral organizations should be there to control globalization, not facilitate it. As one report stressed, globalization is good news for the competitive but not for those who lag behind.

Given the extreme differences which exist between rich and poor countries in the 'starting conditions', globalization is likely to exacerbate cross-national inequality unless conscious action is taken to address these differences. Efforts by developing states to catch up with the industrialized countries in terms of competitiveness may result in falling labour and environmental standards as firms cut costs, thereby resulting in increased environmental degradation, social exclusion and economic exploitation.[17]

This is just the start. In our view, the influence of Keynes will wax even more strongly over the coming years. As the millennium approaches, capitalism is at a crossroads. Either it can continue in the current fashion – the fashion that left a pall of impenetrable fog over Borneo in the autumn of 1997 as fires started deliberately to clear land for big business raged out of control; or it can decide that the globalization process needs to be checked and reconfigured if the world is to reap the same sort of dividend from the new wave of technological advance as it did from the era of Fordist mass production in the aftermath of the Second World War.

There are, of course, plenty of optimists who see Tony Blair as the new Franklin Roosevelt and Bill Gates as the new Henry Ford. But to paraphrase Lloyd Bentsen's damning soundbite against Dan Quayle: 'Prime Minister, you're no Franklin Roosevelt.' At root, Blair is not an interventionist; it was made perfectly clear by the usual Downing Street sources, for example, that he viewed Lionel Jospin, the Socialist victor in the French elections in 1997, as a man with dangerously old-fashioned views. Could Blair do business with Jospin? Yes, but only if he dropped all the silly Keynesian claptrap about protecting jobs and sticking up for the workers. If Blair is essentially a Gladstonian liberal, combining a strong belief in market forces with moral fervour, Bill Gates is more like a nineteenth-century robber baron than Henry Ford. Despite the sneakers and baseball-cap image, Microsoft is as ruthless a multinational as any, and Mr Gates would willingly create a global monopoly in software given half a chance. He is every bit as rich as Ford (probably richer) and, in his geeky way, just as ruthless. But whereas the motor car was an instrument of egalitarianism – indeed, Ford helped to make it one by insisting that his workers should be able to afford to buy the cars they were producing – the personal computer is not, and perhaps never will be. The Internet is essentially elitist, because the capital cost of the computer equipment is high and the bills for surfing the Net can be astronomical.

The spread of the new technology would be hastened by a more egalitarian distribution of income, but even then we are doubtful. Whereas the attraction of the car was that it allowed the working classes to escape from all thoughts of their jobs with a spin in the country or a day at the seaside, the Internet's appeal is really only to those who insist on bringing their work home with them. It may come as a surprise to those who favour home–school contracts and would willingly send a homework police force round to check that seven-year-olds are learning their tables rather than watching videos, but most people endure rather than enjoy education. They do enough to get by, but no more. Given the choice between a night in the pub and an interesting paper from the Internet on aboriginal culture from the University of New South Wales, we would hazard a guess that they would choose the former, even if Mr Blair gave them all a free PC.

Frankly, putting schools online with the help of Bill Gates seems puny when set beside the achievements of Roosevelt, Keynes, Ford and Beveridge in the 1940s. As a critic of Blair's flirtation with stakeholding put it:

Firstly, it is simply not possible to have a socially cohesive, caring, stakeholder society (whatever the reality of that might prove to be) in a country such as contemporary Britain, unless that society is grounded on a high productivity, high wage, egalitarian economy; secondly, such an economy is not possible unless it is built first and foremost on a high-value added manufacturing industry and related services; and thirdly, we will not get to that by waiting for businesses to respond to market signals: there remains a decisive role for the state.[18]

Strategic thought and planning were all but banished in the Thatcherite year zero. Economic policy amounted to reducing inflation, industrial policy to attracting as much Japanese FDI as possible and environmental policy to promoting lead-free petrol and putting a belated curb on out-of-town shop-ping centres. The problem for the right – both in the UK and in the USA – is that it was in power for the downswing of the Kondratieff cycles – fifty- or sixty-year waves in the economy that end in a concatenation of technological exhaustion, rising inequality and over-restrictive monetary policies. If Kondratieff was right – and not every economist is sure he was – the world should now be on the cusp of a new upswing, that would be built on the development of green technology to heal environmental wounds, expan-sionary economic policies and an attack on inequality. Such a strategy would, we feel, attack the root causes of the Age of Insecurity and provide the pro-gressive left with a historic opportunity which may not recur for many years.

The left could certainly seize this opportunity. But we fear that it will take a great deal of persuasion. But since from tiny acorns mighty oaks do grow, we will conclude by trying to surmount the political and practical objections to our ideas. The sense on the left is that environmentalism is bad politics, but this is hardly supported by the survey evidence, which indicates that a red–green alliance already exists. Those who are most concerned about the environment are among those not only most interested in politics but also most likely to support Labour. Moreover, when they state policy prefer-ences, they cite green concerns above living standards.

A MORI poll conducted in the UK before the 1997 election showed that while the environment does not have the same importance as unemployment or health, ten million prospective voters said they put it among the top two or three issues that would help them to make up their mind on whom to vote for at the next election. 'Three people in four across the country, and eight in 10 opposition (at that point Labour) MPs are in agreement that "British companies do not pay enough attention to their treatment of the environ-ment"; this contrasts with the few, recently fewer than one in five Conservative MPs who believe that British companies are lagging in their concern for the environment.'[19]

However, there is a bigger philosophical point. Both Blair and Clinton have tried to put together coalitions that extend well beyond the boundaries of the traditional left; they are, in the words of the Italian Marxist thinker Gramsci, seeking to create a hegemony. This quest has actually been made much easier by the policies followed by the right over the past twenty years, in which the Republicans and the Tories acted like radicals rather than conservatives.

There was a time not so long ago when the Tory paternalists cared about safe-guarding jobs and – in Disraeli's phrase – 'educating our masters', but that all disappeared in the 1980s and 1990s. The right trumpeted a peculiar form of individualistic hedonism, in which people were judged by how well they could stand the full blast of the free market.

A small group of disgruntled greens set themselves up as the Conserver Party in the UK in the mid-1990s, and their manifesto made a lot of sense.

The free market right has almost eradicated the politics of traditional conservatism. The result is that 'conserving' is no longer evident in 'old' conservatism while 'new' con-servatism's pursuit of economic success through a scorched earth policy of profligate consumption is evidence of their disdain for conservation. The acceptance of a need for forms of economic protectionism and a modicum of austerity, and the necessity to be sparing and to live within means, is nowhere to be found in their beliefs. Moderation and restraint are no longer part of their value system.[20]

The Labour Party could stretch out and seize the political prize so wan-tonly abandoned by the Conservatives. However, the first thing the traditional left needs to do is to readjust its vision from the global to the local, from the international to the national.

Our suggestions break down into four categories. First, we look at ways of taking back control of the economy, second, ways of protecting the envi-ronment, third, enhancing security and, finally, deregulating the individual.

(1) TAKING CONTROL

The money system

The key is for the people, through their governments, to restore democratic supervision of capital. When even speculators like George Soros are asking questions about the power of footloose finance, it is time for action. The most obvious reform would be to put curbs on capital, starting with a Tobin tax on foreign exchange speculation. James Tobin believed that a 0.5 per cent levy on all Forex bets would throw sand into the wheels of international finance; given that daily transactions are now well over $1 trillion, it may be that the proposal is too modest. As one American economist put it: 'We may need boulders not sand.'[21]

To bolster the Tobin tax, governments ought to reintroduce controls on capital flows, impose taxes on speculative deals and limit the power of individual banks to create money with hefty reserve requirements on demand deposits. Two arguments will be marshalled against this argument: preventing capital from doing whatsoever it wished would harm the economy, and, in any case, would be impossible to achieve. The first point is not for us to prove. Our case is simple. The performance of the world economy since capital was liberalized has been worse than it was when it was tightly controlled. The people of Mexico and Thailand might dispute that free movement of capital represents some economic nirvana, as might millions of people in the West not fortunate enough to drive around in Ferraris paid for by the annual City Christmas bonus. The second objection looks more of a problem. However, we believe that controlling capital is more a question of political will than of practicalities. In the unlikely event of a war tomorrow between Britain and the USA, would the government allow every last cent of American money in London to be repatriated? Of course not. The state is still the body with ultimate jurisdiction, and it could simply state that any financial institution flouting exchange or capital controls would cease to be protected by English law. Austin Mitchell has suggested such a strategy with regard to offshore activities, and an October 1994 publication from the Institute for Public Policy Research made a similar suggestion in terms of tackling unauthorized foreign-exchange speculation.[22]

We would shift this concept of 'negative enforcement' centre stage, on the impeccably 'market' grounds that its judicial function is one of the nation-state's 'unique selling points'. To all who deal in financial instruments or cash, the message should be simple: if it is not registered here for the purposes of taxation and regulation, then it is not justiciable here. Offshore, overseas transactions – and those on the furthest reaches of the Internet – will be, like gambling liabilities, mere debts of honour, unenforceable in the courts. Such 'negative enforcement' can be even more powerful a deterrent when backed by the new technology – in fact, precisely the sort of technology that is brandished as 'proof' that nation-states have lost control of financial flows. Developments in the fields of 'electronic signatures' and other encryption devices will effectively allow the Bank of England (or whichever is the appropriate agency) to 'de-activate' sterling shifted electronically outside the taxed and regulated area in defiance of British law, rendering such money as useful as an expired cash-machine card. Domestically, the challenge is to re-establish state control over the credit system and, by definition, the money creation system in general. Since Edward Heath's 1971 deregulation package, the misnamed Competition and Credit Control, banks have enjoyed a more or less free rein in credit creation, interrupted only by a brief return to physical controls in the wake of the 'Barber bubble'.

Ideally, we should like to return all credit creation to its proper home, the government, allowing banks to lend only those deposits it takes from the public, as building societies used to do. We should also, in the very long term, phase out one of the most powerful weapons in the financial interest's armoury, compound interest (interest charged on previous interest) and establish serial interest (interest charged only on the principal). But these are, realistically, on a distant time horizon: in the immediate term, we would attack the financial interest with, in addition to the capital controls mentioned above, physical controls on credit and legal limits on interest charges. We should also ensure lenders bear their fair share of the costs of actions for debt recovery and insolvency and reform from top to bottom the laws concerning bailiffs, repossession men and other civil enforcers.

All these measures are about reasserting popular control over the money system, in order that monetary policy may once again be guided in the interests of the economy as a whole. The abolition of exchange control and deregulation of banking and credit brought about the opposite position: the operation of monetary policy in the interest only of the holders of wealth. Capital and credit controls are not advocated in order to clear the way for a Weimar-style inflationary splurge; such a course of action is always self-defeating for governments of the left, because it triggers a stampede into Krugerrands, fine art, vintage cars and rare stamps – in other words, just about the least productive assets imaginable. Rather, the object is to make manageable in the interests of all the system of money and credit – the system whereby tangible claims on national assets are created, moved and executed.

The price system

If the above ideas seem heresy to the free marketeers, they will like our next suggestion even less. Our proposal is simple: to rejig the prices of essential goods and services in such a way as to benefit the poorer levels of society at the expense of wealthier consumers. In essence, heavier consumers would be 'clipped' to subsidize those on average and below-average incomes. HM Government does this already, on a colossal scale, through the National Health Service prescription, with its flat charge which, although it may be waived for certain groups in society, bears no relation to the market price of the particular drugs being dispensed.

Given the vital nature of medical supplies, the 'clipping' mechanism is not explicitly built in to prescription charges. But elsewhere, we believe it could be applied to a range of essential goods: domestic gas and electricity, water, telephone costs, indeed anything that can be metered. Everyone would pay below-market prices for the first chunk of their consumption, up to a notional average. Above that level, prices would rise sharply, allowing those who wish to indulge in three piping hot baths a day followed by an energy-intensive dinner for ten to do so – at an above-market price.

The two great advantages of such a scheme are that it would, first, relieve some of the burden on the welfare system by internalizing transfer payments in the price mechanism and, second, that it would allow, indeed encourage, competitive suppliers to fight for business, as they (supposedly) do now. The only change would be that the state would interpose itself between supplier and consumer, just as it does in the field of prescription medicines. As a third advantage, it reduces the importance of money and takes the sting out of poverty, our first priority.

A variation on this principle can be extended to transport. There seems no justification, now that the railways are privatized, for paying subsidies to the operating companies. Instead, they should be given directly to the consumer, who would get a set amount of free travel on public transport each year. Expansion of public transport would be paid for by higher taxes on petrol and diesel, together with road pricing for every town and city above a certain (relatively small) size. Use of the free bus and rail vouchers would be limited to travel to work areas – no more than thirty or forty miles – in an attempt to cut down sharply the number of short journeys undertaken by car. This measure would be both environmentally friendly and redistributive.

In all, these interventions in the price system would operate like a tax-free allowance for every worker, and would be steeply progressive so that the big users paid substantially more than low users.

Trade and investment

Companies should be told in no uncertain terms that they have to 'site here to sell here', and trade restrictions should be imposed to keep as much activity as possible at the local level. We can imagine the howls of protest the last sentence has occasioned, for we have committed the cardinal heresy and mentioned the P-word, protection. Yet, historically, America's growth and productivity rates were higher when tariffs were steep than when they came down. The key was the fierce internal competition, which ensured that the economy did not follow the Soviet route into ossification and decay. We will be accused of meddling with the market mechanism, but our answer is that the market does not adequately reflect the true cost of trade on the environment. Why, for example, do the shops in the Vale of Evesham, Britain's centre for growing asparagus, import large quantities of the vegetable from Spain? Why does France import its Mars Bars from Slough and export Kit Kats to the UK? Is there any sense in Britain – Europe's great offshore orchard – importing 65 per cent of its apples?

(2) OUR COMMON LIFE

The environment

There are those who feel that our prescription would do immeasurable harm to the world economy. The Australian economist Graeme Snooks says that the world has experienced three technological revolutions so far – the palaeolithic (the use of tools), the neolithic (the use of animals and wind power) and the Industrial Revolution (the use of fossil fuels). A fourth, he says, is about to break over us based on solar power and the only thing that could spoil it would be attempts by eco-warriors to halt growth and progress, because that would result in war and even greater environmental damage.[23]

We are not anti-growth, and would not classify ourselves as eco-warriors. But the Snooks scenario appears extremely remote unless market forces are pushed, prodded and cajoled in that direction. It should be possible greatly to increase the output from a fixed resource use – indeed, one study believes resource productivity could be raised fourfold[24] – but not without active regulatory measures and tax incentives.

At present, the tax system in the UK makes no sense. The government taxes things it wants more of – jobs – while taxing only very lightly something it wants less of – pollution. This imbalance has to be redressed, and could be without any damage to growth according to a study carried out by the Institute for Public Policy Research, a left-leaning think tank.[25] The IPPR put together a package of measures and had them costed by an economist at Cambridge Econometrics. He found that an energy tax starting at $1 in 1997 and rising to $9 by 2005 would raise £10.5 billion in 2005 (the taxes are in USA dollars, as this is the currency in which oil is priced). Raising the landfill tax, currently £7, to £25 by 2005 would raise £2.7 billion. Putting the squeeze on motorists by raising fuel prices by 8 per cent in real terms every year, as opposed to 5 per cent, would net £6.8 billion, a quarrying tax of £9 per tonne £2.4 billion and an office parking tax of £8 per space per week just over £0.5 billion. All the revenue – more than £23 billion – would be spent on reducing the tax on jobs, the national insurance contributions paid by employers when they hire a worker.

The results of the simulations showed substantial cuts in pollution, with carbon emissions down 9 per cent, 6 per cent off sulphur dioxide emissions, 16 per cent less waste disposal and 18 per cent less landfill. Moreover, there would be a significant employment boost in the shape of 717,000 extra jobs in 2005. For all the talk of green taxes damaging growth, gross domestic product would be virtually unchanged.

Tighter regulation would be the second pillar of the attempt to create a greener economy. Car makers in some American states, notably California, are already exploring cleaner technologies following new emission laws, and the same policy should be applied in the UK. Environmental industries will be highly profitable in the next century as the West tries to repair some of the ecological damage it has caused and those that make the breakthroughs will garner monopoly profits. Tighter laws on pollution would lead to higher spending on pollution control technology, while energy-saving dictats would create jobs and diminish pollution.

Andrew Tylecote, author of a book on long economic waves, believes that environmental legislation and regulation could be as big a spur to the economy over the next few years as cheap money was in the 1940s.[26] As he rightly says, cheap money would not go amiss now either, since it would help foster long-term thinking and create the right conditions for investment.

As is obvious from our proposals, this is not a platform likely to win us many friends among the rich. There is a case for raising marginal income tax rates for those who have gained from twenty years of trickle-down economics, particularly if the increase were hypothecated so that half the extra money raised would go to education and half to health. But as Tylecote says, a better and greener way to hit the rich would be through a land tax, which would make hoarding much less lucrative and lead to the stimulation of urban development through the release of land.

The community and social solidarity

Control of land leads neatly to our next point, which concerns reinvestment in communities. And our emphasis is on reinvestment of hard cash and assets, not on gaseous moral uplift about 'rediscovering the community spirit' or similar cost-free waffle. The long withdrawing tide from small and medium-sized communities has left in its wake the debris of closed schools and post offices, axed railway lines and bus routes and shrinking employment opportunities. Inner city and market town alike have been 'hollowed out' by the remorseless operations of the free market. This would matter less were people and businesses coagulating into new communities elsewhere, although it would still mean critical pressure on open countryside and the Green Belt. But all the evidence is of a remorseless drift into what Americans have described as 'linear cities': straggling suburban developments strung out along or near major motorways and other transport gateways. Examples would include the Gatwick–Crawley–Croydon complex and the eastern M4 corridor running from Wokingham and Bracknell through to Slough.

Are these 'communities' in any meaningful sense, or are they, rather, giant anti-communities? Put another way, if achievement of the status and income needed to migrate to one of these 'linear cities' is the one sure and certain way to escape the decaying inner city or the dying market town, then surely the linear cities are ghettos rather than communities, albeit ghettos of the affluent rather than the poor? The essence of community is the living together cheek-by-jowl of a diversity of types, and there is no diversity more important in this context than that of what we used to call class. The narrow spectrum of the linear city ranges all the way from the successful down to the moderately successful, and no further.

It could be, of course, that the inhabitant of linear suburbia, as he nervously eyes his security camera, checks the status of his burglar alarm and awaits the return of his children from school via contract minicab, is ready, willing and able to act as storm-trooper for the new communitarianism preached by New Labour. But we doubt it. When the nearest 'shop' is a huge retail development ten miles away and the 'local' pub is a vast 'big steak' gin-palace ten miles in the opposite direction, 'community' is a somewhat tenuous concept. Indeed, routine human contact in linear suburbia is increasingly confined to officials of the housing development concerned, principally security guards, a neat encapsulation of the triumph of business values. Communities do not spring into being at the behest of uplifting speeches from politicians. Like the natural environment, they need care and nurture; indeed, they could be said to represent the human equivalent of the natural environment, the human ecology. We support small communities not out of some twee Laura Ashley nostalgia, but because they are the soil in which a healthy socio-economic system can flourish. People can matter in a true community in a way they cannot in a linear city. For that reason, we wish to reverse the tide of disinvestment in the community and propose some initial moves to that end.

Transport

To accuse the linear city of having been built around the car is rather like accusing a billiard-ball of being spherical. Writing in the *Guardian* on 15 June 1990, John Whitelegg described the ways in which a combination of high-speed railways and private car use has exacerbated pollution and urban squalor: 'High speed rail creates hyper-mobility for the few and a psychological dependence on other high speed modes to support the rail journey. Most journeys to and from rail-heads are likely to be by . . . high-performance cars because high-speed rail customers strive not to "lose" the benefits of their high speed rail journey by using "slow" modes elsewhere.' Earlier in the same piece, he calls for a shift of resources away from high-speed trains and cars and into 'high quality, local public transport' at speeds of between 20 and 40 kilometres an hour.

We would concur. The public transport challenge at community level is the building not of high-speed but low-speed corridors: tramways, light-rail lines, reliable and affordable bus operations and licensed, regulated Hackney carriage services. The virtuous circle thus created embraces far more than environmental gains; safe, properly staffed railway stations benefit women passengers, the elderly and anyone else likely to be deterred from standing around deserted platforms late at night. The same is clearly true for the trains themselves: the strenuous efforts of the railway companies to manage without guards, conductors and even drivers make no sense whatever. Restaffing of public transport creates steady, responsible jobs – another social plus.

Installations

Communities congregate around the local presences of institutions of all types: post offices, police stations, schools, hospitals. Without them, the community becomes a collection of houses: the linear city. It is nonsensical for statesmen to wax lyrical about decentralization in the context of new regional assemblies and bureaucracies while acquiescing in, for example, the centralization of county constabularies into a handful of fortress-like head-quarters buildings. Such skewing of spending priorities is disinvestment with a vengeance and ought to be met by a vigorous tilting-back of available funds towards community level.

Services

Three thousand bank and building-society branches closed down in the seven years to 1997; in February of that year, the trade-union-backed Alliance for Finance conference heard that the banks' withdrawal from 'unprofitable' communities was leaving poorer people in the hands of loan sharks and pawn-brokers. A separate report at the same time, from the National Consumer Council, said poorer people were being offered such low returns on deposits from financial institutions that they would do as well by stuffing their cash under a mattress. The retreat of the banks is merely part of the wider prob-lem of disinvestment, but it gives the public authorities an opportunity to act decisively on reinvestment in communities. The Girobank concept – killed in 1990, when the state-owned bank was privatized – is an idea whose time has come once more. Indeed, it could be argued that a publicly owned retail bank is needed more urgently now than it ever was when Girobank was launched in the mid-1960s. Britain's big four clearing banks make little secret of the future they seek for their customers, who will be transformed from individual clients into a high-volume mass market 'served' by a minimal branch network, credit-scored by computer and dealt with largely from huge telephone call-centres.

The wealthy will continue to enjoy full banking facilities – everyone else will be treated simply as 'targets' for the selling of dubious 'packaged products' such as pensions, life assurance and unit trusts. A National Bank, with proper branches, managers and advisers, would do far more than rescue the poorest from loan sharks and pawnbrokers. Its branches – authorized to make personal and small-business loans – would act as catalysts for community regeneration. Each would be a centre of expertise, helping customers with budgeting, general insurance, tax, wills, credit matters and foreign exchange. Business advisers would help aspiring entrepreneurs with planning and finance. At the strategic level, the National Bank would be a powerful lever for the promotion of economic policy. But its staff members would be not civil servants but public servants: responsible on a one-to-one basis for each individual client, just as are the managers of the private banks used by those with sufficient wealth to be welcomed.

The catalytic effect of such a bank in the financial field can be replicated by schools and libraries in the intellectual and artistic fields. Wave after wave of closures of such institutions – or 'consolidation', in the jargon – is part of the steady withdrawal of the state from the community and ought to be reversed. Such a reversal would represent genuine municipalism, not the bogus 'regional identity' preached by devolutionists. Indeed, the drive for regional government will exacerbate the problems of communities, not relieve them. Grandiose provincial governments, headed by clapped-out national politicians or slaveringly ambitious young chancers, will contain a built-in bias towards huge 'central' units – be they hospitals, schools, libraries or police stations – and against individual communities.

This is not a reactionary position. On the contrary, devolution and regionalism, by threatening to re-create medieval baronies with their own powers of patronage, are the real engines of reaction.

Similarly – in a final comment on the enhancement of our common life – there is nothing reactionary in resisting demands from big-business organizations that all 'distorting' restrictions in working and trading hours be swept away. Just as the first spelling of a difficult word that comes into one's mind is usually the correct one, so the Labour movement's initial hostility to Sunday and late-night opening was the right response. Both common days of rest (Sundays, bank holidays) and common times of rest (lunchtimes and evenings) are essential features of a common life. Those interests opposed to these features are the enemies of the common life; their aim is an atomized, on-tap workforce and a society in which there are no 'artificial' barriers to business activity. Contrast the fury with which the last Conservative government reacted to Europe's 'working-time directive' (specifying a 48-hour standard week and a rest day, usually Sunday) with its acquiescence in, for example, measures that would devastate the British fishing industry.

We would void in law all deals, contracts and other commercial agreements struck on public holidays, on Sundays or during the hours of darkness. It is not that we wish to protect the home life of the hyperactive tycoon so much as that of the army of secretaries, clerks and messengers who have to dance attendance on him. More important, such a step would send the right signals to society at large: that our country's government has slipped anchor on business values, that financial activity ought to be kept in its place and that such financial activity is a narrow, albeit important, aspect of the human experience, not the whole of life.

(3) SECURITY

The social variety

Nothing has damaged the standing of our welfare system as much as the belief – current and increasing since the end of the 1960s – that, far from representing a large-scale mutual fund, levying and disbursing according to a strict, open set of rules, Beveridge's creation turned into a giant bran-tub of cash, access to which is granted via labyrinthine procedures grasped only by initiates of 'welfare culture'. Jeremy Seabrook has written of one such urban myth – that of the black man who has his fast car expensively refurbished and instructs the garage to send the bill to social security – and of the difficulties encountered by the well-meaning outsider who tries to quash such myths.[27]

The idea that 'everybody knows' the welfare system is a fiddle is as damaging to social security as the idea that 'all policemen are corrupt' is to law and order. In such an atmosphere, it is hardly surprising that New Labour is determined to 'think the unthinkable' on welfare (a euphemism for widespread benefit reductions: such unthinkability rarely involves plans to increase welfare payments). By the end of 1997, the government was embroiled in its first large-scale backbench revolt, triggered by its determination to cut benefits to single parents. Aside from the morality of such reductions at a time of bumper corporate profits and a boardroom pay bonanza, the affair demonstrated the futility of using cuts as a substitute for thought.

Not only was the motor behind the scheme – 'welfare to work' – hardly the most practical of measures, involving, as it did, the shifting of perhaps half a million lone parents into the workplace at a time of fragile labour-market demand, but it was no more morally or even electorally defensible than the pre-existing situation. Henceforth, taxpayers who had been expected to pay single parents to sit at home would now be expected to pay instead for their babysitters (or, to use the approved term, for 'high-quality childcare').

Welfare to work – and New Labour's unthinkably thought welfare reforms in general – look certain to replicate all the vices of the existing system in terms of complexity, illogicality and consequent lack of public support. Worse, the involvement of the private sector in the fields of pensions and long-term care insurance will, we suggest, erode, not bolster, confidence in the system. Not only have we sat through this X-film once already – the 1986 'New Beveridge' package of Mrs Thatcher's Social Security Secretary Norman Fowler – and seen how it ended (with the £4 billion pension mis-selling scandal), but we have also noted a certain divergence in official attitudes to the desirability of betting the farm on the equity market. As turmoil gripped Asian stock exchanges in November 1997, Howard Davies, chairman of the investment regulator the Financial Services Authority, assured a breakfast meeting of the Confederation of British Industry that UK banks, being far less exposed to the equity market, were unlikely to suffer in the same way as their opposite numbers in the Far East. How it could be simultaneously a sign of weakness for banks to be exposed to the vagaries of the stock market and a sign of strength for people's pensions to be similarly exposed has yet to be explained. Nevertheless, the drive to privatize welfare is gathering speed on both sides of the Atlantic. Doug Henwood writes:

Nothing illustrates the severity of the attack on the welfare state better than the emergence into popular discourse in the USA of ideas about privatising the social-security [state pension] system . . . even a commission appointed by a Democratic president . . . [has] signed on to a privatisation agenda that was once an obsession of the libertarian right. When Barry Goldwater suggested in 1964 that social security be made voluntary, it was considered evidence of his madness; now . . . the media are doing the important work of selling the plan to the public.

Since the idea couldn't be sold on its merits – why destroy a system that is universal, successful and deeply popular? – it has to be sold deviously. At the core of the deception is the line that the system faces inevitable bankruptcy . . . about 10 or 20 years into the next century.[28]

Mr Henwood demonstrates later in the same passage that the 'bankruptcy' scare is based on figures assuming a lower average rate of USA economic growth than was achieved during the 1930s Depression. And he sums up in words that have an uncanny echo in British ears: 'It's all very surreal; the financial markets, characterised by nothing if not volatility and scandal, are portrayed as rock solid, and government, which has paid its pensioners without interruption and minimal scandal for over 60 years, is seen as wobbly.'

It is our view that any private-sector involvement in the operations of state pensions and other types of social insurance ought to be strictly limited to essentially administrative tasks. Welfare is properly a governmental function, to be performed within limits laid down openly by Parliament. It sits on the borderline dividing the state's function as a legal framework, within which people can create the circumstances of their own lives, from its function as a 'trust', in which the citizen is alternately contributor and beneficiary. Transparency and a fundamentally non-discretionary nature are the foundation-stones of a properly functioning welfare system: should Parliament vote a £5 broken-leg allowance, then the only qualification for receipt of the £5 ought to be a broken leg. The interposition between benefit and beneficiary of a class of social administrators armed with discretionary powers is a primary cause of the erosion of public confidence in the machinery of welfare.

Nor is welfare properly the province of the law courts. Recent rulings in which judges have sought to confer social benefits on individuals or groups previously thought excluded have done almost as much damage to the idea of social welfare as has the idea that a secretive caste of social workers and civil servants is gaily dishing out millions of pounds to undeserving idlers and con-men. Yet these rulings will be dwarfed by the scale of the judgments that may be passed down if the European Convention on Human Rights is incorporated into British law. The 'mild and provident care' pledged by the early British socialists will have become a monstrous national lottery in which benefits are disbursed seemingly at random to groups able to engage top legal advice.

We believe it would be right to reassert parliamentary – that is, popular – control over the welfare system even if that were likely to mean less generous benefits overall. But we do not believe that would be the probable outcome. On the contrary: in the current litigious, secretive and bureaucratic atmosphere, welfare monies are seen as the property of the state, to be disbursed in accordance with objectives that may never have been thought of at the time the original contributions were forcibly collected. One example would be the 'jobseeker's allowance', a euphemism for a new form of unemployment benefit that is paid out for half as long as the benefit it replaced. An insurance company that tried to renege on its obligations in such a way would find itself having a dialogue with the Fraud Squad.

Welfare is the property of everyone and the business of everyone. It is a form of trust, administered by the state in the general interest. Post-war welfare systems were held up as the pride of Western social democracy; hardly had the Communist rival collapsed than it suddenly emerged that these systems were bankrupt and in need of 'radical surgery' (cuts). We do not agree. But neither do we believe the present levels of welfare payments are a fixed feature of modern life; rather, they have been generated by the unemployment and general social exclusion that are byproducts of 'sound' money policies. Put bluntly, monetarism has knackered the public finances. A healthy economy will make a far smaller call on 'emergency' welfare payments, and it is to some prescriptions for such health that we now turn.

The economic variety

If the welfare system cannot be secured by a series of court cases, then neither can real job security. Nothing has been more depressing in recent years than the sight of trade-union leaders beaming on the steps of the Royal Courts of Justice or House of Lords as they hail another courtroom 'triumph'. As we saw earlier, such 'triumphs' are often nothing of the sort and can actually damage the interests of the union members concerned. But even were each and every favourable ruling on a point of employment law a clear-cut victory for the workers concerned, true security of employment would be not an inch nearer. By definition, a court ruling is narrow and specific, while the modern labour market is an ever-changing kaleidoscope of tasks, conditions, corporate owners and classes of workers. Even in cases where the rulings are widely applicable, the key question is *cui bono?* Prescriptive employment law – judge-made and Parliament-made – acts as a barrier to entry and a reinforcement of the monopoly position of giant companies able to afford office blocks full of lawyers and compliance experts ensuring every action conforms to the rules. By contrast, small and medium-sized businesses enjoy a limited menu of choices. They can throw in the towel (increasing unemployment); they can slip into the black economy (eroding the tax base); they can find substitutes for the act of employment, such as automation or 'outsourcing' (either to the Third World or to our own backyard Third World, the homeworkers).

Above all they – and their bigger brethren – can simply relabel themselves as the customers and the workers as the suppliers, as we saw earlier, through the use of short-term contracts. Once the employee becomes a 'business', then the relationship becomes one of business-to-business. The employer is no more liable for this new 'business' than he would be for ICI.

None of this has anything to do with either the generation of large numbers of jobs or with the core function of the trade union, which is to ensure workers take the largest practicable slice of the company cake, both in terms of income and in terms of time off, working conditions and perks. All the employment regulations in the world cannot create a buoyant labour market in which employees can have the confidence to move jobs, to demand a better deal and – from time to time – to down tools. Only an activist and expansionary economic policy can bring these conditions about, one combined with simplified tax and other paperwork requirements on both employees and employers. True flexibility is our aim: one in which the employee enjoys the same ability to 'up sticks' as does the employer. No law, no verdict, is as liberating for the worker as the certain knowledge that an alternative job is waiting just down the road.

On such a flat playing field, the trade-union official can once again mediate, negotiating pay and benefits packages and working arrangements that are acceptable to both sides. Such deals hold for as long as both sides consider them useful or relevant. By the time of the next negotiations, both the task in hand and many of the personnel involved may have changed. This dynamism is – as we are constantly told – intrinsic to the modern workplace. We agree. But we cannot see why the insecurity that inevitably accompanies this dynamism should fall entirely on the workforce. A 'maximalist' monetary policy redresses in part the balance between the holders of wealth and the sellers of labour. It breeds confidence and security. Its implementation is the true employment protection act.

The national variety

For the big-business vampire, the independent, democractic nation-state is about as welcome as a whiff of garlic and a glimpse of sharpened wooden stake. As Janet Daley wrote in the *Daily Telegraph* on 4 November 1997:

[Big companies] dislike any obstacles that hamper their untrammelled market dominance: national boundaries, cultural diversity, untidy democratic volatility and currency variations are all tedious hindrances to their expansion. What they want, ideally, is a homogenous population with homogenised tastes and predictable habits – an unvarying smooth surface on which to roll out their remorseless market strategies.

As we saw earlier, international capital favours the controlled disintegration of existing nation-states into a much larger number of emasculated municipalities: 'city states', to use the euphemism. Real power will be exercised by the executive organs of capital, such as the World Trade Organization, the European Union and whatever agency polices the proposed Multilateral Agreement on Investment, the 'multinationals' charter'. The left in Britain and elsewhere seems to believe these organs act on behalf of big business only because the left has failed to press the case for change and because, in the right hands, they could become mighty engines for progress.

This is an illusion, comforting but an illusion nonetheless. To banish it, consider one fact: almost all the suggestions we have made here would be struck down as either illegal under EU law or incompatible with Britain's membership of the WTO or other free-trade agreements. Those to whom our ideas are anathema may regard this as an excellent argument for holding fast to such organizations. But for those even vaguely sympathetic, the inability to see through radical ideas ought to be a cause for alarm. Only in an independent democracy do ideas have the slightest chance of being able to result in action; in the absence of an accountable national government, our internal debates on the great issues – freedom, the law, the economy – are merely a form of theatre, taking place within a lavishly appointed arts complex, no doubt, and with superb refreshments available during the interval, but ultimately an interior activity bearing no relation to life outside.

To secure our national home and reassert our control over it, we would suggest a one-clause 'declaration of independence', asserting the supremacy of Parliament over all external courts and legislatures and over all treaty obligations. Not only is this a critically important reclamation of our legal autonomy, it would have also the entirely beneficial effect of bringing down the curtain on the foreign-policy fantasy of 'boxing above our weight'. We do not want Britain to engage in great-power games, either on its own account or as shareholder in the new 'empire in the West', the European Union. We believe, along with Jean-François Revel, that a nation that subordinates foreign to domestic policy is more socialistic than one that behaves in the contrary fashion.[29] Our relations with the world ought to be conditioned not by a desire to 'exercise influence' but by the desire to do good, with particular regard to the twin challenges facing humankind: the moral challenge of feeding the starving and the practical challenge of repairing the environment. Facing these challenges fits neatly with our strategy of orderly, rather than free, trade: reassertion of control over industry and imports would allow discrimination against polluters, while fair-trade agreements allow poorer countries a proper share of the wealth they create.

By contrast, the WTO threatens through its rulings to 'wipe out the bulk of US anti-pollution legislation' and to push poorer countries into the cultivation of opium poppies in order to survive. That is not our prediction, but the gloomy forecast of *Financial Times* columnist Joe Rogaly, writing for the 1–2 November 1997 edition. Of the WTO's founding treaty, he wrote: 'Most participating administrations shape their trade policies according to the needs of their leading companies. . . . Corporate self-interest lies at the heart of both world trade and the organisation that settles disputes between participants.'

(4) 'A GROUP OF ONE':
THE LIFE OF THE INDIVIDUAL

We end with the solitary citizen, not – as is the case with some 'left-wing' tracts – because he is an afterthought, to be wedged in between rousing passages about international solidarity and the brotherhood of man, but because he is, or ought to be, the central figure in any programme for temporal society. We stand four-square for the liberty of the subject, for the Renaissance ideal of the unique potential of each person. Means, not ends, are our priority: the job, the wage-packet, the secure home – creating the conditions in which all these are readily available is the proper task of the state. But come Friday night, when the wages have been handed out and the employees are heading out the door, the state ought similarly to clock off.

By contrast, New Labour and New Democrats wash their hands of the responsibility for the macro-economic environment while taking the keenest of interests in what people get up to in their leisure hours. Tony Blair and his lieutenants have Friday on their minds: your Friday. They are keen to ensure it is spent in low-fat, smoke-free locations with a 'sensible' drinking policy. How you earn your living is your responsibility; how you spend your money is their business. This equation is at the heart of the new command economy: not only is all risk loaded onto ordinary employees and away from capital, but the employee as citizen is to be subjected to ever stricter controls on his behaviour.

Buffeted between his bullying employer and bullying government, the citizen may have trouble distinguishing one from the other. Or, as Alan Clark suggested, writing in the *Spectator* on 5 July 1997, it hardly matters which is doing the pummelling: 'A gap is opening in working-class allegiance, for whom protection from the callous "efficiency" of the multinational or the doctrinal favouritism of a "caring" local authority has become more impor-tant than the freedom to put a polyurethane mahogany front door imported from Korea on their council house.' We would hope to turn this equation on its head, freeing the citizen while clamping controls once more on capital. As we wrote earlier, a firm, admonitory approach to law and order is the antithesis of the control culture. The former is focused on real crimes and real victims, the latter on the invention of notional third parties on whose behalf the state seeks to police behaviour that is in many cases quite legal and in others has no victim other than the perpetrator (the 'war on drugs' being the primary example in this category).

And what goes for the citizen goes for bar and club owners, restaurateurs, hoteliers and other providers of competitive personal services. Whether or not these establishments serve beer in pints, quarts, litres or aerosol tins, or whether or not they set aside large no-smoking areas, is entirely a matter between them and their customers. Closing times, credit arrangements and the publication (or otherwise) of price lists are similarly nothing to do with the authorities.

In short, we would decontrol completely what is currently known as 'leisure' and what we prefer to think of as social life. Not only would we free the citizen once he clocks off work, but would protect him in the workplace from indignities such as drug and alcohol testing and psychiatric assessments. An employee's 'attitudes' are entirely his own affair; the employers' role ought to be confined to ensuring the job in hand is carried out as agreed and that the external appearance and behaviour of employees conform with the company ethos. What happens inside the employee's head is a private matter. Employers have no right to act as compulsory father-confessors or brain-washers.

Nor is it the task of the police to regulate in detail private behaviour. The twenty-year-old 'war on drugs' ought to be abandoned, if only because the record quantities of narcotics now in circulation in this country are proof of its failure. Zero tolerance has bred zero compliance. Whether or not it is practicable to legalize cannabis and permit amphetamines once more to be dispensed by chemists is open to question. What is more important is that the public resources devoted to pursuing drug users ought to be drastically scaled back and the intrusive powers arrogated by the police in the prosecution of this 'war' ought to be removed. Plans for identity cards ought to be abandoned and the occasions upon which a citizen can be required to identify himself should be pared to the minimum. We would sweep away compulsory medicals, AIDS tests, seat-belts, crash helmets and all but the barest essential details on the census. The 'bug and burgle' bill, allowing the police to raid homes and tap telephones without a warrant, would be repealed, as would the rest of the apparatus of surveillance and intrusion erected by cowed ministers at the behest of police chiefs. The requirement to register on the electoral roll would be abolished. Within very broad limits, privacy and anonymity would be respected once again.

Our aim – to paraphrase the former Chancellor, Nigel Lawson – is the greatest practicable degree of freedom within an over-arching framework. The only difference is that he was talking about capital and we are talking about people.

CHAPTER NINE

THE AGE OF SECURITY

'You know, Arrietty,' he went on after a moment, 'as a matter of fact, the less Spiller says the better; this human being . . . this Miss . . . Miss?'
'Menzies.'
'There's one thing that she must never find out — and I really mean NEVER — and that is where we are all living now.'
'I only wanted her to know we were safe . . .'
Peagreen looked back at her. He was smiling his quizzical, one-sided smile.
'Are we?' he said gently. 'Are we? Ever?'

Mary Norton, *The Borrowers Avenged*, Kestrel Books, 1982

The seller of Total Security is a liar and a fraud. In the time it takes to read this book, lives across our country and across the world will have been shattered by the death or injury of a loved one, whether as a result of war or famine or of accidents on the crowded roads of the West. Less tragically, businesses will have collapsed, examinations will have been failed, marriages broken up, jobs lost, dreams dashed. Insecurity is intrinsic to the human condition.

Given that this is so, we believe the human structures we build ought to offer protection against this insecurity; for the laissez-faire economic system to make a virtue out of denying such protection is, to us, as extraordinary, as wilfully stupid and culpably negligent as would be a declaration from the authorities in the Orkneys that they intended to remove all 'artificial' barriers to gale-force winds. This is the madness of the Californian death cult, not the logic of rational economic thought.

We hope we have proved two critical points. First, there is a future for the state, if we want it to have one. Business is not omnipotent and it is time for the myth of the enfeebled state to be challenged.

Second, there is hope. Many of the books written about globalization end with the reader abjectly depressed. We hope that is not the case with this book, for as John Fowles once wrote: 'It is far less nature itself that is yet in true danger than our attitude to it. Already we behave as if we live in a world that holds only a remnant of what there actually is, in a world that may come, but remains a black hypothesis, not a present reality.'[1]

NOTES

INTRODUCTION

1. George Orwell, *Nineteen Eighty-Four*, Penguin, 1954, p. 199.
2. Régis Debray, quoted in the *Guardian*, 15 June 1994.
3. Austin Mitchell, *Competitive Socialism*, Fabian Society, 1989, p. 14.

1 RIGHT ON: THE RISE AND FALL OF ENTERPRISE CULTURE

1. Richard Cockett, *Thinking the Unthinkable*, Fontana, 1995, p. 333.
2. Aneurin Bevan, *In Place of Fear*, Pickering & Chatto, 1996, p. 58.
3. Tom Stoppard, *Arcadia*, Faber & Faber, 1993, pp. 56, 59.
4. J. B. Priestley, *Men in Three Suits*, quoted in Charles Barr, *Ealing Studios*, Cameron & Tayleur, 1977, p. 50.
5. Neville Cardus, quoted in Barr, *Ealing Studios*, p. 97.
6. Hugh Dalton, *The Fateful Years*, Muller, 1957, quoted in Ben Pimlott, *Hugh Dalton*, Macmillan, 1985, p. 425.
7. Pimlott, *Hugh Dalton*, p. 457.
8. Kenneth Morgan, *Labour in Power*, Oxford University Press, 1984, p. 180.
9. Ibid., p. 370.
10. Barr, *Ealing Studios*, p. 103.
11. Richard Hoggart, *The Uses of Literacy*, Chatto & Windus, 1957; Penguin edn, p. 246.
12. Betty Friedan, *The Feminine Mystique*, W. W. Norton, 1963; Penguin edn, p. 13.
13. Ian McDonald, *Revolution in the Head*, Fourth Estate, 1994, p. 7.
14. Ibid., p. 177.
15. Ibid., p. 25.
16. George Melly, *Revolt into Style*, Penguin, 1970, p. 98.
17. John le Carré, *Tinker Tailor Soldier Spy*, Pan, 1974, p. 173.
18. Ibid., p. 136.
19. Alexander Walker, *National Heroes*, Harrap, 1985, pp. 15–16.
20. Michael Pye and Lynda Myles, *The Movie Brats*, Faber & Faber, 1979, p. 211.

2 CASH IS FACT OR HOW I LEARNED TO STOP WORRYING AND LOVE BIG BUSINESS

1. Auberon Waugh, *A Bed of Flowers*, Michael Joseph, 1972, p. 32.
2. Robert Heilbroner, *Business Civilization in Decline*, Marion Boyars, 1976, p. 13.
3. David Marsland, *Seeds of Bankruptcy*, Claridge Press, 1988, p. 1.
4. Arthur Hailey, *The Moneychangers*, Michael Joseph, 1975.
5. Jeffrey Archer, *Not a Penny More, not a Penny Less*, Cape, 1976.
6. Frederick Forsyth, *The Dogs of War*, Hutchinson, 1974.
7. Heilbroner, *Business Civilization in Decline*, p. 47.
8. N. H. Stacey, *Journal of Economic Affairs*, 1981.
9. Marsland, *Seeds of Bankruptcy*, pp. 24–5.
10. Ian Angell, Address to Conference on Financial Crime, Lisbon, June 1997.
11. Jim Slater, *Return to Go*, Weidenfeld & Nicolson, 1977, p. 199.
12. Tony Benn, *Against the Tide: Diaries 1973–76*, Hutchinson, 1989, p. 421.
13. Arnold Wesker, *Journey into Journalism*, Writers and Readers Publishing Co-operative, 1977, p. 73.
14. Fritz Schumacher, *Small is Beautiful*, Abacus, 1974, pp. 24–5.
15. Tony Benn, *Arguments for Socialism*, Cape, 1979, pp. 148–9.
16. Jimmy Reid, quoted in Peter Evans, *The Protest Virus*, Pitman, 1974, p. 131.
17. Schumacher, *Small is Beautiful*, p. 11.
18. Anthony Burgess, *1985*, Arrow, 1980.
19. Benn, *Arguments for Socialism*, p. 67.
20. Andrew Swarbrick, *Out of Reach*, Macmillan, 1995, pp. 122–5.
21. Christopher Booker, *The Seventies*, Allen Lane, 1980.
22. Sir John Hicks, 'The Permissive Economy', in *Crisis '75*, Institute of Economic Affairs, 1975.
23. Evans, *The Protest Virus*.
24. Sir Michael Edwardes, *Back from the Brink*, Collins, 1983, pp. 75–7.
25. Tom Baistow, *Fourth-Rate Estate*, Comedia, 1985, p. 67.
26. Martin Pawsey, *The Private Future*, Pan, p. 156.

3 SYSTEM FAILURE: THE FREE MARKET UNDER BATTLE CONDITIONS

1. Milton Friedman, *Free to Choose*, Pelican, 1980, p. 67.
2. Susan Crosland, *Tony Crosland*, Pelican, 1980, p. 25.
3. Robert Moss, *The Collapse of Democracy*, Temple Smith, 1975, p. 118.
4. Rodney Atkinson, *The Failure of the State*, Compuprint Publishing, 1989, p. 87.
5. Sir Michael Edwardes, *Back from the Brink*, Collins, 1983, p. 52.
6. David Graham and Peter Clarke, *The New Enlightenment*, Macmillan, 1986, p. 50.
7. Thomas Hoving, *False Impressions*, Deutsch, 1996, p. 22.
8. Christopher Lasch, *The Revolt of the Elites*, Norton, 1995, p. 6.

9. Ibid., p. 28.
10. Jonathan Cohn, 'Perrier in the Newsroom', *The American Prospect*, Spring 1995.
11. Roy Greenslade, *Maxwell's Fall*, Simon & Schuster, 1992, p. 1.
12. Joshua Wolf Shenk, 'Hidden Kingdom: Disney's Political Blueprint', *The American Prospect*, Spring 1995.
13. Paul Johnson, *Enemies of Society*, Weidenfeld, 1977, p. 258.
14. Jane Jacobs, *Systems of Survival*, Hodder & Stoughton, 1992, pp. 23–4.

4 A LONGING LOOK ABROAD (1): THE BRITISH LEFT AND THE UNITED STATES

1. Gerald Fairtlough, 'Focussing the DTI on Networks', *Demos Quarterly*, Issue 8, 1996, p. 50.
2. See the *Guardian*, 31 July 1997.
3. George Orwell, 'The Lion and the Unicorn', *The Penguin Essays of George Orwell*, Penguin, 1984, p. 151.
4. Margaret Thatcher, *The Downing Street Years*, HarperCollins, 1993, p. 626.
5. Nigel Lawson, *The View from Number 11*, Bantam, 1992, p. 1035.
6. Robert Hughes, *The Culture of Complaint*, Oxford University Press, 1993, p. 5.
7. Edward Luttwak, 'Buchanan Has It Right', *London Review of Books*, May 1996.
8. Rudi Dornbusch, *Centrepiece*, October 1996.
9. Paul Krugman, *Peddling Prosperity*, W. W. Norton, 1994, p. 191.
10. Robin Ramsay, *Lobster*, no. 33, Summer 1997.
11. Lester Thurow, *The Future of Capitalism*, Nicholas Brealey, 1996, p. 257.

5 A LONGING LOOK ABROAD (2): THE BRITISH LEFT AND THE EUROPEAN UNION

1. Philip Willan, *Puppetmasters*, Constable, 1991.
2. Charles Grant, *Delors: Inside the House that Jacques Built*, Brealey Publishing, 1994, p. 219.
3. Will Podmore and Phil Katz, *Sovereignty for What?: Why Stopping European Monetary Union is Just the Start*, Podmore, 1997.
4. John Laughland, *The Tainted Source*, Little, Brown, 1997.
5. Grant, *Delors*, p. 159.
6. Podmore and Katz, *Sovereignty for What?*.
7. Richard Hoggart and Douglas Johnson, *An Idea of Europe*, Chatto & Windus, 1987, p. 123.
8. *Daily Telegraph*, 23 April 1997.
9. *A Dictionary of Politics*, 7th edn, Penguin, 1973.
10. Robert Jackson, *Tradition and Reality: Conservative Philosophy and European Integration*, undated.
11. Benn, *Arguments for Socialism*, p. 93.
12. Eric Deakins, *What Future for Labour?*, Hilary Shipman, 1988, p. 167.
13. Treasury Select Committee Report on Preparations for EMU, 1996.

14. Ibid.
15. Barbara Tuchman, *The March of Folly*, Michael Joseph, 1984.
16. Podmore and Katz, *Sovereignty for What?*

6 NO HIGHWAY: THE LEFT'S MYSTERY TOUR DOWN TWO BLIND ALLEYS

1. Anthony Arblaster, *Socialism and the Common Good*, Frank Cass, 1996, pp. 3–4.
2. Booker, *The Seventies*.
3. David Owen, *Negotiate and Survive*, Campaign for a Labour Victory, 1980.
4. James Buchan, *Heart's Journey in Winter*, Harvill, 1995, p. 102.
5. *Evening Standard*, 14 March 1995.
6. Will Hutton, *The State We're In*, Cape, 1995.
7. Anthony Howard, *Sunday Times*, 27 August 1995.
8. Andrew Marr, *Ruling Britannia*, Michael Joseph, 1995.
9. Simon Jenkins, *Accountable to None*, Hamish Hamilton, 1995.
10. Clive James, *From the Land of Shadows*, Picador, 1983, pp. 196–7.
11. Brian Walden, *Sunday Times*, 8 July 1990.
12. Laughland, *The Tainted Source*, pp. 174–5.
13. Bernard Connolly, *The Rotten Heart of Europe*, Faber, 1995, p. 225.
14. Anthony Crosland, *A Social-Democratic Britain*, Fabian Tract 404, 1971.
15. Tony Parsons, *The Times*, 3 October 1992.
16. Martin Amis, *London Fields*, Cape, 1990.

7 LET'S HEAR IT FOR KARL MARX: INEQUALITY AND INSTABILITY IN THE MARKET ORDER

1. David Korten, *When Corporations Rule the World*, Kumarian Press, 1995. Quoted figures from various pages.
2. Karl Popper, *The Open Society and Its Enemies*, 2 vols, Routledge & Kegan Paul, 1945.
3. Ibid.
4. Frederick Engels, *Condition of the Working Class in England*, Blackwell, 1971.
5. John Stuart Mill, *Principles of Political Economy*, Kelley, 1970.
6. Ibid.
7. Eugene Varga, *Changes in the Economy of Capitalism Resulting from World War II*, quoted in William Barber, *A History of Economic Thought*, Pelican, 1967, pp. 156–7.
8. George Soros, 'The Capitalist Threat', *Atlantic Monthly*, February 1997.
9. John Maynard Keynes, 'Economic Possibilities for Our Grandchildren', quoted in Kevin Jackson, ed., *The Oxford Book of Money*, Oxford University Press, 1995, p. 465.
10. Alissa Goodman, Paul Johnson and Stevan Webb, *Inequality in the UK*, Oxford University Press, 1997, p. 91.

11. Oxfam, *Growth with Equity: an Agenda for Poverty Reduction*, 1997.
12. William Carrington, 'Wage Losses for Displaced Workers: Is It Really the Firm that Matters?', *Journal of Human Resources*, 1993, p. 454.
13. Richard Freeman, 'Growth and Behaviour', *Centre Piece,* Issue 3, October 1996.
14. Luttwak, 'Buchanan Has It Right'.
15. Peter Robinson, 'Literacy and Numeracy and Economic Performance', paper for the Centre for Economic Performance, September 1997.
16. Thurow, *The Future of Capitalism*, pp. 246–57.
17. Eric Shaw, *The Labour Party since 1945*, Blackwell, 1996, pp. 227–8.
18. Warren Petersen, *Silent Depression*, Basic Books, 1994.
19. Luttwak, 'Buchanan Has It Right'.
20. Ajit Singh, 'Liberalization and Globalization', paper at the conference 'Full Employment without Inflation', Robinson College, Cambridge, 1996.

8 THE BIG ALTERNATIVE

1. Charles Handy, *The Hungry Spirit*, Hutchinson, 1997.
2. Gandhi, quoted in Fritz Schumacher, *Small is Beautiful*, Abacus, 1974, pp. 27–8.
3. Richard Freeman, 'A Hard-Headed Look at Labour Standards', paper for the Centre of Economic Performance, 1996.
4. Lasch, *Revolt of the Elites*, p. 93.
5. Amitai Etzioni, *The Spirit of Community,* Fontana, 1993.
6. HM Treasury, *An Action Plan for Jobs*, HMSO, London, 1997.
7. Milton Friedman, quoted in Lasch, *Revolt of the Elites.*
8. J. K. Galbraith, *The Culture of Contentment,* Sinclair Stevenson, 1992.
9. Lasch, *Revolt of the Elites*, p. 95.
10. Linda Weiss, 'Globalization and the Myth of the Powerless State', *New Left Review,* no. 225, September/October 1997.
11. William Greider, *One World Ready or Not*, Simon & Schuster, 1997, p. 11.
12. John Maynard Keynes, Dublin lecture, April 1933.
13. Nexus Group, 'The Politics of Globalization', *Renewal*, vol. 5, no. 2, 1997.
14. David Korten, *When Corporations Rule the World*, Kumarian Press, 1995, p. 13.
15. Weiss, 'Globalization and the Myth of the Powerless State'.
16. Colin Hines and Tim Lang, *The New Protectionism*, Earthscan, 1992.
17. Nexus Group, 'The Politics of Globalization'.
18. Jeffrey Henderson, 'Whatever Happened to Industrial Strategy', *Renewal*, vol. 5, no. 2, 1997.
19. MORI poll cited in Robert Worcester, paper for 'Greening the Millennium' conference, September 1996.
20. Robert Johnston, 'Escaping from Childishness; The Need for a "Conserver Party"', April 1994.
21. Paul Davidson, 'We May Need Boulders, Not Sand', *Economic Journal*, no. 107, 1997.
22. Dan Atkinson and Ruth Kelly, *The Wrecker's Lamp*, Institute for Public Policy Research, October 1994.
23. Graeme Snooks, *The Dynamic Society*, Routledge, 1996.

24. Ernest von Weizsacker, Amory B. Lovins and L. Hunter Lovins, *Factor Four*, Earthscan, 1997.

25. Institute for Public Policy Research, *Green Taxes*, 1996.

26. Andrew Tylecote, *The Long Wave in the World Economy*, Routledge, 1992.

27. Jeremy Seabrook, *What Went Wrong?*, Gollancz, 1978, pp. 73–4.

28. Doug Henwood, *Wall Street*, Verso, 1997, p. 303.

29. Jean-François Revel, *The Totalitarian Temptation*, Secker & Warburg, 1977, pp. 20–21.

9 THE AGE OF SECURITY

1. John Fowles, *The Tree*, The Sumach Press, 1979.

INDEX